Voice in the American West

ANDY WILKINSON
Series Editor

COWBOY'S LAMENT

COWBOY'S

LAMENT

A Life on the Open Range

EDITED AND
INTRODUCED BY
JIM HOY

FOREWORD BY
DAVID STANLEY

Frank Maynard

TEXAS TECH UNIVERSITY PRESS

This book is typeset in Monotype Albertina. The paper used in this book
meets the minimum requirements of ANSI/NISO Z39.48–1992 (R1997). ∞

Designed by Lindsay Starr

LIBRARY OF CONGRESS CATALOGING-IN-PUBLICATION DATA
Maynard, Francis Henry, 1853–1926.
    Cowboy's lament : a life on the open range / Frank Maynard ; edited and
Introduced by Jim Hoy.
        p. cm. — (Voice in the American West)
    Includes bibliographical references and index.
    Summary: "In memoir, poetry, and prose, describes the adventures of
Frank Maynard, an open range cowboy whose ten-year career coincided
with the peak of the Great Plains trail-drive era. Folklore scholars credit
Maynard with adapting Irish ballad 'The Unfortunate Rake' from its
American version to the well known 'The Cowboy's Lament'"—Provided by
publisher.
    ISBN 978-0-89672-705-2 (hardcover : alk. paper) 1. Maynard, Francis
Henry, 1853–1926. 2. Cowboys' writings, American. 3. Authors, American—
20th century—Biography. 4. Cowboys—West (U.S.)—Biography.
5. Cowboys—Poetry. 6. West (U.S.)—Poetry. 7. West (U.S.)—History—19th
century. 8. Great Plains—History—19th century. 9. Frontier and pioneer
life—West (U.S.)—History. I. Hoy, James F. II. Title. III. Title: Life on the
open range.
    PS3525.A9775Z46 2010
    818'.409—dc22   2010016620

PRINTED IN THE UNITED STATES OF AMERICA
10 11 12 13 14 15 16 17 18 / 9 8 7 6 5 4 3 2 1

TEXAS TECH UNIVERSITY PRESS
Box 41037, Lubbock, Texas 79409-1037 USA
800.832.4042 | ttup@ttu.edu | www.ttupress.org

Dedicated to all the old-time cowboys
whose stories didn't get told.

Contents

Part 3
Maynard's Journalism   175

Illustrations

Foreword

W HEN FRANK MAYNARD sat down, probably in 1888, to record his reminiscences of life on the open range, the American West had already undergone tremendous change since the trail-driving days of the 1870s. Maynard himself had recently relocated from Kansas to Colorado Springs, Colorado, where he built a career as a successful carpenter, living with his wife in a succession of ever-larger homes that reflected their improving economic and social status. Meanwhile, he pursued a second career as a freelance writer, trying out the memoir, the historical sketch, and cowboy poetry as possible avenues to a modest reputation. That his remarkable writings, which give such a vivid portrayal of the western plains of the 1870s, survive at all is testimony to the dedication of Maynard's relatives, who kept them intact, and to the perseverance and alertness of Jim Hoy, who saw them through to publication.

By the time Maynard began writing, the terrible winter of 1886–87, "the Great Die-Up," had made it clear that cattle could no longer be wintered on the northern ranges of the West without supplemental feed. Furthermore, the expansion of homesteads, the advent of barbed wire, and the fencing of water sources had pronounced the end of the open range, and the expansion of railroads throughout the West had made cattle drives largely unnecessary.

These changes triggered others, all creating a national consciousness that something vital had been lost, that the West was no longer a place of endless vistas and endless opportunities, no longer an arena for adventure and experiment or for the pursuit of the dream of sudden riches, respect, and social status that preoccupied the gold miner, rancher, and dry-goods merchant alike. This pervasive sense of loss led to the dime novel—a small, cheaply produced short fiction that sold for a dime or less—and its cowboy hero, albeit one who often combined the detective and the lover with the figure of the horseman.

Another version of the cowboy hero emerged in the person of William "Buffalo Bill" Cody, whose true-life exploits as buffalo hunter, scout, and Indian fighter were the subject of novels, biographies, and dramas. By 1883 he had developed the great circuslike show that he called "Buffalo Bill's Wild West," and by 1887 he was touring Europe. The show was later to be renamed the "Congress of Rough Riders of the World," but in its earlier form it was a deliberate attempt to represent the spectacle and the drama of the history of the West as Cody interpreted it—the Indian attacks, the cavalry rescues, the stagecoach holdups, the heroic range rider in the person of Cody himself.

The nostalgia for a place and a way of life widely viewed as passing, disappearing, or already gone led to biographies, autobiographies, and reminiscent essays in gentlemen's magazines that were read by urban dwellers throughout the country. In contrast to the derring-do of the cowboy hero of the dime novels, these memoirs and reminiscences by working cowboys, ranchers, and travelers in the West represented themselves as factual, with Mark Twain's *Roughing It* (1872) among the earliest. The first great memoir of the livestock business, published in 1874, was Joseph G. McCoy's *Historic Sketches of the Cattle Trade of the West and Southwest*, though McCoy was no cowboy; rather, he was an entrepreneur who spent most of his working life trying to establish shipping points for livestock along the Kansas railways. The popularity of such writing eventually spawned full-length fictional treatments as well, beginning with Owen Wister's novel *The Virginian* (1902) and Andy Adams's somewhat fictionalized memoir, *The Log of a Cowboy* (1903). Within the same year, 1903, William Sydney Porter had shot the first feature film in the United States, *The Great Train Robbery*—twenty minutes in length, and filmed in New Jersey. One of the most remarkable aspects of Frank Maynard's memoir is the way it anticipates so many works that described, romanticized, and eventually reinvented an American West only marginally resembling the hurly-burly of the twenty years (1866–86) of the open range and the trail drives, the West that Maynard lived.

Ever since autobiography began to be seriously evaluated as a literary genre in the 1970s, it has become a truism to assert that autobiography is always a fiction and that the process of memory, selectivity, emphasis, and aesthetic ordering creates an artistic construct very different from the day-to-day experiences that are the autobiography's raw material. So it is with Maynard. His memoir is tremendously valuable for its descriptions of the working life of a youthful farmhand, tyro buffalo hunter, and itinerant cowboy, moving from job to job, returning to his home town occasionally, wondering about his future, his prospects for marriage and family, his career. It is valuable, too, for its description of the complexities of life on the border, that tenuous area encompassing southern Kansas, the Cherokee Strip, Indian Territory (Oklahoma), and north Texas. This was contested ground from before the Civil War and it continued to be so during the trail-driving days, when taking cattle across Indian Territory was perilous, with hostile Missouri farmers, afraid of Texas fever, to the east; the Comanches to the west; and a mélange of forcibly resettled Native American peoples in between. The frequent conflicts with Native Americans in Maynard's memoir testify to the uncertainties of that time and that place.

Maynard's narrative also reflects remarkably the literary culture of the nineteenth century. Here was a young man with a third-grade education who grew up in a home with few books, worked in the out-of-doors for months at a time, yet somehow managed to absorb the literary conventions of the period. Here is part of his description of camping out in a blizzard with a skunk during the buffalo hunt of 1871:

> We had traveled in a circle, lost in a blizzard. Again we started, giving the ponies their heads. The sagacious animals soon came to a halt in front of our tent. Opening the flap, we were greeted by an unpleasant visitor. A large polecat was in full possession. Try as we would to frighten him out, he would run toward us, stamping the ground and showing his teeth. Exasperated, I said, "I'll fix him." Grabbing a rifle from the wagon, I fired at him point-blank, fairly pulverizing him; but alas! He was victorious even in death, for he opened his vanity case and scattered its contents in all directions. It was not filled with heliotrope nor sweet mignonette. Some of it struck our one sack of flour, so we had to subsist on parched corn and buffalo meat for the next three days. (p. 62)

From the understatement of "unpleasant" and the coyness of "alas!" to the elaborated metaphor of a skunk's "vanity case" and the mock-heroic allusion to the skunk's victory, Maynard shows all the influences of extensive reading in the popular works of literary Victorianism. Heliotrope and mignonette, after all, are fragrances rarely encountered on the buffalo range. Considering that Maynard was only about thirty-five years old when he wrote this passage, it stands as a testimony to his intelligence, self-education, and love for language, as well as to the pervasiveness of the written word even on the open range of that era.

Maynard's narrative is also replete with violence, confrontation, and the imminence of death, incidents that he reports matter-of-factly as part of everyday life. One of the first narrated episodes of his new life in Kansas involves passing by, unknowingly, the frozen corpses of five hunters, and the specter of death continues to loom over the narrative: trailing cattle with the murderous outlaw Dave Rudebaugh, standoffs with Indians, a prairie fire, a confrontation with German homesteaders, gunfights, and the Cheyenne Breakout of 1878 and the killing of his friend, Tom Murray. The prevalence of violence in Maynard's narrative may reflect the popular literature of the day—the dime novels, sensational stories in journals like *The Police Gazette*, and early memoirs such as Charles A. Siringo's *A Texas Cowboy, or Fifteen Years on the Hurricane Deck of a Spanish Pony* (1885), although it is worth noting that Siringo emphasized frontier violence and outlawry far more abundantly in his later work, *Riata and Spurs* (1927).

Maynard, then, was clearly aware of and responsive to the sensationalized portrayal of the cowboy of popular culture. It seems that he chose to include in his memoir whatever incidents of violence—personally observed or simply reported to him—that he could recall, including occurrences with which he had only the most marginal association. The frozen hunters in the wagons, the shooting of Jim Ayers by "Little Jim" and his subsequent lynching, and the frequent secondhand stories of rustlers, outlaws, and Indians testify to Maynard's awareness of the popularity of violence in the written depictions of the West in the late nineteenth century. That doesn't mean that Maynard toyed with truth or bent the facts, but it does suggest how conscious Maynard was of the literary conventions of his time.

Despite his wish to be part of what would fast become a substantial American literary enterprise, incorporating fiction, nonfiction, history, poetry, and song (Wister's *The Virginian*, 1902; Adams's *Log of a Cowboy*, 1903; James W. Freeman's *Prose and Poetry of the Live Stock Industry of the United States*, 1905; N. Howard "Jack" Thorp's *Songs of the Cowboys*, 1908; John Lomax's

Cowboy Songs and Other Frontier Ballads, 1910; and *Songs of the Cattle Trail and Cow Camp,* 1919), Maynard maintained a substantial degree of self-awareness, often tinged with irony if not self-mockery. Describing his herding work during the winter of 1874–75, he says, "Among the advantages presented by my location were the following: the post-office was very convenient; the woods were full of wild turkeys, and right on the line of my beat lived a family who had several bright-eyed daughters. They had a large old fashioned stone fireplace in the cabin, and I found it a capital place to stop and get warm, and it is a singular fact that I got cold on some very warm days" (p. 92).

Despite the disappearance of a few pages and parts of pages at the end of the manuscript, Maynard's intention for the end of his memoir is clear: he concludes with a sense of loss, of regret. The Indians waste away on their allotments, the soldiers grow fat, many of the "old time boys are lying beneath the sod" and "the free rover of the plains is no more" (p. 134). Maynard concludes with a tribute to his wife and says, somewhat wistfully, "On the margin of the sun-kissed plains over which I once galloped so recklessly, yet almost under the shadows of the snow-capped peaks of the Rockies we have pitched our camp, and life passes quietly and peacefully" (p. 134). Just as he has moved from the plains to the mountains, so too does he recognize that his life has passed from the old wild times to his adult life of carpentry and freelance writing, from remembered experience to its selective representation.

DAVID STANLEY

Preface

THE PLEASURES
OF SERENDIPITY

I N THE FALL OF 1991 I WAS INVITED down to the old cow-town of Caldwell, Kansas, to help the community kick off a series of programs and events that would culminate two years later in the centennial celebration of the opening for settlement of the Cherokee Outlet, better known as the Cherokee Strip Land Run. After an evening that included a fund-raising auction, a barbecue dinner, and some cowboy poems and songs, a man named Don White, who lived halfway between Caldwell and Hunnewell on a wheat farm that bordered Oklahoma, came up and asked if I'd like to see a copy of the cowboy poems his great-uncle had written. "Sure," I said, and gave him my address.

A couple of months passed, then one day I received in the mail an envelope from White with a note: "Enclosed is a copy of a book of rhymes by Maynard. He was married to an aunt of my father's. He was a real cowboy in his younger days. I'm sorry it has taken so long to send this to you since your visit to Caldwell. Better late than never, I guess." Accompanying his note was a photocopy of a small book of poetry published in 1911, the title page of which read: "*Rhymes of the Range and Trail* by F. H. Maynard, an Old-time Cowboy." I glanced at a couple of them and thought, definitely better late than never.

The first poem, "On the Trail," presented a composite view of a drive up the Western Trail, while the second, "Bill Springer's Hand," described an exciting card game in old Dodge City. Pretty good stuff—better than a lot of cowboy poetry, I thought, as I flipped briefly through the rest of the manuscript, then stuck the copy back into the envelope, tossed it among the clutter that resides more or less permanently on my desk, and picked up a pile of student essays. It was the middle of finals week: work came before fun.

Christmas intervened, and the beginning of a new semester. Then about the last of January 1992 I uncovered a corner of Don White's envelope on my desk. I pulled it free, excavated the contents, and started to read Maynard's rhymes. Here was a poem about Billy the Kid, one that seemed to have stuck surprisingly close to the facts without romanticizing the young sociopath. Here was another on the excitement and the disappointments of prospecting in Colorado; a poignant, frightening one about a young cowboy ambushed by Indians; and a short, humorous piece about hauling a cat to a line camp to thin out the mice that played atop the cowboy's bed as he tried to sleep.

About midway through the nineteen poems I spotted the title "The Dying Cowboy" and under that the word *song*. A first glance told me, or so I thought, that Maynard had included one of the popular cowboy songs of his day in with his own verses, for it read: "As I rode down by Tom Sherman's bar-room, Tom Sherman's bar-room so early one day," the opening line of one of the variants of "The Cowboy's Lament." I read through the familiar verses, then browsed the rest of the volume. There followed poems about rovers, horse thieves, and reckless cowboys, then poems more pensive and introspective about the end of the frontier and about bidding farewell to the plains. Maynard closed his booklet with two poems for his wife.

Reading through the entire book reinforced my initial response of two months earlier, that Maynard was more talented in prosody than many other cowboy poets; his poems scanned well, the syntax was smooth, and the rhymes generally were unforced. But when, a couple of days later, I turned to Lomax and other collectors of cowboy songs, trying to find other versions of "The Cowboy's Lament" that began at the door of one of Dodge City's rowdiest saloons instead of on the hot, dusty streets of Laredo, I made an even more exciting discovery: Francis Henry Maynard claimed to have written new words to an old ballad, resulting in what is perhaps the most famous of all the old-time cowboy folk songs. If his claim was true, then the poem I had in my possession was undoubtedly the earliest printed version of the song—printed, at least, as Maynard had wanted it printed. I began to do some digging.

The first two collections of cowboy verse and lyrics ever published, by Jack Thorp in 1908 and John Lomax in 1910, contain "The Cowboy's Lament," although neither has Maynard's particular version, which is distinguished by calling the dying man a ranger (that is, one who rides the range, not a law-man). Neither did they mention Maynard as the author, nor did any of the other popular collections I thumbed through. Thorp, a working cowboy who, thank goodness, took it upon himself to collect some of the songs he had heard in the cow camps of the Southwest, gave Troy Hale, a Nebraska cowboy, credit for writing it in 1886. No help there for Maynard's claim.

So, moving deeper into the library, I delved into the professional journals, where scholars deal in the coin of esoterica. Sure enough, Ina Sires in 1928 noted Maynard's claim to authorship, and that finding was repeated in 1934 by Phillips Barry. Austin and Alta Fife, in their 1966 annotated edition of Thorp, also mentioned Maynard's claim along with those of several others, as did, more recently, Jim Bob Tinsley (1981) and Guy Logsdon (1989). But none of the many versions of the song that I had seen in my digging through the stacks had printed the song as Maynard had written it, while only one obscure variant, from Colorado Springs (Maynard's home after his roving cowboy days ended), used the central figure of a ranger. It was beginning to look as if I had lucked into a nice little find. Serendipity: the scholar's most exciting, if not always his most dependable, friend.

What about *Rhymes of the Range and Trail* itself? How widespread was the distribution of that little volume? I pulled down Hal Cannon's *Cowboy Poetry: A Gathering*, the anthology that derived from the first modern cowboy poetry gathering, organized in substantial part by Cannon and held at Elko, Nevada, in late January 1985; that event not only occasioned the public rediscovery of cowboy poetry but also was directly responsible for its phenomenal outburst of popularity in the succeeding decades. Cannon's book has a thorough bibliography of published collections of cowboy verse, both historical and contemporary, well known and obscure. Maynard, however, was not listed. Through letters and phone calls to libraries, and with the help of colleagues who knew how to use the Internet better than I, I had the holdings of likely archives searched for references to Maynard and his book. The search turned up nothing in Colorado Springs (Maynard's home for over forty years) or Denver; nothing at the Kansas State Historical Society (the state in which Maynard was living when he wrote the song); and nothing at major repositories of Western Americana nor at the Library of Congress, even though Maynard had copyrighted his book. This was a rare volume, indeed.

So I called Don White and arranged to drive down for a visit about his great-uncle and maybe get a firsthand look at *Rhymes of the Range and Trail*. Don and Gloria White greeted me warmly and led me to their good-sized family room, the west half of which was as neat as the pins that Mrs. White

F. H. Maynard,
Colorado Springs, Colo. Title of book:
Rhymes of the Range and Trail.
By F. H. Maynard.

Copies received *Nov. 20*, 1911. Date of publication *Nov. 11*, 1911.

Affidavit received *Nov. 20*, 1911. Entry: Class A, XXc., No. *302 249*

[SEAL]

Thorvald Solberg
Register of Copyrights.

A

COPYRIGHT OFFICE OF THE UNITED STATES OF AMERICA
Library of Congress—Washington
❊ ❊ ❊
CERTIFICATE OF COPYRIGHT REGISTRATION

This is to certify, in conformity with section 55 of the Act to Amend and Consolidate the Acts respecting Copyright approved March 4, 1909, that TWO copies of the BOOK named herein have been deposited in this Office under the provisions of the said Act, together with the AFFIDAVIT prescribed in section 16 thereof; and that registration for copyright for the first term of 28 years from the date of publication of said book has been duly made in the name of

[OVER]

Copyright registration card for Rhymes of the Range and Trail. *Courtesy of Arlynn Anderson.*

was using in her sewing that afternoon. The east half, however, was crammed with filing cabinets and tables, every surface piled high with papers and boxes and photographs. There was even a photocopier squeezed into Don's half of the room. Don, you see, just happened to be the family genealogist. Serendipity had struck again.

He pulled out the Maynard file, which looked a bit on the thin side, and we sat down for a talk. Maynard's wife, Flora Vienna Longstreth, was a sister of Myrtie Elizabeth Longstreth, Don's paternal grandmother. The Longstreth family had lived near Towanda in Butler County, Kansas, during the late nineteenth century. Don handed me a photograph of Maynard that he had had copied from the original studio portrait. He also gave me a photocopy of the Maynards' marriage license, dated April 24, 1881. And he handed me a typewritten sheet, with data largely taken from the family Bible, that list-ed the names of brothers and sisters, birth dates and places, marriage dates and partners, and children resulting from the various unions (none from the Maynards). And that was about it. Don had never seen Maynard (who died several years before his great-nephew's birth). Don's younger brother Duane, however, who lived in suburban Johnson County, had somehow or other acquired Maynard's old Winchester rifle. Other than that, despite the bulging files on other, more prolific family members, the Maynard cupboard was disappointingly bare.

Even more disappointing, however, was Don's next bit of news: he could not find his copy of *Rhymes of the Range and Trail*. He might have misfiled it, he thought, or, worse, he might have accidentally tossed it after making a photo-copy. Still, a photocopy of a photocopy, which is what he had sent to me, was much better than a mere typed, or handwritten, transcription of the original. I drove back to Emporia well satisfied, thinking about the next move.

Jim Bob Tinsley had mentioned in his chapter on "The Cowboy's Lament" an article about Maynard that had appeared in the *Colorado Springs Gazette and Telegraph* on January 27, 1924. In mid-January, a week or so before I had read through the copy of Maynard's poems, my wife and I had taught, in Denver, the first segment of a weekend-intensive course for Emporia State University, part of the School of Library and Information Management's distance educa-tion program, which Cathy at the time directed. We were to meet the class for the second full weekend (Friday night, all day Saturday, and Sunday morn-ing) in early March after students had had time to complete assignments and work on their research projects.

Then, for the third time serendipity reared its lovely head. One of the women in the class just happened to work in the local history room of the Colorado Springs Public Library, and, needless to say, she was more than happy to help out when I wrote to see if she could get me a copy of the 1924 article from the *Gazette and Telegraph*. Not only did I receive, in short order, a photocopy of the article (about which more later) but also a newspaper feature article ("Maynard's Western Tales") that Maynard himself had written in January 1925, information about the house the Maynards had lived in on historic Cheyenne Boulevard, and copies of several different pages of city directories from both Denver and Colorado Springs listing men named Frank Maynard (the Denver listings were of someone else). A little more correspondence, as well as a stint in the Colorado Springs library, resulted in three more "Western Tales" stories from the newspaper and copies of obituaries for Maynard and his wife (who survived him some five years).

This new information, combined with data from the Butler County censuses for 1870, 1875, 1880, and 1885, began to give shape to Maynard's life. I knew, for example, that he had been born in Iowa in 1853; that he had run away from home to join a freighting crew on the Oregon Trail when he was sixteen, an adventure that lasted only a couple of months; that he had moved to an aunt's house at Towanda in early 1870, a few months before his father moved the rest of the family there from Iowa; that he had soon after gone off buffalo hunting and Indian trading; and that by the spring of 1872 he had begun working as a cowboy. I knew that he and Flora had married in 1881 and that by at least 1888 they had moved to Colorado Springs, where Frank worked as a carpenter and building contractor for the remainder of his life.

When I sent copies of this new information to Don White for his genealogy files, he told me that he had been in communication with other family members, trying to see if he could locate a copy of *Rhymes of the Range and Trail*. He had had no immediate luck, but one of his cousins, Arlynn Anderson from Grand Junction, Colorado, another great-nephew of Maynard's, wrote back that while going through his recently deceased mother's effects he had found a box marked "Maynard." Arlynn offered to share the information with me once he had had a chance to look everything over, so we arranged for him to stop at the Whites' on his trip to Georgia in the fall of 1993. I arrived a few minutes ahead of the Andersons, and when Arlynn walked in he was carrying a good-sized cardboard box filled with all sorts of envelopes, letters, newspaper clippings, handwritten manuscripts, photographs—and a copy of *Rhymes of the Range and Trail*. Ironically, Don White had recently discovered his own copy of the book, which had been in a file folder that had gotten placed backwards in the cabinet. After arranging to redeliver the materials to Don, who would get them back to Arlynn after I had finished with them, I once more headed back to Emporia, there to sort through the trove.

Although gaps in Maynard's life remained (such as his whereabouts and activities between the time of his marriage in Towanda and his appearance in Colorado Springs by the late 1880s), many more got filled in. Two additional "Western Tales" surfaced, one of them clipped from an undated issue of the *Gazette and Telegraph*, the other an unpublished manuscript in pencil on lined paper. Several photographs were in the box: two showing Maynard as a young cowboy in the mid-1870s, some of camping trips in the mountains with his wife, and others of himself in later years posing with his Winchester and with a suitcase. Among the newspaper clippings were obituaries of Bill Tilghman, whom Maynard had known in the 1870s, and Buffalo Bill Cody, whose family had sent a black-edged card of thanks to Maynard in response to his expressions of sympathy on the death of the famous plainsman. There were also several packets of letters: some from other old cowboys; some from an Oregon writer who was seeking information about Dodge City in its glory days; some from Elmo Scott Watson, author of the 1924 newspaper feature piece that had brought Maynard into the public eye at Colorado Springs; one, in French, from the secretary of the Queen of Belgium, responding to a spirited poem that Maynard had composed and sent to King Albert when Germany had invaded Belgium at the beginning of the Great War; and one from Jack London, written aboard the *Snark* and offering advice on publishing, obviously in response to a query from Maynard. I learned also that Maynard belonged to the Junior Order of United American Mechanics and the Modern Woodmen of America and that he had been part owner of a syndicate that sold stock in a Colorado gold mining venture.

But most intriguing among these documents was a sheaf of onionskin typing paper (the kind often used to make carbon copies) loosely bound between blue oilcloth covers (of a kind often used to enclose legal documents in an earlier day), the bundle held together in a roll by a rubber band. There was no marking visible on the cover, but when I spread the bundle on a table and opened it, the first page read as follows: "Reminiscences of wild life and adventure among the cowboys, outlaws, and Indians of the southwestern border, by F. H. Maynard, an old-time cowboy." Just below was a dedication:

"To those that have gathered around the same campfires, who have faced the same wild storms, and who have shared the same wild adventures, this volume is affectionately dedicated."

There followed over sixty single-spaced typewritten pages describing grand adventures of buffalo hunting, Indian trading, and cowboying throughout the decade of the 1870s. I started reading, fascinated by the detail, the matter-of-fact tone, the sheer adventure of it all.

I read through the manuscript at a sitting, although it took some doing. Maynard had obviously paid to have someone, perhaps (considering the binding) a legal secretary, type these memoirs from his handwritten copy, if the several handwritten manuscripts of the "Western Tales" articles were any indication. Sometimes I could barely make out the dim imprint of the words, and several times I had to hold a blank white sheet behind a page to make it legible. To save wear on the original, I decided to make a copy, but because the pages were so flimsy and the staples binding them so rusted in, I could not make a photocopy. Instead, I had to read the manuscript aloud into a tape recorder, then transcribe the tape, then compare the transcription with the original to make corrections. It was an arduous process but worth the effort.

Here was the real thing, a working cowboy's memoirs during the very heart of the era of the open range. Not a fence does he mention nor a gate does he open. Occasionally he encounters a famous frontiersman (Bat Masterson and his brother Ed, Prairie Dog Dave Morrow, Bill Tilghman), and occasionally he refers to well-known historical events (the killing of Ed Masterson, the Cheyenne Outbreak of 1878) and famous cow-towns and rivers (Dodge City, Ellsworth, Wichita, Ogallala, the Red, the Arkansas, the Cimarron). But for the most part the names dropped in his narrative are of ordinary people (ranchers, working cowboys, small-time outlaws, friends, relatives), the events he documents are the details of daily life (driving cattle, roundups, riding bad horses) or, for the times and the job, of quotidian adventures (hunting cattle rustlers, chasing horse thieves, dealing with potentially hostile Indians), and the places he names are ones seldom found on maps (Griffin's Ranch, Fort Woodward, Big Mule Creek, Flag Springs, Short Creek). Here was primary source material for the open range of the 1870s, written in 1888 (according to an internal reference) and never before published.

Maynard's account is particularly important because it sheds light on an often overlooked aspect of the open-range era. We tend to associate the origin of the Great American Cowboy of popular culture with the years of the

Texas-to-Kansas trail drives. These trail drivers called themselves "drovers," a term that gave way to "cowboy" during the decade of the '70s, Maynard's decade. But trail driving was only one of the occupations that provided the genesis of the cowboy: in addition to drovers there were also herders. Drovers trailed cattle to the cow towns; herders looked after cattle on the open range. Undoubtedly some Texas herders stayed home with the cow-herds when drovers took cattle to market, just as some drovers may have made a career of trail driving, never working as ranch hands. But many, like Maynard, were both trail drivers and herders. Although illness forestalled Maynard's one venture trailing cattle to the Dakotas, he did work as a drover taking horses from Kansas to Texas, moving cattle from Kansas to Colorado, and meeting herds in Indian Territory and taking them on to the railhead at Ellsworth. He also worked extensively as a herder, watching over cattle grazing in various parts of Kansas, particularly near Medicine Lodge, and on down into Indian Territory. A herder working on the open range was also sometimes called a range rider, which likely explains Maynard's use of the term "ranger" rather than "cowboy" in the verses of his song, which he titled "The Dying Cowboy."

We often think of the cattle ranches as being primarily in Texas at this time period, but large ranches were also established in the open-range country of Indian Territory and Kansas. In addition to the herds on those ranges, many Texas steers would arrive in Kansas in late spring or early summer but would be grazed there, or in Indian Territory, before being shipped out from the cow towns in the autumn, or even the next spring. Thus Maynard's recollections of his life on the open range are particularly important because they reflect both the more widely known occupation of drover as well as the less often considered herder.

Maynard, I think, had wanted to have his story published. His 1907 query to Jack London about publishing his poems and his later query to Elmo Scott Watson about publishing his article on Adobe Walls indicate his desire to get into print, as do the five "Western Tales" that appeared in the newspaper between his "discovery" by Watson in January 1924 and his death on March 29, 1926. So, too, does the handbill (p. 18), date and place blank, that was included in the materials loaned to me by Arlynn Anderson. I have no idea whether Maynard ever took his show on the road, nor do I know just when he composed his lecture. It could have followed the publicity he received from the Watson article, or it may have been a dozen years earlier when he published his book of poems.

The Maynard tombstone in Evergreen Cemetery, Colorado Springs. Courtesy of Judy Hopkins.

A final bit of serendipity occurred in July 2009 when one evening I received a phone call from a woman in Arizona. Judy Hopkins, it transpired, was the great-granddaughter of May Maynard Miles, Frank Maynard's youngest sister. Judy, like Don and Duane White, has delved deeply into the genealogy of her family. Having learned through the Internet of my interest in Maynard, she phoned to offer further family information about the Maynards, including, among other things, photographs of Flora, diary entries from his sister Nettie, and photocopies of a tribute Frank had written about his mother for a 1925 magazine contest. Of special interest in these materials were some poems, a short one written by Nettie to her fiancé, George Ross, and two by his father. It would seem that the proclivity to compose verse ran strong in the Maynard family.

One of Horace Maynard's poems, "Battle of Cedar Creek," was published (although I don't know where or when), for the copy I received from Judy Hopkins had been photocopied from a book (she does not know the source). Below the title are these words: "By H. Maynard, Co. 'E,' 28th Iowa, Vols. Tune—'Star Spangled Banner.'" In ten stanzas the poem describes this major battle in Virginia's Shenandoah Valley, which was being lost by Union forces until General Sheridan arrived from Winchester and rallied his troops to victory. (A personal note: This battle inspired a more famous poem, Thomas Buchanan Read's "Sheridan's Ride," which my father used to recite from memory, along with "The Ride of Jenny McNeal" and "Charlotte the Frozen Girl," as he and my sister and I would ride pastures.)

Also in the materials sent by Judy Hopkins was a letter Maynard had written to his brother Lon in May 1925. In the letter Maynard tells of a recent illness, myocarditis, that involved inflammation of muscles and membranes surrounding the heart. The symptoms he describes, "a great pain all around my heart," sound like a heart attack. It was brought on, the doctor told him, by rheumatism and strain, so he said, "I see I must find some lighter occupation." He finished the letter a few days later, reporting that the doctor had said that the inflammation was gone and that it had been "a passing attack, with no organic trouble of a chronic nature." The trouble was, however, chronic, and less than a year later, on March 28, 1926, Frank Maynard died at age seventy-three. "Plains Bard and Pioneer of Earliest Cowboy Days Is Dead" was the headline on his obituary in the March 31, 1926, *Denver Post*.

Maynard must have been a spellbinding speaker, with a fount of tales to relate. It's too bad that videotape was not yet available to capture one of his lectures, if he ever gave one, or to preserve the yarns he could tell around a campfire. But even in print his lively prose and verse are more than adequate to transport a modern reader back to the days of the open range.

JIM HOY
from the Flint Hills of Kansas

Acknowledgments

I AM GREATLY INDEBTED to the relatives of Frank Maynard who so generously opened their homes and their file cabinets to me. Had I not met Don White, I would never have known about his great-uncle Frank's book of cowboy poetry—nor, considering its rarity, would hardly anyone else outside the family. My appreciation for the hospitality of Don and Gloria, and that of Duane and Jackie White, is deep. I am pleased that Arlynn Anderson made a detour on his trip from Colorado to Georgia to come by Kansas and share with me the letters, photographs, and especially the memoirs of his great-uncle. My conversations with Gerald Rose were invaluable in obtaining insight into his uncle's post-cowboy life in Colorado Springs. Judy Hopkins, the great-granddaughter of Maynard's youngest sister, May, provided hitherto unknown information about Frank's parents and siblings as well as photographs of Flora Longstreth Maynard.

All photographs, except as noted, have been provided by and used with the permission of the above family members. I am grateful to Susan Brinkman (assistant director of the Center for Great Plains Studies at Emporia State University) and Jason Brinkman (instructor of design at Flint Hills Technical College), who provided technical assistance with the illustrations, and to Megan Flory and Kary Reznicek, students at Emporia State University, who created the maps. I want to thank Pam Bella for permission to include here materials previously published in the *Colorado Springs Gazette*.

I also thank Andy Wilkinson of the Southwest Collection of Texas Tech University for his initial encouragement of this project and for his sound advice. Judith Keeling, Joanna Conrad, Karen Medlin, and Barbara Werden of Texas Tech University Press and Noel Parsons all helped to shepherd it through the publication process. David Stanley's suggestions, based on his considerable expertise in cowboy poetry and western history, strengthened the manuscript significantly. Finally, thanks to my wife, Cathy, for her support, her encouragement, and her good editorial eye.

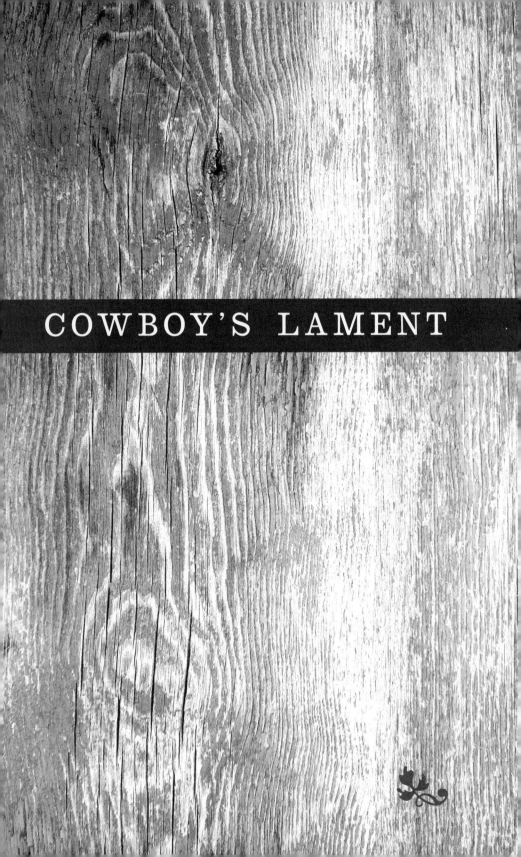

COWBOY'S LAMENT

Frank Maynard, 1904. Courtesy of Arlynn Anderson.

Introduction

A BRIEF LIFE OF
FRANCIS HENRY
MAYNARD

The Years of Adventure

RANCIS HENRY "FRANK" MAYNARD was born December 16, 1853, in Iowa City, Iowa, the second child of Horace and Georgiana Maynard. Two sisters, Mary Annette (Nettie), three years older, and Emma Carrie (Carrie), seven years younger, and one brother, Alonzo (Lon), thirteen years younger, were born in Iowa, while his third sister, Marion Luella (May), eighteen years younger, was born in Kansas.

At sixteen Maynard left home and elementary school to look for adventure, working for three months as a freighter along the Platte River before getting his fill of the rigors of bull whacking. He returned home for a few months, then left Iowa for good in early 1870 to go to Towanda, a small town in Butler County, Kansas, where he lived with a widowed maternal aunt, Martha Cole. The rest of the family followed him to Towanda later that same year, settling in the same general region as J. R. Mead, an Indian trader who was one of the founders of Wichita. After spending his first few months hunting, fishing, and working as a farm hand, Maynard joined his father in hauling freight from the railroad at Emporia to the newly forming city of Wichita.

In the fall of 1871 Maynard, accompanied by his father and half a dozen other men in three wagons, went on his first buffalo hunt in present-day Kingman County. The stated purpose was to acquire winter meat for their families, but Maynard was primarily motivated by his desire for adventure. After enduring a couple of blizzards, in one of which five men in another hunting party froze to death, Maynard's group returned home safely.

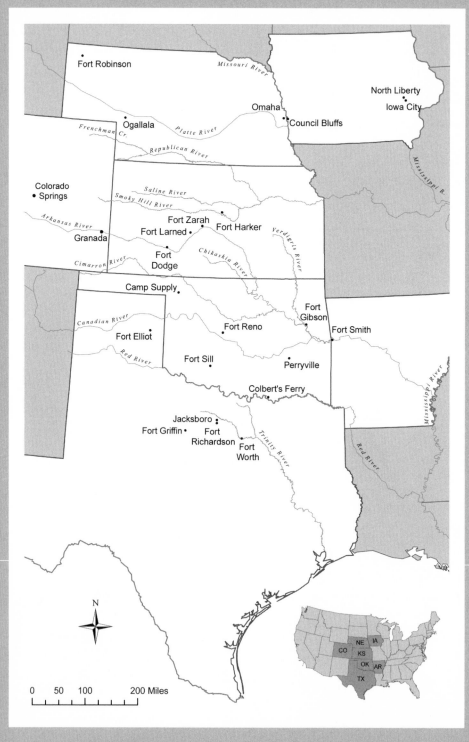

Central and Southern Plains. Map by Kary Reznicek.

In February 1872 Maynard and two companions went to the Gypsum Hills country of what is now Barber County to trade with Indians and hunt buffalo. After trading trinkets, groceries, and dry goods for hides and furs with a party of Osages, the three young men went through the new town of Medicine Lodge on their way to the buffalo range, where they killed enough bison to fill out their load with meat and hides before returning home after their month-long adventure.

In the spring of 1872 Maynard became a cowboy, a following he would pursue until his marriage in the spring of 1881. His first job, from March until early summer 1872, was helping to drive a herd of horses, which had been wintered in Kansas, to Jacksboro, Texas, so that they could be used to deliver a herd of longhorns north to the cow-towns. The horses and cattle were owned by Wiley Robbins, a less than savory character (from Maynard's perspective, at least). One of the cowhands on the drive was Rube Arp, a native Texan who nonetheless befriended the young northerner, the son of a Union veteran, and helped to protect him from threatened harm from others of the crew who were unreconstructed Confederate sympathizers. Among this latter number was a man known to Maynard only as "Slusher," from his habit of slushing down large quantities of rotgut whisky. After some trouble on the trail (which occurred when Maynard followed through on his threat to kill a kicking horse that belonged to Slusher), after a number of lightly veiled references to revenge by Slusher, and after a warning from Rube Arp that the others were planning to kill him, Maynard sneaked away from camp in the middle of the night, taking refuge first at Fort Richardson and then with various farmers and ranchers. After a short stint at breaking horses in Fort Worth, Maynard became ill and started north for home, getting into the Choctaw (or possibly the Chickasaw) Nation before collapsing from fever. After two weeks of being tended to by a kindhearted Choctaw (or Chickasaw) family, Maynard again set forth, this time reaching Perryville, then the terminus of the Missouri, Kansas & Texas Railroad (the Katy) and a hotbed of outlawry, before collapsing again. At Perryville, Maynard was nursed back to partial health by a young man named Thomas Wall. Maynard finally arrived home in early summer 1872 but did not attain full health until autumn.

After some buffalo hunting and a final session of formal schooling during the winter of 1872–73, Maynard took a job in the spring helping to trail a small herd of cattle west from Towanda, where the owner, Jim Graham, had camped while on his way to eastern Colorado. Graham, Maynard, and

Area of Maynard's Activities in Kansas and Indian Territory. Map by Megan Flory.

a young cowboy named John Sullivan drove the herd, while the cook and chuckwagon driver was Dave Rudebaugh, a youngster from Greenwood County who would later become a notorious outlaw and member of Billy the Kid's gang. In fact, he is said to have been the only man of whom Billy was afraid. Rudebaugh's proclivities toward violence became evident on the trip when, in an altercation on the Fourth of July 1873, he beat Graham with his fists, then tried to attack him with an ax. Graham picked up a gun, but both combatants were restrained by Maynard and Sullivan, and the quarrel smoothed over.

Later that month, after Graham had located his cattle on open range near Granada, Colorado, Maynard returned to Dodge City, where he took a job night-herding horses for a hay contractor. That job ended with the hay season in late summer, and Maynard next herded cattle near Great Bend for Peter Moore. There he was able to repay the kindness shown him the previous year by Thomas Wall. When Maynard spotted Wall walking back to Saint Joseph, Missouri, after having lost all his money prospecting in Colorado, he arranged for Wall to hire on as cook for the Moore outfit.

After a brief visit home in mid-December 1873, Maynard again went to work for Moore in February, driving his cattle from the prairies near Hutchinson to the Gypsum Hills near Medicine Lodge, where he then remained as a herder. During that job, which lasted until mid-July 1874, some buffalo hunters from Sun City rousted a gang of horse thieves; some Indians stole some cattle from a cattleman named Evans; John Coon, a young farm boy in the area, was killed by Indians; the local militia at Medicine Lodge attacked a group of Osages; and Peter Moore faked the theft of a number of his own cattle in order to avoid paying a lien. Maynard had trailed the missing cattle from the range to the Chisholm Trail, where their tracks merged with thousands of others, before discovering that the cattle had been taken intentionally. Losing confidence in his employer both for this reason and for late pay, Maynard quit in midsummer and spent the remainder of the season helping to herd and ship range cattle near Great Bend.

During the fall of 1874 Maynard began a year-long job with a cattle owner named Dr. Simmons, herding near Wichita, then moving the stock to winter range in the Gypsum Hills (where Simmons joined a number of other owners in pooling labor and material resources). Following spring roundup, the cattle were fattened on summer grass closer to Wichita and then shipped in the late summer. During this job Maynard had several adventures, including a couple of Indian scares and a couple of standoffs with cattle and horse thieves. He also became ill, but some medicine prescribed by his physician employer soon cured him.

From the fall of 1875 through the spring of 1876 Maynard worked for W. B. Grimes wintering cattle in the Medicine Lodge country. Indians again caused trouble for the cowboys, and after repeated skirmishes in which the cattle-men refused to give over any beef, the Indians set fire to the prairie in an ef-fort to burn the cattlemen out. Those who had been wintering below the line in the Cherokee Outlet were forced to move their herds out of Indian Terri-tory and back into Kansas. That was the winter, by the way, during which Maynard wrote his version of "The Cowboy's Lament."

In April 1876 Maynard headed toward Texas to find employment as a drover. In Indian Territory he met up with a Millett and Mabry herd and was hired by the trail boss, William Lockridge. As they approached Ellsworth, a storm scattered the cattle and those of a following herd owned by Jesse Driskill, whose family was heavily involved in the cattle business. Lock-ridge sent Maynard to the shorthanded Driskill crew to help recover their cattle, some of which had been confiscated by German settlers for damage to crops. In a tense standoff, trail boss Till Driskill and Maynard faced down the homesteaders and ran the cattle back to their herd. The next day Driskill sent Maynard to Ellsworth with a letter, both of them knowing that the young cowboy would be chased by the irate settlers, whom he managed to outrun. Maynard then returned to the Millett and Mabry herd and helped move the cattle onto summer pasture near Kanopolis, where he next took a job with Driskill, herding cattle near Ellsworth during midsummer of 1876.

After encountering more hostility from homesteaders, Maynard decided to move toward less settled country. During the fall of that year he helped to drive a herd of cattle from Wichita to Sun City, then he visited the Grimes headquarters, where he witnessed a shooting between two Mexican cow-boys, before finally moving on west to the Cimarron country south of Dodge City, where he helped to winter cattle for Budd Driskill.

Maynard returned to Towanda after the death of his oldest sister, Nettie, who had died on May 1, 1877, a week after giving birth to a son who sur-vived her only four months. Nettie was married to George Ross, Maynard's old buffalo-hunting and Indian-trading companion. Not long after Nettie's death, Ross disappeared while on a cattle buying trip and was never heard from again. After a few days Maynard returned to Dodge City, where he

Cowboys and cattle on the W. B. Grimes ranch, Oklahoma Territory, 1897. In 1876, the year he wrote "The Cowboy's Lament," Maynard was riding for Grimes in this border region of Kansas and Indian Territory. Photograph by F. M. Steele, courtesy of the Kansas Historical Society.

joined a crew taking cattle to the Sioux at the Red Cloud Agency in Dakota Territory. However, he became sick just north of Ogallala, Nebraska, and had to return to Dodge City. In late summer and fall he herded cattle for Dennis Sheedy near Lakin, then he returned to Dodge City in early November just in time to see City Marshal Ed Masterson get wounded in a gunfight.

Maynard's obituaries mention his service as a deputy sheriff in an unspecified location, although it is most likely that any law enforcement experience he may have had would have been as a posse member or during some special situation. Family tradition links him with Wyatt Earp and some sort of trouble in Dodge City, but there is no documentary evidence of a connection, nor is there any mention of it in his memoirs.

After hunting stray cattle west of Dodge City for a short while in November 1877, Maynard decided to return home to visit old friends. While there he met and fell in love with Flora Longstreth. Flora, however, heeding warnings about wild young cowboys from what Maynard called "meddlesome old ladies," did not at once requite his feelings; in fact, it took him nearly three years to win her affections. So in April 1878 Maynard joined the Driskill crew for spring roundup south of Dodge City.

He quit after only a month, however, to go back to see Flora. Again receiving small encouragement, he headed to Fort Reno, Indian Territory, in July 1878 and got work with a hay contractor. In early September he was recovering from an attack of fever when between 300 and 350 men, women, and children of the Northern Cheyenne tribe left the nearby Cheyenne-Arapaho Agency in their storied attempt to return to the Powder River country. Despite the efforts of thousands of troops and volunteers, the Indians managed to reach northern Nebraska before splitting into two groups. A very few in the smaller party, led by Little Wolf, made it back to Montana, but those in Dull Knife's party were captured and held at Fort Robinson in Nebraska. During an abortive attempt to escape from Fort Robinson in order to avoid being returned to Indian Territory, more than sixty of the Cheyennes were killed. Eventually a reservation in southeastern Montana was granted to the Northern Cheyennes. Maynard's account of the episode is obviously not based on firsthand observation, but he was acquainted with Tom Murray, a young cowboy who was one of the forty settlers killed by the Cheyennes in Kansas. Maynard's poem "The Ranger's Last Ride" was written in tribute to Murray.

*Flora Vienna Longstreth
Maynard, ca. 1900.
Courtesy of Judy
Hopkins.*

Later that winter, while herding cattle near the Cheyenne-Arapaho agency, Maynard helped fight a prairie fire. After another illness, and after partak-
ing of some of the cultural life among the Cheyennes and Arapahos at the
agency, including a chuckaway dance, Maynard returned to Towanda, where
he eventually overcame Flora Longstreth's reluctance to commit herself to
him. They were married on April 24, 1881, and by the late 1880s (1887, according to his obituary) they had moved to Colorado Springs, where they
spent the remainder of their lives. The events in the Maynards' first few years
of marriage are unknown. Their names are not in the 1885 census for Butler
County, but neither does Maynard show up on a Colorado Springs directory
until 1888, at which time he is listed as a carpenter, a trade he followed for the
rest of his working life.

11

Life in Colorado Springs

Just where and when Maynard learned carpentry is not known, but, as is obvious from his memoirs, his was an adaptable nature, one ready to try new ventures. He was responsible, entrusted with cattle herds by their owners, and afraid of neither danger nor difficult work. Maynard is remembered by his nephew, Gerald Rose, as mechanically inclined, good with handwork, and capable with tools. Colorado Springs was the right location for a hard-working, ambitious young man with a new wife, one who encouraged ambition.

Despite his cowboy years of carefree living, Maynard adapted well to settled life in a growing city. His carpentry business seems to have prospered, and his social and professional contacts grew. He joined both the Junior Order of United American Mechanics and the Pikes Peak chapter of Modern Woodmen of America, in which by 1890 he had been elected treasurer ("Excellent Banker"), a position that required a thousand-dollar bond.

Maynard seems to have been nearly as adventuresome in his business dealings as he was as a ranger of the prairies. Fewer than ten years after moving to Colorado Springs he had become a partner in the Buckeye Gold Mining and Milling Company, apparently a speculative venture that held title to five claims about fifteen miles southeast of Cripple Creek. According to a prospectus issued in 1896 for the purpose of selling a hundred thousand shares of stock at a dollar a share, the company owned three contiguous claims—the South Seneca, the Independence, and the Golden Treasure—with assays that varied from $2.00 to $21.50 per ton, while the outcroppings of the nearby Mountain Maid assayed at $3.00 per ton. Touted as their best prospect was the gold- and copper-bearing Mineral Hill claim, located a quarter of a mile southwest of "the celebrated Big Four mine," which was negotiating for the building of a concentrator for extracting gold from the low-grade ore that was prevalent in the area. Prospective investors were enticed by descriptions that pointed out the physical similarity of the terrain of the Buckeye property with that of Cripple Creek and by the promise that the company intended "to push development work as fast as practicable."

No one knows today just how many shares of stock Maynard held in the company, which was capitalized for a million shares and had a quarter of a million dollars in the treasury at the time the prospectus was issued, but his investment was probably sizable, because he is listed on the cover of the prospectus as president of the company. Nor is it known whether the venture

PROSPECTUS

- OF -

The Buckeye Gold Mining and Milling Co.

Incorporated Under the Laws of the State of Colo.

CAPITALIZATION 1,000,000 SHARES.
Par Value $1 Each, Full Paid, Non-assessable.

F. H. MAYNARD,	- -	*President.*
IRA J. MORSE, -	*Vice-Pres. and Treas.*	
JNO. R. TAGGART,	- -	*Secretary.*

Cover of the Buckeye Mining prospectus. Courtesy of Arlynn Anderson.

was profitable, either in producing gold or in selling stock or in unloading the entire company for a capital gain, but if Maynard's poem "Colorado Joy" is any indication, then chances are good that the partners did not get rich. They may, in fact, have been happy if they just broke even.

As late as 1920, when Maynard was well into his sixties, he was apparently still risking venture capital, if a letter found by Arlynn Anderson in the Maynard effects is an accurate indication. Maynard never lived outside Colorado Springs after moving there in the 1880s, but he does mention being in Wichita Falls, near the oil fields being served by the refineries at Grandfield, in 1920. (He was in Oklahoma, in fact, when he learned by letter of his mother's death at age ninety-one.) On March 30 of that year the Sellers-Brown Coffee Company of Saint Louis sent a cover letter for an express shipment of "your regular Peaberry Blend of Coffee" to Pentecost & Maynard, Oil City Cafe, Grandfield, Oklahoma. While he might not have been personally running the restaurant, nevertheless he may very well have invested in a business that, next to a saloon, was guaranteed to be one of the biggest money makers in an oil boom town.

Maynard does not seem to have grown rich, but he certainly did well in his new home and profession. He and Flora also seem to have moved with some frequency during their first years in Colorado Springs, a not uncommon occurrence for members of his profession. Carpenters in general have a tendency, it seems, to build an attractive house for themselves, then sell it and build another, usually moving up the status scale in the process. This apparently was the case with the Maynards, who lived on South Weber Street in their first years in town. By 1890 they had moved to West Kiowa, then in 1894 to North Walnut and in 1898 to Cheyenne Road in the popular Ivywild section of town. Two or three years later they made their final move, deeper into the Ivywild district at 420 Cheyenne Boulevard. Although their house was not one of the area's conspicuous showplaces, it was a well-crafted cottage with a hipped roof and dormer windows and a full porch typical of the district's architecture, which is now considered of historic value. Both Maynard houses in Ivywild are still occupied as of this writing.

This upward mobility in housing was not done solely for the purpose of showing off Maynard's skill at carpentry; it had in it an element of social climbing. Flora Longstreth Maynard, according to her nephew, Gerald Rose, had in common with her sisters a tendency to "put on airs." Rose's mother, Blanche, had been born in Kansas in 1878, shortly after the Longstreth family

Maynard with suitcase, ca. 1920. Courtesy of Arlynn Anderson.

The Maynards' house at 420 Cheyenne Boulevard, built by Frank Maynard ca. 1903 and still occupied over a century later. Photograph, ca. 2005, courtesy of Duane White.

had moved to Towanda from Meigs County, Ohio. She was the youngest of six sisters, eighteen years the junior of Flora, the eldest. Life on a pioneer farmstead was hard, and Rose believes that the Longstreth girls were particularly interested in future husbands whose professions tended toward genteel city life. Flora, the eldest, had not set a good pattern for her sisters in marrying a wild young cowboy, which may well have explained her hesitance in accepting his initial protestations of love. Perhaps Frank's footloose past helps to explain Flora's vanity in their having the biggest car in the family (an Overland) while her sisters' husbands drove Model Ts, or her pride in having one of the first Victrolas in Colorado Springs. "Aunt Flora would brag about that," Rose told me. Flora liked to impress others with her china, her linen, her house, its furnishings.

The Maynards belonged to Trinity Methodist Church in Colorado Springs, even though from 1920 through 1924 Blanche's husband, Forrest Rose, was minister to a much smaller Methodist congregation a couple of miles closer to them. That did not bother his father, Gerald Rose said, but it did irk his mother that her sister had to go to "the big church" instead of the one her husband served. Maynard, Rose told me, led a good Christian life but without outward religious forms; he didn't have to do any pious posturing. "He had a consistent goal: helping people," according to his nephew. It is probably significant that Forrest Rose liked his brother-in-law very much, Blanche less so.

In truth, the Longstreth women, particularly Flora, did not like to be reminded that Frank Maynard had been a rough, tough cowboy in the past. Sometime, probably between 1910 and 1925, he had toyed with the idea of giving public lectures about his adventures, although there is no record of an actual performance. When in 1924 he began to get some notoriety in the local press and even subsequently published his own accounts of outlaws, horse thieves, and lynchings on the plains, he did so, according to Gerald Rose, in the face of the "moderate, unstated resistance of the Longstreth women." But Forrest Rose liked the stories and the attention that his brother-in-law was getting.

Gerald Rose recalls that he always felt a kind of stiffness in relations between his uncle and his aunt. Apparently there was never any definite rupture in their marriage, as one might possibly infer from the final two poems in Maynard's collection, "To My Wife" and the overly sentimental "Come Home." Rather, Rose remembers an ongoing, unarticulated tenseness or

The Winning of the Wild

Come and hear F. H. Maynard in his thrilling and realistic description of life in the Middle West, when the West was young. Reminiscences of life and adventures among the Indians, Outlaws, Cowboys and Settlers of the border.

Incidents tragic, pathetic and humorous, yet always pointing a good moral.

Mr. Maynard was for many years a ranger of the great plains, as hunter and cowboy.

_____Evening____o'clock

At_____

Admission: Adults, 25c; Children, 10c

Poster for Maynard's public presentation, "The Winning of the Wild," ca. 1915. Courtesy of Arlynn Anderson.

reserve. Flora was dominating, especially about the house, and she was vocal, not diplomatic, about her wants and demands, Rose said. She liked indoor, social affairs, while Frank preferred the outdoors. Two photographs survive showing a group of women on a mountain trail up Pikes Peak, mounted on burros, with Frank acting as guide. Another shows a small camp wagon set up in a mountain valley near Steamboat Springs with Frank skinning a deer he has just shot, while another shows Flora working at the back of the wagon. But these occasions must have been rare, for Rose remembers that the little camping wagon was parked and falling apart, never once moved during his many youthful visits to the Maynards. He had the impression that his Uncle Frank may have liked camping, but his Aunt Flora did not. It is not surprising, then, that Frank took refuge in the carpentry workshop behind the house, which he had remodeled from the stable that had once held their carriage horses. Moreover, in his poems and histories he could relive the freedom of his youth.

Despite their differences, however, there seems to have evolved a loving relationship that worked for them. As an exchange of letters in 1904 between Flora and her sister Blanche indicates, Flora had affection for her husband. Blanche had received a letter in which Flora had lamented Frank's extended absence on a construction project in Grand Junction, and in response Blanche noted, "You must be real homesick to see him." Maynard, despite the formality that Gerald Rose noted, was not henpecked. Although he

Frank and Flora Maynard (on the right) with unidentified women on a burro ride up Pikes Peak, 1906. Courtesy of Arlynn Anderson.

19

Maynard skinning a deer on a camping trip near Steamboat Springs, ca. 1900. Courtesy of Arlynn Anderson.

*Flora Maynard cooking at the camping wagon near Steamboat
Springs, ca. 1900. Courtesy of Arlynn Anderson.*

Maynard cooking over a campfire, ca. 1910. Courtesy of Arlynn Anderson.

acquiesced to Flora in most things, especially those relating to the household, he did not do so in a cowed or submissive fashion, according to his nephew. Rather he maintained his dignity through a kind of imperturbability.

With his nephew, however, Maynard was warm and open, especially once he learned that the youngster was interested in working with wood. He would often take Gerald into the shop to show him tools or to make things, or they would go down to the lake below the house to catch fish, happily whiling away the hours until Flora called from the house, wondering what Frank was doing so long in the shop. Gerald Rose, born in 1914, was six years old when his family moved to within a mile of the Maynards in 1920, and his family stayed in Colorado Springs until 1924.

Rose remembers Frank Maynard well because he spent many hours there between the ages of six and ten. "He had more influence on me at that time than my own father," Rose recalled. "Dad was busy, but Uncle Frank was sort of retired and had lots of time to spend with me. I'd go down there every chance I got. My parents would say, 'Don't be bothering Uncle Frank,' but he never indicated in any way that I was a bother. I think now that I was the son he never had." Rose regrets that Maynard didn't live longer so that the two of them could have had even more time together.

He recalls that his uncle was a "damned good carpenter" and furniture repairman who had made a good living at his trade. He remembers Maynard as "a heck of a nice guy, very friendly," who didn't go into detail about his accomplishments, much less brag or boast about them: "He was a remarkable man who didn't have to tell others how remarkable he was." Thus many people, even family members, never found out just how extraordinary he really was.

Maynard's education seems to have stopped shortly after grade school, with only a few months of high school attendance in Iowa and Kansas. Based on the evidence of his writing, he was most likely a reader (Rose recalls that there were quite a few books in the Maynard household, but he remembers with certainty only those on carpentry, which was what he himself was most interested in as a boy), and he was alert to current events. Forrest Rose, who had a college education, as did his wife and others in the Longstreth family, was favorably impressed with Maynard's command of language. Whatever the limits of his formal education, Maynard wrote and spoke well, more than holding his own in conversations and exchanges of ideas. Gerald Rose was surprised when he found out that his uncle wrote verse, even though now he realizes that "poetry fit his quiet nature."

Rose said that his uncle did not talk much about his experiences in the West, but he does remember being shown some of the guns that Maynard had used, one of which was a Winchester rifle in a saddle scabbard. This same gun is now in the possession of a great-nephew, Duane White, who lives in Prairie Village, Kansas. Rose also recalls some two or three Colt revolvers, including one with nickel plating that Maynard said was "pretty, but I wouldn't use it much." It was too fancy for his taste. As far as Rose knows, Maynard never shot or shot at anyone.

One time Maynard gave Rose one of a pair of brass knuckles, telling him "we don't use these anymore." Soon after moving from Colorado Springs to Littleton, when Rose was in either seventh or eighth grade, he took the brass knuckles to school to show to some of his new friends. Someone told a teacher, and he was hauled into the principal's office and his parents were notified, which, given his Methodist-minister father's position in the community, was

Maynard with his Winchester rifle, ca. 1924. Courtesy of Arlynn Anderson.

highly embarrassing. The teacher did not return the knuckles, nor did his father offer to ask for them, so Rose lost his one material memento of his relationship with his uncle.

Remembering the Past

Although Frank Maynard gave up the roving life of a cowboy to win the fair hand of Flora Longstreth, taking up the settled and remunerative life of a carpenter to keep it, he seems never to have lost his sense of being, at heart, a cowboy, still roving the southwestern plains, if only in his mind's eye. He may not have been overly talkative or boastful about his exploits, even to impressionable young boys eager to hang on his every word, and he may not have been a showman such as Buffalo Bill, even if he did at one time develop a public lecture of his reminiscences of adventures "among the Indians, Outlaws, Cowboys and Settlers of the border," but he was nevertheless keen on recording his memories of the old days and on making those memories public.

By 1888, for example, he had written down his recollections of the 1870s, and sometime after that, whether weeks or years is not known, he had paid to have his handwritten account transcribed by a professional typist. No evidence survives to indicate that he explicitly tried to have these memoirs published, but it was this source that he later drew upon in composing "Maynard's Western Tales" for the *Colorado Springs Gazette and Telegraph*.

Maynard had begun to write verses based on his decade of adventure as early as 1876, which is the year that he put new words to "The Bad Girl's Lament," thus turning it into the classic "The Cowboy's Lament." Five poems are included in his unpublished memoirs of 1888, but not "The Cowboy's Lament." Four of these poems are original narratives or lyrics, while the fifth is a two-quatrain dirge that he says was sung over Ed Masterson's grave after the popular marshal of Dodge City was killed in a gunfight.

Sometime not long after the turn of the century Maynard had written enough poems for a collection and was wanting to have them published. He was also writing prose pieces about his experiences on the range. Several of his handwritten manuscripts (most of which are in pencil on lined tablet paper) have word totals listed, indicating his awareness of submission protocol. On April 12, 1907, he wrote to Jack London, sending him copies of his verses and seeking advice on publication. One month to the day later, in a typewritten letter marked "On Board the Snark," London answered, as follows:

> This is in reply to yours of April 12, and will probably be mailed to you from Honolulu. Am sending you herewith the poems, which I have just finished reading.
>
> I thank you for the privilege of letting me see the poems, and I have enjoyed them very much; all of which has nothing to do with the advice I am about to give you. I am going to give you practical advice, which is, namely, that you must never pay any publisher for the privilege of bringing your poems out in book-form. Publish them, by all means, if you can get a publisher to bring them out, with no risk to you. But watch out for the publisher who makes you pay for bringing out the book. Such a publisher is a robber, and will skin you or anybody.
>
> I would give you the same advice concerning the collection of short stories you mention. If I were you, I'd try the magazines with my short stories, before entertaining any thought of bringing them out in book-form.
>
> Regretting my inability to be of more practical assistance to you, Sincerely yours,

London had signed the letter in a hand as firm as his advice, advice which, like most cowboy poets, Maynard was undoubtedly forced to ignore if he wanted to see his work in print.

On November 11, 1911, Maynard brought out *Rhymes of the Range and Trail*, copyrighted but with no publisher or place of publication listed. The paperback booklet was small, about four by seven inches, with nineteen poems included within its twenty-six pages. Maynard's photograph graced the cover just below the title and just above his name: "By F. H. Maynard, An Old-Time Cowboy." A brief preface on the first page dedicated the poems to his fellow plainsmen.

Flora Maynard was probably less than pleased with any public attention that derived from her husband's cowboy poems, although her concern with status may have caused her to react more favorably to his next recorded poetic endeavor. In late 1914, following the German invasion of Belgium, Maynard wrote a poem, "The Night that Follows 'The Day,'" which he published in the *Gazette and Telegraph* on December 21. The poem's subject matter projected the consequences that Germany could expect for its aggression once

A Texas Trip
By F. H. Maynard.

In March, 1872, I had just returned from a hunting, trading trip as related in my last article, when there came an opportunity to go to Texas with a bunch of cow-ponies that had wintered in Kan's where feed was cheap. In our outfit was Reub, Arp a dark, slim young Texan who was "capitan", or foreman, a big back-woodsman from Ark, called Slusher, a gouty gentleman who secured passage in the chuck wagon hoping the trip might benefit his health, and very important, Andrew Jackson of African extraction who drove the chuck-wagon and acted as cook. Last your humble servant. We had 35 saddle horses besides horses for the chuck wagon. We took the eastern (or Baxter Springs) trail across the Indian Territory.

Autograph copy of "A Trip to Texas," pencil on lined tablet paper. Courtesy of Arlynn Anderson.

the allies had been stirred to action, while its title referred to the toast ("Der Tag") reputedly popular with German officers, who anticipated eagerly "the day" when their troops would meet those of England in battle.

A few weeks after the poem had appeared in print, Maynard on a whim sent a copy to Belgium's King Albert. In a letter dated May 9, 1915, he received a reply, handwritten in French and signed by one J. Bergenbery, secretary to the king and queen. A news story about the occurrence, including a translation of the letter and a reprinting of the poem, appeared in the October 3, 1915, *Gazette and Telegraph*. My translation of the letter reads as follows:

> It is with joy that the King has read your kind letter and the poetry that was enclosed. Her majesty was very much touched by the expression of your sentiments and I am pleased to be able to tell you that she has directed me to convey her appreciation to you. Receive, I pray you, sir, the assurance of my distinguished consideration.

It is doubtful that either Flora or Frank was aware of the implications of the subtle shift in pronoun usage in the letter. Certainly the newspaper wasn't, for its published translation maintained the masculine throughout. It would seem that protocol allowed the king to be pleased by Maynard's letter and poem, but it was more the queen's place to direct, through the royal secretary, the response to this American commoner's expression of concern and outrage. Whatever the case, he seemed pleased with the reaction, and Flora most likely was also.

No other evidence from that period exists to suggest any further attempts at writing by Maynard, although the handbill for "The Winning of the Wild" most likely was produced at that time. That he was aware of the potential public interest in his experiences, however, is suggested by the obituary of Buffalo Bill Cody found among his effects, along with an envelope edged in black, postmarked January 22, 1917, containing an engraved card, also edged in black, from Cody's widow and three daughters expressing appreciation for Maynard's kind expressions of sympathy. Maynard had obviously sent a letter or card of sympathy at the time of the great showman's death.

Rediscovery and Local Fame

At the time that Gerald Rose was part of his uncle's life, 1920 through 1924, Frank Maynard was nearly, if not fully, retired. Given what Gerald Rose perceived as the stiff relationship that existed between Maynard and his wife, as well as her complete control over the household and its furnishings, one can imagine that Maynard probably spent much of his time during retirement either in his workshop or among friends in the town. He also seems to have taken an interest in the annual Pikes Peak or Bust rodeo, for it was during the 1923 performance of this well-known show that Elmo Scott Watson, a young journalism instructor from the University of Illinois, discovered the old-time cowpuncher serving as a nightwatchman at the rodeo grounds and learned of his claim of authorship of "The Cowboy's Lament." Maynard had taken the job not for the money, but simply to be near rodeo cowboys, horned cattle, and bucking horses, a reminder of his years as an open-range cowboy. Perhaps Watson might actually have overheard Maynard singing his famous song, then decided to ask the old-timer for an interview. Whatever the circumstances, Watson's article, which appeared in the *Gazette and Telegraph* on January 27, 1924, brought Maynard into the local spotlight and gave him the opportunity to publish some of his prose reminiscences.

Maynard could not have been interviewed by a more appropriate reporter, for Watson, then young and seeking to make a name for himself, later became the most widely read historical feature writer in the country, according to his syndicator, the Western Newspaper Union. Watson, a native of Illinois, had taken a bachelor's degree at Colorado College in 1916, then joined the staff of the *Gazette and Telegraph* for two years before becoming an instructor of journalism at the University of Illinois. While at Illinois (1918–24) he manifested his ambition by writing one book, eight newspaper and magazine articles, and 394 syndicated newspaper features, most of them on western history. This burst of productivity took him to a position at Northwestern, where he remained until 1947. For the next three years he taught at Illinois Wesleyan in Bloomington, which put him closer to the family farm, where he planned eventually to retire. In June 1950, however, he was lured back to the Rocky Mountains as chairman of the journalism faculty at the University of Denver. He died on May 6 of the following year at age fifty-nine.

Watson was a productive writer and an active professional in academic journalism who was also deeply interested in western history, an interest enhanced by his residence in Colorado. He is even reputed to have managed the Colorado Springs rodeo one year (perhaps the year that he wrote about Maynard). He was also, along with Leland Case in Chicago in 1944, a cofounder of Westerners International, the premiere nonacademic interest group in the history of the American West.

Watson's article not only described the genesis and popularity of "The Cowboy's Lament," but it also provided some biographical background about Maynard, listed some of the notorious characters he had encountered, and hinted briefly at some of the exciting adventures he had experienced. Maynard seems to have been ready to take advantage of this opportunity to publish, for fewer than two weeks after Watson's article had appeared, Maynard had written to Watson to express his approval of the story and to seek help in placing an article he proposed to write about the Battle of Adobe Walls, the major confrontation on the southern plains between buffalo hunters and various Indian tribes that had occurred fifty years earlier. He apparently had mentioned to Watson his desire to write and had hoped that Watson could help Maynard get his work picked up by Watson's syndicate, the Western Newspaper Union. Watson, in a letter dated February 8, 1924, offered to query his syndicate on Maynard's behalf but also suggested a more practical possibility: "May I suggest that you write up some stuff, such as you mentioned to me at the time of our interview, and try to sell it to the *Gazette and Telegraph?*" While this approach might not be as lucrative, he said, it would probably be the most likely venue for a series of personal history reminiscences.

Maynard wasted little time in following up on his advantage, for on February 14 he published a poem, "The Passing of the Old Frontier," in the *Gazette and Telegraph,* and shortly thereafter he sent Watson a handwritten copy of his article about Adobe Walls. Watson's reply, on March 11, 1924, might have dampened the powder of a less stalwart plainsman, but instead it seems to have provided just the resolve Maynard needed to set his authorial sights on the possible (that is, on the local rather than the national media). After complimenting Maynard on his poem and asking him to send, at Watson's expense, a copy of *Rhymes of the Range and Trail* to a couple of old-time cowboys in New Mexico and Nevada, Watson got down to cases:

> Now, as to the manuscript you sent me. I believe you would prefer to
> have me be very frank and tell you that I don't believe it is salable in its
> present form rather than for me to say that it is great stuff and tell you
> that I felt confident that I could find a market for you and then not be
> able to do so. So that is what I am saying—my frank opinion is that it
> is not salable in its present form. As I see it, it is much too general in its
> tone and in the facts it contains. But I reckon you are more concerned

with how it can be improved so as to make it salable rather than what's wrong with it now, so I beg to offer this suggestion.

Watson then made not one but two suggestions. The first was to narrow the scope, both spatially and temporally, to the Battle of Adobe Walls itself instead of providing so much background material. His second suggestion, the one followed by Maynard in the published version, "1874 an Epochal Year," was to make it a personal narrative, setting the events of Adobe Walls into those of his own life at the time. Watson closed with the caveat that his critical assessment could be wrong and that he would try to sell Maynard's manuscript unchanged if that is how the old cowboy wanted to try it. He also listed three outdoor magazines that Maynard could send his work to directly, if he wished to do so.

Between the time of his "rediscovery" by Watson in January 1924 and his death a little over two years later (March 29, 1926), Maynard published some five reminiscences in the local paper, all under the title "Maynard's Western Tales." A sixth, in a handwritten copy, was found among his papers. All but the Adobe Walls piece replicate to some degree, but with altered order and added details, episodes in his memoirs.

Watson's article, even though published only in the *Gazette and Telegraph* instead of through one of his syndicated series, seems to have brought Maynard more public attention than had his book of verses. Undoubtedly the article had more readers than had the poems, and it also had the advantage of timing: by the 1920s the nation was growing nostalgic for the Wild West. Among the Maynard papers are sets of correspondence with three men that most likely typify the reaction Maynard received. Two men were old-time cowboys themselves, one of whom had ridden the same range as had Maynard, while the other commented on Maynard's song. The third was of a newer generation, a budding author and avid fan of the Western mystique.

Apparently, soon after the Watson article appeared, a young man living in Colorado Springs contacted Maynard to tell him that his father, R. R. Rea of Liberal, Kansas, had also been a cowboy in the Gypsum Hills near Medicine Lodge in the 1870s. Maynard wrote to Rea and received a reply dated March 11, 1924. Although the two men had not met as open-range cowboys, they did share several acquaintances, among them cowboys Barney O'Connor (who at the time Rea wrote was living near Garden City and active in the Kansas Livestock Association), Bill Dunlap, Jim Temple, Clark Bunton, Tom

Barney O'Connor on his BOC Ranch, Grant County, Kansas, ca. 1900.
Photograph by F. M. Steele, courtesy of David and Carolyn Meyer.

Cowboys in Wichita, 1876. Clockwise from lower right: Clark Bunton, Charley Green, Cy Davidson, Jim Temple, Frank Maynard. Courtesy of Arlynn Anderson.

Murray, John Mosely, Frank McAlester, and Cy Davidson, along with cattle-men Grimes, Quinlan, and Drum. Rea also mentioned several other cow-boys and cattlemen: J. R. Mead, L. C. Faris, Lou Parker, Updegraff, Matt Frost, Beach, Bill Nicholson, Bill McMilon, Hackney, and Charley Rankin. And he told how Enos Mosely, one of his fellow cowboys, was shot by a Texan who mistakenly believed that his brother had been killed by Mosely. Rea closed his letter by promising to meet with Maynard when he came out to Colorado Springs to visit his son. One can only imagine the wonderful tales that must have been told if indeed the two men got together.

The second old-timer to write to Maynard, on April 25, 1924, was E. D. Baker of McGill, Nevada, one of the two men (the other was James Gill) to whom Maynard had sent a copy of his book of poems, as requested by Elmo Scott Watson. In response to Maynard's communication, Baker made the following lengthy and imaginatively spelled and punctuated typewritten re-sponse, which I reprint here in full and in its original form for its historical value, for its ingenuous but accurate commentary on the way that folksongs are transmitted, and, not least, for its considerable, if rough-hewn, charm:

Dear Sir:

Yours of March 18, to hand in due time, but I have neglected answer-ing it, so long, that I am ashamed to write now; But will try and do the best I can, byt I fear that will be very little, as I had no schooling at all, and am unable to compose, punctuate, or spell. so I hope you will over look the same. I was more than pleased to reseave a letter from you as I am all wase glad to hear from any old time, especualy, old Cow Punch-ers. As it brings back memories of days gone by; days that I remember with moisened eyes and melting heart; and your little booklet of your poems and song struck a cord in my heart as nothing elce could of done. For it brought back memories of days and places and old timers that I knew when the west was young and filled with men that was men. The trail of Texas and of old Dodge City, days gives me a sure anough thrill, and I hope I will not live long anough to for get them. My hat is off to the van guards. I made my first trip to Texas in 1876, and made several trips north in the next few following years, with cattle, and being only a kid I was the day rangler, and say! I had some sport chaseing Antilope and shooting at them with my pistol and some times I would go to far and by the time I got back to my horses they would be scatered all over the land scape and before I would get them rounded up, and get to where the Hurd was camped, it would be dark and they had no fresh horses to go on first guard with, and say, maby the boss wouldent rave some, he finley fired me, but the punchers wouldent stand for it, they wanted me to stick, so I could sing to them; I never could sing much, but I could skin most of them, you know how the average puncher could sing, well as soon as we had chuck, and the boys had rolled out their beds, they would say; well Kid, sing "Sam Bass" or "the "key Hole In The Door" or "The Cow Boys Lament" etc. So you are the author of "The Rangers Lament", I have often wondered who wrote it, I knew the original, "The H——S, lament, long before I heard the parody, and used to sing it to the boys, and one night, in a dance hall; I heard a girl sing the parody. And I sure went after her and learned it, and the next night, in camp, I sang it to the boys, and they near went nuts. There was an other cowboy song I heard once, and didnot get a chance to learn it, and I have been sory every since, as I would liked to know it, maby you know it, and if so I would apreciate it very much if you would write it off for me; it is a parody on the old song that goes like this,

> *Last night as I layed on my pillow*
> *Last night as I lade on my bed*
> *Last night as I layed on my pillow*
> *I dreamed that my Bonnie was dead.*

It has the same tune and the first verse, as near as I remember it, goes like this.

> *Last night as I lay on the prairie*
> *Looking up at the stars in the sky*
> *I wondered if ever a cow boy*
> *Would get to the sweet by and by.*

I never attempt to sing any more, but I like to have some of the old favorites. I do a great deal of resiteing for the diferent lodges at smokers and socals and card parties, etc. I went to a smoker, last month, given by the Masons, at Ely Nevada, and resited eight long poems, all pertaining to the old west, so you see if I keep that up, I will run out of stuff, so I am all wase glad to get hold of stuff like your book, that you sent me, contains, for that is the only kind of stuff I memorise.

I reseaved the coppy of the Colorado Springs Gazette, thet Mr. Watson sent allso a copy of the song "the cow boys lament". Say I memorised a song or poem years ago, intitled "on the trail from a punchers point of view" that I think is a dandy, for it tells all about it, I thaught you might like to have a coppy of it, if so let me know and I will write it off for you, the best I can.

Well as you ask for some information, on this country, I will indever to tell you all there is here, and that is very little, for it is a desert pure and simple. The Nevada Consolidated Copper Co, has all there is here, it consistes of a concentrator, which has a copasity of 15,000, tons of ore per day, and a smelter. The mines are located, about 25 miles from here, and they hall the ore down on trains, as there is no water there to treate the ore, as it takes about five tons of water to one ton of ore, so you see it takes some water. They have all the water from duck creek, bird creek berrie creek, and a repumping sistem, that handles 15,000, galons per minuit. so by that they have suficent water. But oweing to the light fall of snow in the mountains, they are expecting a shortage of water this sumer.

The County Seat, is 15 miles from here, it is oneley a small place, in fact Nevada is sparsley settled all over. I put in four years around Rhyolite, which is situated in the Bull Frog district, and about twenty miles from Death Valley; and beleave me that is some desert.

Yes you have been some buisey yourself since you quit the cow range. I think you fortinate to learn a trade; I wish I had learned something besides what I did; but I guess it is human nature to go against the least resistence. I got broke in a small inland town, and had every thing in soke except my six shooter, and a saloon keeper ofered me a job tending bar, so I took him up and that was the starter of my disapated carear. I soon learned to deal the games and of a consiquence I followed the vocation of saloon keeper and gambler all my life untill I came here, and seeing the finish of that buisness in sight, I went to work for the Nev C C Co, and have worked for them for 14 years. I was in Cripple Creek in the spring of 1894.

Well I dont know of any think to write that would be of interest to you, so I will close for this time, thanking you again for the book, and

hopeing to hear from you again in the near future, and again apoligise-
ing for poor spelling and punctuations,
   I am yours truley
   E. D. Baker

Of particular interest in Baker's letter are his memories of life on the trail,
which in their detail match the authenticity of Maynard's own memoirs.
Moreover, his accounts of reciting poetry and singing around the campfire
for entertainment and of how he first learned the words to "The Cowboy's
Lament" provide a firsthand account of oral transmission that adds to that
given by Maynard himself.

Whether Maynard was able to supply the words to "The Grand Roundup"
or any additional poems for Baker to recite, I do not know, but he did write
back and apparently ask for copies of some of Baker's poems. After a number
of months had elapsed, Baker wrote back on January 13, 1925, and sent copies
of eight narrative poems to Maynard. He also mentioned the names of ten
others, including two of Robert W. Service's most popular, "The Shooting of
Dan McGrew" and "The Cremation of Sam McGee." How many, if any, of
Baker's poems were original is hard to say.

Rea and Baker enjoyed sharing memories of old times with Maynard, but
Joe E. Milner of Portland, Oregon, was more interested in gathering information about the sensationalized Wild West of popular culture. Milner, the
grandson of "California Joe" Milner, sent at least ten letters between August
30, 1925, and February 5, 1926, most of them entreating Maynard for "stories"
of famous lawmen, outlaws, and gunfights at old Dodge City. (Milner, by the
way, did publish, in 1935, a biography of his grandfather. See Bibliography.) In
his first letter, enthusiasm bubbling, Milner styled himself "one of the biggest
cranks on Frontier History that you ever knew." And, although his intentions
were to write only "true and authentic stories and try to stick to facts and
truth," eschewing the romantic and fanciful, he was obviously both capti-
vated by the romantic and fanciful myth of the Wild West and eager to add
to it. For example, he wanted "real facts" about gunfights in Dodge City that
had not only occurred in other cowtowns, but that he had dated several years
before they actually transpired. He also misnamed some "famous gunmen,"
such as giving "Rowdy Joe" Lowe the new surname of Hunt.

Maynard's role in Milner's plan was to provide firsthand accounts of
cow-town violence, which Milner would then write into "stories" to sell to

Joe Milner, ca. 1925. Courtesy of Arlynn Anderson.

magazines, never mind that Maynard was himself trying to publish his own work. Luckily for Milner, Maynard suffered neither from selfishness nor an inflated ego, and he freely corresponded with the younger writer. In a letter of October 9, 1925, Milner thanked Maynard for the information he had sent, which included a newspaper article about Bat Masterson that Maynard had saved. In this letter, as in later correspondence, Milner offered to return any loaned materials to Maynard via registered mail with the contents insured for a hundred dollars, a not inconsiderable sum for the times. He also offered to send copies of what he considered rare photographs of Western personages as a gesture of appreciation for Maynard's generosity. One such photograph, of eight members of the Dodge City constabulary, including Wyatt Earp, Luke Short, and Bat Masterson, Milner identifies as having been taken in 1871 when it was actually made in 1883. Among specific questions Milner put to Maynard were how many men had been shot in Dodge City and how many were buried on Boot Hill. He also asked about two incidents said to have occurred in 1868 (four years after Fort Dodge was established, and four years before Dodge City was platted). One, obviously wrong, was about a shooting in Tom Sherman's dance hall in which five men had been killed, one-third of the total supposedly killed in that one evening by a vigilante group called the "regulators." The other incident involved Nellie Rivers, a dance-hall girl whose loose talk had caused five men to be killed. As a result, a kangaroo court in Handsome Harry's saloon sentenced her to be hanged, but Harry and Fancy Pat Monahan spirited her out of town. Both these tales had been told to Milner by "a man who was in Dodge City in 1868" and, to Milner's credit, he had "always wanted to get the story verified." Interestingly, Milner refers to E. D. Baker, with whom he had been corresponding for two years, as "my good friend" but then states in the next sentence that he had never met him. As a researcher who relies on the kindness of old-timers myself, I cannot completely fault Milner for his enthusiasm, although his moments of credulousness seem excessive, to say the least.

On December 8, 1925, Maynard's brother-in-law, Methodist missionary Oscar Huddleston, sent a postcard telling Milner that Maynard had been sick but wanted to send some materials that he did not want to get lost. Maynard himself added a line advising Milner to contact old-timer H. M. Bell at Dodge City for "possible data." Milner, who had been in Lewiston, Idaho, for a few weeks, responded eagerly on December 15, promising to take special care of any items received and to return them by registered, insured mail. As of December 29 Milner had not yet received the promised material, so he wrote again, fearful that his earlier letter might have been lost in the Christmas rush. He repeated his desire to write a book about Dodge City, if he could get enough stories from the "good Old Timers" who saw the cowboy capital in its "Palmy Days." "There has [sic] been so many outreageous [sic] stories written on Dodge City, that I want my story to be as true and authentic as can be gotten, at this late day."

On January 13, 1926, Milner received a shipment of books from Maynard and immediately wrote a letter of thanks, mentioning in the process that H. M. Bell had not yet responded to his query and that another Dodge City history correspondent, O. S. Clark of Attica, Indiana, had told him that Robert Wright's book about Dodge City was to be reprinted. He also mentions a recently deceased neighbor, Harry S. Young, who had lived in Dodge City when "it was in its glory." Young had written a rather sensational book, *Hard Knocks*, about his experiences there.

Two days later Milner received a "most interesting long letter" from Maynard, who was suffering from what would be his final illness. This letter was apparently filled with just the sort of firsthand information that Milner had been craving, according to his response to it: "Your letter certainly has a historical ring to it, and contains so much of information that I want. I have for several years been trying to gather data and truth about Dodge City and its famous characters, to put into a book. If I succeed in doing this, I will certainly give you special mention and put a long chapter or more if I can, giving your experience and information."

Milner then immediately segued into a series of questions about the gunfight in Rowdy Joe Hunt's [sic] saloon (was it in Newton or Dodge City?) and a fight between Texas and Kansas cowboys in Newton in which fourteen men were killed. This latter story, included in Harry Young's book *Hard Knocks*, had been contradicted by so many other sources that even Milner had grown doubtful about its authenticity: "I rather think and believe Mr. Young was a little overdrawn in this article, also several other articles which have been contradicted by old time cowboys who have written to me and said they never heard of some of the articles which are in Mr. Young's book." Milner closed this letter by expressing concern for Maynard's health and suggesting that perhaps the high altitude of Colorado Springs might not be good for his heart.

Exactly one week later Milner wrote to Maynard to say that he had mailed back his "valuable papers" and book, but was keeping the "rare newspaper with the article about Bat Masterson." He expressed thanks for the interest Maynard had shown and the help he had given and wished him "a speedy recovery."

The last letter from Milner among Maynard's papers was dated February 5, 1926, and contains a handwritten list of more than eighty historical photographs that he had collected and that the curator of the Oregon Historical Society had urged him to donate to the museum. Included in the letter (with a clearly stated caveat not to let anyone make copies of them) were a number of these photographs, including Rowdy Joe, Diamond Dick, Charlie Siringo, and "Green [sic] River" Tom Smith, marshal of Abilene, Kansas, offered in appreciation for "your many favors in sending me such rare historical writings," which he promised to care for and return in a few days. Toward the end of his letter, Milner makes the following observations:

Your articles are very interesting and certainly have the historical ring to them. I only wish I was as an expressive writer as you are, and had the given talent as a writer that you are. I could make a fortune in writing stories pretaining [sic] to the Old West. There is not a doubt in the world, but a book written by you would be a big success. You could string it out to some length by writing of the famous characters of whom you knew and came into contact with, in your life's experience. You could easily write a couple of thousand words a day for a month, that would make a book of 60,000 words. Well my friend I will close for this time, and I do hope this letter finds you improved in health.

I believe that the writings that Milner refers to in this letter are copies of Maynard's "Western Tales," not unpublished materials. And while Maynard might not have been able to "make a fortune" writing western tales, there is no doubt that Milner was correct in his assessment of Maynard as an expressive and talented writer—certainly a far better stylist than Milner, and better, too, than many others who tried to re-create the Wild West. In fact, Maynard wrote very well indeed when one considerers that his education ended after only a few years of elementary school. In general his prose exhibits clear syntax, good grammar and spelling, and diction only slightly marred by an occasional Victorian flourish of "high" style.

Like many of the cowboys spoken of by J. Frank Dobie in his 1950 introduction to Charlie Siringo's *A Texas Cowboy, or Fifteen Years on the Hurricane Deck of a Spanish Pony,* Maynard must have been an inveterate reader. He makes direct allusions to Poe and Shakespeare, he corresponded with Jack London, and his poetry shows the influence of popular poets of the day, such as Rudyard Kipling and Robert W. Service. His prose is generally straightforward, and while not as boisterous as Siringo's, neither is it as polished as that found in *The Log of a Cowboy* or *We Pointed Them North.* Andy Adams was, after all, a professional writer, as was Helena Huntington Smith, who co-wrote Teddy Blue Abbott's memoirs.

Maynard's memoir, like Siringo's but unlike the writings of Abbott and Adams, was composed within a few years after his days as a cowboy, not decades later. Adams's novel, published in 1903, tells of a trail drive from Texas to Montana in 1882, while Teddy Blue's recollections, primarily from 1879 and the 1880s, were published in 1939. Siringo's book, on the other hand, first came out in limited numbers in 1885, with a more widely distributed edition issued the following year. Maynard's account of his adventures in the 1870s was written in 1888; one wonders if he might not have been inspired to write his own story by Siringo's book.

Both Siringo and Maynard were aware of the popular image of the cowboy as it was manifested in dime novels and Buffalo Bill Cody's Wild West, and neither writer shies away from accenting some of the more exciting events he experienced. Like all memoirists, Maynard had to choose from his experiences for his topics, in both prose and poetry. Although his recollections include many mundane details of cowboy life, his story, if limited to these details, would have had limited appeal for the general reader. Accounts of chasing outlaws, being chased by irate homesteaders, gunfights, and other such sensational occurrences would, on the other hand, have had much greater popular appeal. For the most part, however, Maynard eschews the excesses of the overly romanticized and sensationalized Wild West depicted by popular culture.

It is likely that Helena Huntington Smith smoothed off some of Teddy Blue's rough edges and thus may be responsible for the lack of overt racism in Abbott that one finds in Maynard, Adams, and Siringo. While jarring to the ears of today's readers, such terms as "greaser" and "darky" would not have offended the majority of Maynard's contemporaries. His characterization of Indians as savages, Mexicans as vengeful, and African Americans as speaking in minstrel-show dialect are consonant with the commonly held, if biased, assumptions of his times.

Unfortunately for Maynard, back in the early twentieth century old-time cowboys with good stories to tell were a dime a dozen: there was little market for memoirs such as his. Today, however, a century later on, firsthand accounts of daily life and exciting times on the southwestern plains of the 1870s are a rare commodity. Fortunately for us, we can vicariously experience those times through the memoirs of Frank Maynard, which are printed on the following pages just as he wrote them in 1888.

Part 1
The Recollections
of F. H. Maynard

BEING THE ADVENTURES OF
FRANK MAYNARD ON THE
SOUTHWESTERN PLAINS,
1870–1880

*Reminiscences of wild life and adventure among the cowboys,
outlaws, and Indians of the southwestern border, by F. H.
Maynard, an old-time cowboy. To those that have gathered
around the same campfires, who have faced the same wild
storms, and who have shared the same wild adventures, this
volume is affectionately dedicated.*

Preface

It is not to strive to win the applause of the public nor with any idea of winning bright laurels of fame that the author presents this little volume, but
knowing that one of the greatest pleasures of bordermen is, when gathered
around the campfire, or wherever met, to recount the trials and adventures
of bygone days, the object has been to present a plain, unvarnished narration
of facts as they occurred, many of them under the Author's own eyes.

While there might be much to criticize in these pages, if viewed with a
critic's eye, it is earnestly hoped that they may find a warm appreciation in
the hearts of those to whom they are dedicated.

THE AUTHOR

*Facing: Frank Maynard at twenty-three, Wichita, 1876.
Courtesy of Arlynn Anderson.*

Chapter 1

I WAS BORN ON THE sixteenth day of December, 1853, in Iowa City, Iowa, close by the banks of the river that bears the same name.

Among my earliest recollections is that of starting to school at the Third Ward School in the North part of the city. The school was presided over by one, Professor Wells. One of my most distinct recollections of this gentleman is of being led around the room by him with a pair of tongs clasped on my nose, as a punishment for some trifling misdemeanor on my part. I did not remain long in this school, for it was soon after I made my debut as a student that the great financial crash of '57 and '58 engulfed the country. My father, who was a retail grocery man, was among the unfortunates who lost their all in the terrible vortex of ruin.

I used to delight in spending my leisure hours in the old grocery, on account of the nuts and candy and other dainties that often fell to my lot. In the rear of the store was quite a large wareroom, in which the bulkier articles were stored. On one occasion, while in this room, my attention was attracted to a faucet and a large hogshead of Orleans molasses. Prompted by curiosity I turned the faucet, and immediately a flood of sweetness came pouring out on the floor. In alarm I fled through the backdoor and never stopped until I reached home. Imagine my father's feelings when he opened the door and found the floor completely covered with molasses. I will drop a curtain upon the scene that followed when he next had the pleasure of meeting me.

After my father's failure, he moved from our pleasant home in the city, to a small village about eight miles north, where he succeeded in renting a small cottage. Then the poor man managed by teaching district schools in the winter and toiling among the farmers through the summer, to provide for the wants of his little family. This was during the good (?) ol' days of Buchanan's administration, when the wages for a good harvest hand was fifty cents per day. It was not long until the Civil War broke out. How well I remember how anxiously my father watched the course of events. Soon came Lincoln's call for volunteers. One day my father returned from the city, and I saw that his face wore a grayer and sterner expression than usual. As he met my mother at the door, he said, "Georgia, I've enlisted." "Oh, Horace," was all the poor woman could say, as she clung to him while her eyes filled with tears. He had joined the 28th regiment of Iowa Volunteer Infantry, and with other regiments, they were stationed at Camp Pope, in the suburbs of Iowa City, where they were drilled preparatory to going into active service. I had quite a martial turn, and spent a great deal of time drilling with a wooden gun; and was never so delighted as when permitted to visit my father at the "barracks." I was always making unfortunate blunders. On one occasion while at the barracks on a very hot day, I wanted a drink of water, and seeing what I supposed was water in a bucket I dipped in a tin cup and took a large swallow. Imagine my disgust when I discovered it was lard, which being melted had the appearance of being water. During father's absence I attended school winters and found employment among the farmers in summer. Many were the quarrels among the schoolboys on account of political differences, and many the hard fought battles. In these I received scars which I will carry to my grave, for even in loyal Iowa the sons of the "Knights of the Golden Circle" were taught to hate anything loyal, and a word of rejoicing over a Union victory was often sufficient cause to bring about a battle, where nature's weapons were freely used. When Lincoln and Douglas were running for president, in my ignorance, I would sometimes call out to the passers by, "Hurray for Douglas." My mother hearing me one day, said, "Frank, if I hear you say that again I will wash your mouth with soap suds." I soon forgot myself, and my mother was as good as her word. I give this incident merely as an instance of her intense loyalty.

At the close of the war father returned in very poor health; in fact, he took to his bed, where he remained for about a year. In the meantime he had purchased a small farm about six miles north of the city where we were living when he returned from the war. He was only just able to be about after his long illness, when one Sabbath he, in company with my eldest sister, went to North Liberty, a village about two miles away, to attend church. During their absence our house caught fire and burned to the ground with nearly all its contents.

Nothing daunted by all these streaks of bad luck my father ventured into a timbered land speculation, which proved so successful that he was able to pay off some old debts that had hung over him since the mercantile failure and have a few hundred dollars left. Time passed on with little happening worthy of note until the autumn of '69, when I was nearly sixteen years of age. At this time my oldest sister and myself set up housekeeping in Iowa City with the intention of attending school. For a long time I had been reading glowing accounts of the wonderful wealth and the exciting adventures in the "Wild West," and had often expressed the desire to go and see for myself; but my parents thought I was too young and had better wait awhile. I had saved a small sum of money from my summer's wages, and I secretly determined to start west at the first favorable opportunity. I had not long to wait, for one Friday evening my sister went home to remain until Monday morning. Now was my time, so purchasing a valise I packed my little outfit of clothing, etc., and wrote a few lines to my sister. They ran about as follows:

My dear sister: —E're you see this I will be hundreds of miles away. Tell the folks not to worry about me for I am going to try to do the best I can for myself. Good-bye. Frank.

Pinning this note to the table, I hastened to the "Rock Island" depot, where I purchased a ticket and boarded the first train for Omaha. Arriving at Council Bluffs I had to transfer about one mile by stage over to Omaha as the river was not yet bridged at that point. The coach was so crowded that I was obliged to take a seat on top. I found a bitter cold wind blowing from the Northwest, and great cakes of ice were flowing down the Missouri, which was crossed by ferry. I thought I would freeze and began to think I had made a foolish break. However, I determined not to yield to discouragement on such short notice. I found a hotel kept by some old friends where I remained three days, when I found some men who were freighting to a point on the Platte River. I hired to them to drive a mule team, and to work on the ranch when we reached our destination. I suffered considerably with a cold on those bleak prairies, and more than once wished I was safe at home with my kind parents who I knew would be grieving over my escapade. Between two and three months had elapsed when I resolved to "Arise and go to my father." In the meantime my father had moved into the city, and was living in the house from whence I had taken my flight.

It was on a Sabbath day, and a bitter cold one, when I arrived at my father's door. I stood outside for some time with palpitating heart hardly knowing what kind of reception to expect. I finally mustered courage to rap, when my sister came and opened the door. Her first exclamation was, "Kill the prodigal. The calf has returned." I found them all overjoyed to see me. I had to bear a great deal of twitting from some of my old schoolmates. Others were very kind to me, and seemed to understand and appreciate the spirit of adventure that had led me astray. Among these were two sisters, Misses May and Emma Wilson, whom I will ever hold in grateful remembrance, and to whose gentle and refining influence I owe much, for in the wild stormy years that followed I kept up a correspondence with them that was a wonderful help to me when temptations gathered thickest. It was near the beginning of the new year, '70, when I arrived at home, and I started to school almost immediately. The longing for adventure was not yet dead, and I fear the wild west held more charms for me than my studies. However, the winter passed very pleasantly, for there was no end to parties among the young people, and yet there came the rub. I was poor, and many of my companions were the sons and daughters of wealthy parents. Although they treated me kindly and I had many friends, I still felt my poverty keenly, and by the time spring had rolled around I had resolved to go west again, this time with my parents' consent.

So on the fourth day of April, 1870, I started for Butler County, Kansas, where my mother had two sisters living. As the train which carried me away passed the schoolhouse, my teacher and schoolmates were out en masse, waving me a good-bye. They soon faded from my vision, and although nearly twenty years have passed I have never met but two of them since. Arriving in Kansas I found a comparatively new country, nearly all the settlers living in rude log cabins or houses built of sod. I refer particularly to that part of Kansas where my relatives were living, Butler and adjacent counties.

My first summer was passed there quietly enough, part of the time being employed among the settlers, and when I failed to find other employment I spent most of my time in hunting and fishing, being passionately fond of these pursuits.

In the fall my father emigrated with his family, arriving in Butler County in November. During the following winter father and I engaged in freighting from Emporia to Wichita. The latter place was just beginning to build, and Emporia was the nearest railroad point, being the terminus of the Atchison, Topeka and the Santa Fe road, nearly 100 miles northeast of Wichita.

We camped out during the most severe winter weather, sometimes awaking in the morning to find our blankets covered with snow. Often we would have plenty of company, there being great numbers of freighters on the road who would make for the same camping ground. Many of them were freighting into the Indian territory to the various military posts and Indian agencies.

Here I met many typical frontiersmen, light, wiry fellows. Some of them clad in buckskin, and nearly all wearing broad-brimmed sombreros, and carrying the inevitable six-shooter. It was a hard, rough life, but nevertheless I found much enjoyment in it. The new scenes, the excitement, and bustle peculiar to new towns in the West all had their charms for me.

In the spring of '71 the "Santa Fe" road was extended westward, being completed as far as Newton, if I remember rightly, sometime in June. In the meantime father had taken a homestead near Towanda, a small town in Butler County, while I still followed freighting. I would load at the terminus of the road and deliver the freight to the nearest town beyond. When the road reached Newton there were thousands of Texas cattle in the vicinity awaiting shipment. As far as the eye could see in any direction there were vast herds grazing, and it required a great many men to handle such numbers of cattle. Here it was that I first made the acquaintance of the Texas cowboy in all his glory. It was no uncommon thing to see them leaving Newton filled with bad whiskey, mounted on a fleet footed mustang with the bridle rein hanging loosely on the pony's neck, a six-shooter in each hand, firing at random and yelling like Comanche Indians. Sometimes they would be followed by the city marshal or his deputies, brought back and fined for their misdemeanor.

During the summer of '71 there were many shooting affrays, and many a man died in Newton with his boots on. Need we wonder at this when we consider it was the headquarters for great numbers of gamblers and prostitutes, besides the railroaders who were employed in the construction of the AT&SF Road. In addition to these was the small army of cowboys, made up of almost every grade and nationality; among them were college graduates, men who were fitted by education for almost any position in life, yet who had, for reasons best known to themselves, chosen the wild life they were following. There were Mexican "Greasers," with their fierce revengeful natures, half-breed Indians, men from the backwoods of "Arkansaw" and the frontiers of Texas; in fact they were from everywhere, and while there were many brave whole-souled fellows among them, there were many who were just the opposite. It was no uncommon thing for a man to ride into a saloon and call for the drinks, the call being emphasized by the click of a pistol.

Any old settlers will remember the terrible fights which took place in "Rowdy Joe's" dance hall. It was between the cowboys and the railroaders, and in it there were eleven men killed or badly wounded.

Today Newton is a peaceful city. Schoolhouses and churches have taken the place of the dance hall and the gambling hell, and where the longhorned cattle fed and fattened the farmer feeds his shorthorns, and comfortable homes may be seen in any direction.

Chapter 2

A T THE TIME I ARRIVED IN KANSAS the whole western part of the state was literally alive with buffaloes, and it had long been my ambition to indulge in a buffalo hunt. In the autumn of '71 this ambition was gratified. My father, a Mr. Richards and myself, loaded our "traps" into a wagon and accompanied by three other wagons, with about the same number of men to each wagon, pulled for the buffalo range. After about three days drive we arrived at a point on the South Ninnescah River, not far above where the flourishing city of Kingman now stands. Here we saw our first buffaloes, but it was late in the evening so we could not do very much hunting. However, Mr. Richards and myself took our guns and sallied forth to see what we could do. The buffaloes we had first sighted were too far away to think of reaching them that day, but as we wandered along and raised the top of a little knoll we discovered two dark objects lying stretched out on a smooth grassy plain in front of us. We journeyed on towards them and saw that they were buffaloes. We approached within 75 yards of them, and they lay so still that I began to think that they were dead, but suddenly they arose and shook their huge frames and glared at us through their tangled manes as much as to say, "What means this intrusion?" I frankly confess that I was considerably startled. Turning to Mr. Richards, I said, "Shall I shoot?" Before he had time to reply they turned and went galloping across the prairie. By the time we were ready to shoot they were so far away that our shots had no effect. I secretly determined to do better the next time.

In the morning I started out by myself. I had not gone very far when I spied a large bull quietly grazing in a little nook among the hills. Taking advantage of the ground and the wind current I crawled within about 100 yards of him, where I took a position in a small "buffalo wallow." I was armed with a sixteen-shooting Henry rifle. Taking deliberate aim behind the shoulder I fired. My shot struck a little too far back to bring him down, and not seeing where it came from, the huge beast happened to take his flight directly towards me. I was somewhat alarmed but I poured shot after shot into him. He finally caught sight of me, and shaking his great head in his fury he charged right for me. At this point I heard the crack of a rifle to my left, and an instant later the heavy thud of a ball hitting the buffalo. It caused him to stop and wheel around, broad side to me, I took advantage of this and fired two or three more shots into him in rapid succession, while once more I heard the rifle to my left. Soon the buffalo began to sway to and fro, and then sank to the ground, gave one or two convulsive shudders, and the monarch of the prairie was dead. Then Mr. Richards, who had fired the two shots at my left, approached and we proceeded to skin our game. During this operation we discovered no less than fourteen bullet wounds. This will give the reader some idea of the buffalo's wonderful tenacity of life when wounded and enraged. Since then I have often killed them with one shot, but to do so one must know just where to aim. The most vulnerable point is just behind the shoulder or at the butt of the ear.

On the same day that I had the above mentioned adventure I met with another of quite a startling nature. I was on my way down the South Ninnescah River towards camp, when I spied a large yearling buffalo coming down from the hills at a break-neck speed. It was headed for the river, and its course would lead it about one hundred yards in front of me. I quickly dropped flat on the ground, and when it came opposite took the best aim I could, considering its rapid motion, and fired. I heard the bullet strike plainly, but my game kept on its course and crossed the river, which here was quite shallow. It had run probably a quarter of a mile when to my gratification I saw it fall, and lie stretched out on its side. I started at once, and not heeding the river splashed right through, and then boldly up to the prostrate animal. I was perhaps within three yards of it, when it suddenly sprang to its feet and made for me with wonderful rapidity. Jumping quickly to one side I was nearly in a position to fire when it struck my gun, knocking it out of my hands and sending it end over end through the air. As soon as the buffalo could turn it came back at me. I pulled a Colt's six-shooter from my belt and fired right in its face. So close was it that the powder burned and blackened all around the wound. The buffalo dropped dead in the twinkling of an eye. I felt proud over my success, but I have ever since been cautious about dead buffaloes, whether large or small.

On this my first buffalo expedition I killed five of them. Later in the fall I went on another hunt. This time our company went further out on the plains to the head waters of Elm Creek, a tributary of the Medicine Lodge, in what is now Barber County, Kansas. Between Wichita and Elm Creek is a stretch of prairie eighty miles in extent, with no timber, and hunting parties depend on buffalo chips a great deal for fuel. In wet or snowy weather they are very poor dependence, as they become so saturated that they will scarcely burn at all.

On the Great Plains severe storms often arise, with scarcely any notice of their approach, and men have frequently suffered loss of life or limb by an overtaking "blizzard" on the bleak prairies. One afternoon, when we were within about twenty-five miles of Elm Creek, the wind suddenly arose with such force as to tear the covers from two of our wagons, while at the same time a great black cloud came rolling up from the southwest. The lightning flashed fiercely athwart the sky, and the heavy rumble of thunder echoed over the vast prairie. Before we had succeeded in replacing our wagon covers the storm was upon us in all its fury. The rain seemed to come in great sheets, and our bedding, and in fact everything in the wagons was deluged. Soon the rain changed to sleet and the sleet to snow, while the wind whipped around from the southwest to the northwest, and it became intensely cold. We journeyed perhaps three or four miles until we reached the head of the Chikaskia River, which here was only a very small brook with no timber. It being near night we prepared to camp in this dreary place, making a corral of our wagons, we placed our horses inside, blanketed and fed the poor creatures, and then prepared ourselves a hasty meal. After we had eaten, having but little fuel, we got into our wagons and tried to make ourselves comfortable as possible with our wet and frozen blankets. I suffered a great deal that night, frequently thinking that my time had come. My father, who bunked with me would rub and chafe my benumbed limbs and speak encouraging words, and so the long night wore away, and morning dawned clear and cold. The earth was wrapped in a white mantle of snow. We bustled around and gave our horses a good meal, and then hitched up and pulled for timber. We saw large packs of grey wolves and coyotes, but were too cold to give them much attention. We traveled on until about two o'clock in the afternoon, when to our great joy, upon reaching the top of a hill, we discovered only

a short distance ahead a stream thickly bordered with timber, while on beyond, the whole country presented a broken appearance, scores of ravines
intersecting each other, most of them well supplied with timber. Only those
that have traveled over bleak, sterile plains in the winter season can fully appreciate our feeling as this beautiful scene dawned upon us.

We hastened to the nearest point of timber, and selecting a well sheltered
place, went into camp, and after gathering up dry wood soon had a bountiful
fire blazing, and cheering all with its warmth. After preparing and enjoying
a good meal, some of the younger members of our party, myself included,
sallied forth to see what was in the country, in other words to look for fresh
meat. We went by twos, and my partner and I had not gone far when we
discovered a herd of buffaloes about a mile distant. We hastened towards
them, and had nearly arrived within good shooting distance, when some of
the other boys approached from the opposite direction and frightened our
game, causing them to go thundering away pell mell, helter skelter. We all
opened fire at the fugitives and had the satisfaction of seeing a fine two year
old drop to the ground. As it was nearing night we cut off a ham and some
of the choicest pieces of meat and took them into camp. One of the boys
carried a shotgun and took in quite a number of quail and rabbits, which
abounded here.

We had a jolly time in camp that night, singing songs and spinning yarns
around the campfire. On the following morning we started out for a good
day's hunt, leaving my father in camp to look after the horses and prepare dinner for the outfit. We found plenty of fresh signs but no buffaloes. It seemed
that for some unaccountable reason they had left that part of the country,
nearly all going north as their trails indicated. This was a great disappoint-
ment, as our object was to load our wagons with meat. In the language of
the professional hunters, who slaughtered thousands of buffaloes for their
hides only, we were "meat pilgrims," or "cornfield sailors," as the cowboys
and other plainsmen dubbed the homesteaders who would go out and kill
six or eight buffaloes for "winter meat." We dreaded to leave our well sheltered camp, and follow the game onto the dreary plain that stretched away
to the northwest, so we returned to the camp in the evening tired and somewhat depressed in spirit after a fruitless day's hunt. I found that my father had
met with a painful accident during our absence. It was somewhat amusing;
seeing a flock of quails near camp, he took a double barrel shotgun, which I
had loaded heavily with buckshot. Not knowing its content he held the gun

loosely and fired. The quail flew away unharmed, while Father landed on his back in a clump of bushes and the gun several feet beyond. He escaped with a bruised shoulder, which was all right after a few days.

I resolved to hunt by myself on the following day, and started out determined, if there were any buffaloes in reach, that I would have some of them. After hunting nearly all day without success, I had the good fortune to come across a herd of seven buffaloes only a short distance away. The ground being broken I crawled within seventy-five yards of them, then after taking a short breathing spell, I opened fire. My first shot brought down a buffalo. The others seemed so bewildered that they scarcely knew what to do; they would smell their fallen comrade, and put their heads together very much after the manner of domestic cattle under like circumstances. Taking careful and deliberate aim I fired in all seven shots, and had six buffaloes stretched out on a very small space of ground. The seventh seemed to think that it was no place for him, for he skedaddled away.

Some of the boys came to me, having been attracted by my firing. We sent one to camp for the wagons, while the rest set to work to dress our game. We worked far into the night before this was completed. In the meantime the wagons had arrived so we loaded our meat, also the hides and pulled for camp. The howling of wolves told us plainly that had we left the game on the prairie until morning there would have been nothing but bones left.

The next day we devoted to hunting smaller game, and succeeded in taking several wild turkeys, some rabbits and quail. Along towards evening our horses, which had been turned out on the prairie to graze, became frightened, probably at wolves, and came tearing down to camp. One belonging to my father, ran down a steep hill and ran into a miry place which lay at the foot of it. Although we succeeded in extricating him, he had suffered an internal strain, and the poor creature died in a short time. In later years I have seen buffaloes and cattle dead in this mire. It is situated right at the head timber of Spring Creek, one of the main tributaries of Elm Creek.

One of our party happened to have a light wagon, so after removing the tongue, we improvised a rude pair of shafts and on our homeward journey we worked one horse to the light wagon, and still had two for our heavy one.

When about half way across the eighty mile prairie we were again overtaken by a blizzard, but we decided to travel night and day until we reached the timber on Cowskin Creek. We broke camp at about eleven o'clock at night, and keeping a man ahead to pick the trail we "rolled out." Soon after daybreak we passed an outfit of five wagons which were corralled, with the horses blanketed within the enclosure. Supposing the men were sleeping inside the wagons we passed on, but a day or two later the whole party consisting of five men were found frozen stark and stiff.

We reached the Cowskin about three o'clock in the afternoon and soon had a cheerful fire of dry logs which were plenty. Some of our party, myself among the number, had their toes nipped by the frost, but all felt fortunate in faring as well as we did.

In the early part of January, 1872, a party consisting of Volney P. Mooney (now clerk of the District Court of Butler County, Kansas), George Ross, and the writer started from the little town of Towanda for the Medicine Lodge country. Our object was to trade with the Indians and buffalo hunters, as well as to enjoy a hunt ourselves. We had a sturdy team of ponies and a covered wagon well laden with the remnants of a dry goods and grocery store, calico, beads, buttons, needles, thread, sugar, coffee, tobacco and many other articles that were likely to appeal to the needs of buffalo hunters and Indians, besides a small tent and other camp outfit. The first night out we camped on the bank of Chisholm creek, where now stands part of the flourishing city of Wichita. In the morning we passed thru Wichita and on to Cowskin creek, a fine timbered stream about 10 miles west and on the extreme border of the sparse settlement. Crossing Cowskin, we proceeded a few miles further and encamped for dinner, then on to the westward, making camp for the night about four miles east of the North Ninnescah river.

During the night a fierce north wind sprang up, and by daylight it was bitterly cold. After a hot breakfast we rolled out and soon reached the Ninnescah. We found the stream about two-thirds covered with ice and there was no alternative but to cut a way thru wide enough for the team and wagon. The water was about thigh deep, but I waded in and in about half an hour had a passage way completed. Then the "boys" wrapped me in blankets and we again proceeded on our way.

We had not gone far until we met three hard-bitten individuals heavily armed and driving a bunch of spotted ponies. We exchanged ordinary greetings and proceeded on our respective ways. We had gone probably 10 miles when we met Old Hard Rope (usually known as Hard Robe) and 10 husky warriors. With them was Buckskin Joe, a long-haired buckskin clad plainsman, who acted as interpreter.

He inquired if we had met anyone driving ponies and how far ahead they were, etc. They left us vowing a terrible vengeance upon the rustlers if they could overtake them before they reached Wichita. We subsequently learned that the rustlers reached Wichita and had almost closed the sale of the ponies when their pursuers arrived. Luckily for them (the rustlers) that they were not overtaken where they were "beyond the law." Their names were Wolsey, Cord and Omett. They were given 10 years in prison for the theft of the ponies.

The next day we passed near where Kingman is now located. There were only dim trails to follow. In another day's travel we had arrived in buffalo country. We found a few small hunting camps, and of course, we obtained plenty of fresh meat. The hunters were glad to replenish their scant supplies from our stock.

We struck the Medicine Lodge at Griffin's Ranch, where Sun City is now located. Griffin had established a hunting camp and trading post there, which was a headquarters for the buffalo hunters. Two or three large log buildings were used for smoking and drying meat, which was destined for the eastern markets. The meat was brought in vast quantities by the hunters and exchanged for cash, provisions, ammunition and whiskey. Andy Griffin, altho handicapped by a wooden leg, was a skillful hunter, but for the most part he would ride out to locate the game and direct his hunters, of which he employed a large force, to the most favorable localities for their purpose. In the spring of '72 he was found dead, lying behind his dead pony, at the mouth of Soldier Creek, 10 miles west of his camp, while thickly strewn around him were empty cartridge shells which told the story of his desperate battle for life. The Indian casualties were unknown, as always, when possible, they would remove their dead.

We were quite successful in disposing of some of our stock at Griffin's camp, but were quite anxious to try our luck trading with the Indians, so we moved on to the southwest for the head of Salt Fork, where we were informed there was a large camp of Cheyennes and Arapahos, who had a reputation for making fine buffalo robes, soft and pliable. At Big Mule creek we passed the camp of a hunter named Cole. After exchanging the usual civilities we resumed our journey. We were soon in a trackless wilderness, passing through a country literally alive with game, buffaloes, antelopes, and wolves in every direction. One buffalo came directly towards us. Mooney and I opened fire on him and brought him down. When we approached him we were somewhat surprised to see an arrow protruding from his side. We looked in every direction expecting to see the dusky owner of the arrow coming to claim his game, but in vain.

Reaching the head of Salt Fork we found plenty of Indian signs; arches made of willows with both ends sharpened and stuck in the ground on which they had been drying meat, and the smoldering remains of campfires, but no Indians were to be seen. A broad trail, leading down the stream, showed plainly the direction they had taken. We went into camp on a high knoll, which commanded a fair few of the surrounding country. Leaving my companions in camp, I mounted one of our horses and followed the trail down the Salt Fork, hoping to find the Indians and a new camp a few miles off, but in this I was disappointed. I rode until late in the afternoon but saw no signs of a camp, so I concluded to retrace my steps. Before doing so I rode to the top of a high round knob, crested with cedars, and found a magnificent panorama of nature spread out before me. The waters of the Salt Fork shimmering in the sun, the hills and valleys covered with a luxuriant growth of buffalo grass, with here and there a small herd of buffaloes quietly grazing, while antelopes and wolves were to be seen in almost any direction. As I gazed on this glorious picture a flock of crows flew over me, some of them alighting in the cedars just over my head, where they commenced a furious cawing as if they resented my intrusion. They seemed to me like an omen of evil, and visions of Indian ambushes came into my head. However, I reached camp just at dusk, and found the boys glad to see me back safely, as they had grown uneasy at my long absence.

Disappointed at not finding Cheyennes and Arapahos we concluded to go back to the Medicine Lodge and visit Hard Robe's band of Big Hill Osages, who were in camp six miles below Griffin's Ranch, near the present site of Lake City. After travelling at a moderate rate for a day and a half we reached the camp and were greeted by the usual chorus of barking curs. Numbers of half naked savages, of both sexes and all sizes, gathered around our wagon when our business became known. We had quite a lively time for two or three hours, Ross and Mooney doing the trading, while I was kept busy watching the poor Indian "with the untutored mind" to see that he did not steal anything. Three pints of green coffee would get in exchange a good buffalo robe. One pint, a buckskin. They brought out moccasins, buckskins, rawhide lariats and pelts of various kinds, and received in return beads, buttons, needles, thread, coffee, rice, sugar and many other things too numerous to mention.

60

Hard Robe, the head chief, with ten braves and a white scout called Buckskin Joe had gone to Wichita in pursuit of some white men who had stolen some of their ponies. A sub-chief, who had control of affairs during Hard Robe's absence, did not like the bargains that were being made, so he tried to get rid of us by saying, "Good-bye, Good-bye," at the same time motioning for us to depart. We were not to be hurried off in that style, but stayed as long as they brought out anything to trade. I must here state that Mooney was quite smitten with the charms of a dusky maiden, who was arrayed in a charming negligee toilet, A la Mode Osage. We managed to get him away however, and in a few days he was himself again. When we were leaving, and were about two hundred yards from the camp a cunning looking Indian overtook us, and said, "Say, you fellers got any whiskey?" We told him that we were not allowed to bring whiskey into the Indian country. He replied, "I believe you got some. You all look like d——n wild cases." We assured him that there was no whiskey to be had, and making him some trifling present bade him good-bye and rolled out down the river.

We travelled about ten miles and encamped for the night. We were somewhat uneasy for fear that the Indians might follow us, and try to steal our ponies, as well as the goods they had traded us. The night passed without any adventure, and the following morning about nine o'clock we drove into the infant city of Medicine Lodge which then consisted of a few log cabins scattered here and there while the principal streets were covered with a rich growth of buffalo grass.

After taking an observation of the town, and making a few sales, and purchasing feed for the ponies we pulled out for the plains, heading northeasterly to the head of the Chikaskia river. There we turned to the northwest to make a final hunt on the South Ninnescah. On this stream we pitched our tent where it was only a tiny rivulet, so near were we to its source. Leaving Ross and Mooney in camp, I started out to get meat and hides to fill out our load, which, so far, consisted of light articles procured from the Osages. About a mile from camp I came upon two fine 3-year-old buffalo. I soon had them down and returned to camp to report. Leaving our tent, we drove to the carcasses and were soon busy skinning and cutting up meat. So far the day had been pleasant, and the sun shining, although a peculiar haze pervaded the atmosphere.

Almost without warning, a north wind sprang up, a great black mass of clouds came scudding from the north. By the time our work was completed a howling blizzard was on with the air filled with snow. We started for camp and drove until we thought we surely had gone far enough to reach camp, when suddenly we found ourselves back where we had started from. We had traveled in a circle, lost in a blizzard. Again we started, giving the ponies their heads. The sagacious animals soon came to a halt in front of our tent. Opening the flap, we were greeted by an unpleasant visitor. A large polecat was in full possession. Try as we would to frighten him out, he would run toward us, stamping the ground and showing his teeth. Exasperated, I said: "I'll fix him." Grabbing a rifle from the wagon, I fired at him point-blank, fairly pulverizing him; but alas! He was victorious even in death, for he opened his vanity case and scattered its contents in all directions. It was not filled with heliotrope nor sweet migonette. Some of it struck our one sack of flour, so we had to subsist on parched corn and buffalo meat for the next three days.

The blizzard increased in fury. We were in the lee of a six-foot bank. We led the ponies on the sheltered side of the wagon, with a blanket and buffalo robe securely tied on each one; then, pulling robes and blankets over and under ourselves, we were soon sleeping the sleep of the just, despite the all-pervading odor from our late visitor.

By morning, the storm had abated, while the earth was wrapped in a mantle of snow. I was first to arise, and as I opened the tent flap, a wonderful sight met my eyes. A great bunch of buffalo had bedded not over 100 yards from camp, in almost a perfect circle, with the cows and young ones inside and the bulls outside, as a protection not only from the storm, but from wolves and coyotes. We had completed our load, so left them in peace until they arose and shook off the snow, when they moved slowly away toward the south. We then proceeded to Wichita, where we disposed of most of our stock in trade, and the next day arrived home in Butler County "fat, ragged and saucy." We had had a month of roughing it on the plains and in the canons. Here I will leave this line of my subject, and proceed to my next chapter, where I merge into a "Texas cowboy."

Chapter 3

THE WANDERINGS and adventures that I have narrated were far from satisfying me and only made me anxious to see more, and try new fields of adventure.

In the early part of March '72 I found a chance to go to Texas with an outfit of cow-ponies; the object being to use the ponies in driving cattle from Texas to Wichita, Kansas, by way of the "Chisholm Trail." The ponies had come up from Texas the previous season, and had wintered on a ranch in Kansas, on account of the low price of feed.

Our outfit consisted of a Texan, "Rube" Arp by name, who was "boss" or foreman of the outfit, an Arkansas "chap," who rejoiced in the nom de plume of Slusher, probably from his capacity for slugging down bad whiskey, a gouty gentleman from Leavenworth, who took the trip overland hoping to benefit his health, a gentleman "of color," a namesake of the illustrious Andrew Jackson, who drove a wagon containing our bedding, provisions and the aforementioned gentleman from Leavenworth, and lastly your humble servant. Andrew Jackson besides being teamster, also had charge of the culinary department, not a very heavy responsibility perhaps, as our diet consisted mainly of cornbread baked in an old fashioned dutch oven, bacon and strong black coffee, varied by what game we could shoot along the route.

From Augusta, Kansas, our route lay over a high rolling prairie in a southeasterly direction until we reached the head of Elk River, and thence down its beautiful valley, passing through Howard Center, Elk Falls, Elk City, Longton, Independence, Coffeyville and reaching the line of the Indian territory at the town of Parker. Nothing worthy of note occurred thus far, but I enjoyed the trip immensely. Rube, Slusher and I drove the loose horses, about twenty-five in number, ahead of the wagon. Each had a number of horses set aside to ride and care for, and so we had a fresh mount every day.

Leaving Parker we entered the Cherokee Nation. On Big Creek we reached the first Indian settlement, some Delawares, many of which tribe live upon the Cherokee Reservation. We reached the Verdigris River, which had to be crossed by a ferry. An Indian with a big feather in his hat had charge of the old scow which answered for a ferry boat. After some trouble we succeeded in getting part of the ponies on board and had almost reached the middle of the stream when one of them ran and leaped overboard, into the swiftly running waters. Down he went entirely out of sight, but in a few seconds his head appeared alongside the boat, and pulling for the shore he gained it some distance in advance of his comrades on the scow.

Rube and Slusher being Southerners their sympathies were with the "lost cause," and they were very bitter against the d——n "Yankees," as they termed all loyal people of the North. Rube had been raised on the Texas frontier, amid the wildest surroundings, where even his sisters carried "Winchesters" when they went in search of the cattle, or to the spring for a pail of water, for the frequent forays of the Kiowas and Comanches made life very uncertain in the early settlement of northwestern Texas. He was very illiterate, yet a man of natural keen perceptions, one who was brave, generous and reckless to the last degree. Although we differed in our views in many respects, I learned to admire the dark flashing eyes, the steady nerve and the unerring aim that could send a pistol ball through the cork of a bottle at fifty yards without breaking the bottle. Instinctively a warm friendship sprang up between us, which afterwards served me well in time of need.

Slusher was a man of altogether a different turn; born and bred in the backwoods of Arkansas, he had a natural love for whiskey, and was full of brag and bluster. He frequently said in my presence that a Yankee wouldn't fight. He made much sport of "shorthorns," as green hands on the trail were called; and I knew that his slurs were meant indirectly for myself. However, I took everything quietly, yet had my mind made up, that if ever occasion required I would do the best I could to sustain the Yankee reputation.

Reaching a point called Honey Springs, about twenty miles below Fort Gibson, we made a halt of about forty eight hours to rest the stock. Slusher took advantage of this to go on a visit to his friends in Arkansas and when he returned again we had nearly reached the Red River. When he came up he was leading a small roan pony, which he had traded for among the Choctaw

Indians. It proved to be an unfortunate trade in more ways than one. When the new pony was turned loose among the others, he was not long in showing a very vicious disposition, kicking at everything that came within reach. Frequently he would lag behind the others, and when we would try to urge him on we would be saluted by a series of wicked kicks. It was not long until he had two of our ponies seriously crippled, one of them being a saddle pony of mine. I was very angry, and declared that if he ever kicked me I would kill him. Here I will leave him to return further on.

Arriving at Red River we crossed it at Colbert's Ferry, and we had reached the sunny land of Texas. Then for about a week our route lay through a beautiful country, with fine old plantations on every hand, with old fashioned mansions, after the southern style of architecture, with broad verandas, and surrounded by the inevitable "darky shanties." Now the scene begins to change and the country is more unsettled, log cabins take the place of the mansions, and we finally come into a timbered country known as the "cross timbers." Here we commenced to stand guard over our stock nightly, for only recently there had been a raid by the Comanches, and settlers had been killed, and many horses driven off.

One Saturday evening Rube informed us that we would reach his father's home, and that we would rest there over Sunday. We reached the place about sundown, and were cordially greeted by the family. It consisted of old Mr. Arp, who was past seventy, but still hale and hearty, Rube's brother "Hub," a tall, strapping specimen of frontier manhood, and last, but not least in the writer's estimation, the three sisters ranging in age from ten to eighteen years.

The old home where these children of the forest were born and reared was a long, double log cabin, with a roofed passageway between. All sides were provided with loopholes for Indian defense. Each room had a large, old fashioned fireplace and around the walls were hung a great variety of firearms. The young ladies had never seen a cook-stove, a boat of any kind nor a steam engine; the nearest railroad being probably 100 miles distant. Their cookery was all prepared in the old fashioned style, on the fireplace. A small stream ran within a few miles of the cabin, while nearby was a spring of pure, cold water. A vast body of timber stretched away in every direction. Its density being broken by occasional openings which were covered with a fine growth of mesquite grass. East of the cabin was a range of high, steep hills, forming an almost entire circle about half a mile in diameter. The enclosure was only accessible to cattle or horses by means of a stairway cut down the rocky banks of the creek, which formed the western boundary of this natural pasture. About two years before my visit to this interesting place old Mr. Arp detected some Comanches trying to scale the hillside mounted on his ponies. He hastened out, rifle in hand, and succeeded in getting within shooting distance. The wily savages, true to their custom, threw themselves nearly out of sight on the opposite side of the animals they rode. The old man took a careful aim and fired, shooting a pony through the neck and killing the Indian on the other side. The others abandoned the ponies and escaped on foot.

I was deeply interested in these wild and romantic surroundings, and time flew swiftly. Monday morning dawned bright and beautiful, and bidding adieu to our hospitable friends we set out for Jacksboro, which was our final destination. Our employer had preceded us, making the trip by rail and stage. Hub Arp accompanied us as a reinforcement in case of Indian attack.

We had reached a point known as "Ten Mile Prairie," about fifteen miles east of Jacksboro before anything occurred worthy of note. As we came into this opening it seemed fairly alive with the wild denizens of the forest, which surrounded it. Deer and turkeys went scurrying for the timber as we came in sight, but the center of interest was a herd of wild horses with long, flowing manes, and tails which swept the ground, as they circled around us with heads erect and full of curiosity to know who or what the intruders were. Rube and Hub quickly uncoiled their lariats, and dashed away in hot pursuit. The chase was very exciting, but the wild horses finally distanced their pursuers.

While the race was going on Slusher and I still kept driving the stock along, one of us on either side of the little herd, while Andrew Jackson brought up the rear with the mess wagon. While my attention was drawn to the chase, I suddenly felt a tremendous blow on my left shin, and the vicious little roan pony went trotting off shaking his head, with ears tucked back, after the manner of angry horses. Remembering the promise I had made I whipped out a Colt six-shooter remarking, "Now you have got to die." Taking a quick aim I sent a ball crashing clear through him just behind the shoulder. In an instant I realized my own life might be in peril, and looking towards Slusher, I saw that he had partially drawn a huge pistol. Holding my still smoking revolver, I looked him squarely in the eye. No word passed between us, but after a short pause he slowly tucked his weapon back in its scabbard, and I did the same with mine. After a brief halt we drove on, leaving the dead pony stretched out on the "Ten Mile Prairie."

There may be some events in this narrative that I would fain pass over without mention, but having started out to tell a true story, I will only ask the kind reader to cast the broad mantle of charity over any faults that may stand out too prominently.

When Rube and Hub rejoined us one of them asked, "Who killed the little roan?" Slusher nodded towards me, and no further comment was made about the matter at this time. In about two hours we went into camp for the night.

The next morning Rube and Hub left us and went on ahead to Jacksboro, instructing us to let the ponies graze slowly along, so as to reach town in the afternoon. Once during the day I detected Slusher with pistol in hand partially concealed under the blue cavalry overcoat, which he wore in spite of the Yankees. Seeing that he was observed he turned around and replaced the weapon. I knew from this that in the future I must be on my guard.

Arriving in the vicinity of Jacksboro we held the stock out to graze until about dusk when we drove them into town, and corralled them in a high stockade, which had a ponderous gate with a good lock; hence we were free from duty for the first time since entering the Indian country, excepting the two nights at Arp's.

After supper our employer came around to see us. He was highly elated over the good condition of the ponies after their long trip. I noticed that he was under the influence of liquor. He addressed us, "Well, fellers come around and I will introduce you to the boys." We followed him, and he led the way through the city post-office into a back room, where there was a bar and about a half dozen as desperate and reckless appearing men as it has ever been my lot to meet. He introduced our party one by one, winding up with your humble servant after this style, "Gentlemen, this is a little red headed devil I brought down from Kansas." A drunken ruffian by the name of Vandeberg started towards me, declaring that he could whip any g——d d——n man from Kansas. I seized a large bottle which stood on a barrel near by intending to use it if compelled to, in self defense. Some of his friends came between us and pacified him by telling him that I was all right.

It did not take me long to discover that my lot was cast with a hard outfit; most of them indulged in whiskey very freely. In the course of the evening Wiley Robbins, my employer, came around to me and said, "So you shot Slusher's pony?" I replied, "Yes." "Well," he said, "You've got him to pay for. It will cost you sixty dollars, and instead of giving you thirty per month up the trail you will only get twenty. I'll learn you to shoot horses." All this accompanied by a volley of oaths. I resolved that he should not have things all his own way. I would have been willing to pay Slusher twenty dollars for his pony, for that was about what it cost him. After giving me this interesting information Robbins left me and returned to his whiskey, and by midnight was so drunk that he had to be carried to his lodging place. Some of his boon companions were not much better off.

In the morning when they had become sober enough, they resolved to drive the ponies out about seven miles northwest, to a point on the West Fork of the Trinity, called Flag Springs, where there would be better grazing for them. We arrived there about eleven o'clock in the morning, and encamped in a beautiful spot, with plenty of shade, and near the banks of the Trinity. After dinner some of our party went out hunting and fishing, while the others remained at home to look after the stock. I neglected to mention that Robbins' crowd from the saloon went out with us, to get thoroughly sober I presume. About two o'clock two of them came into camp greatly excited. They had seen two Indians dodging stealthily around among the trees. Robbins himself soon afterwards came in, having seen moccasin tracks in the sand along the stream. The rest of the fellows were signaled in, and the team hitched to the mess wagon, the ponies rounded up, and in a very short time were being driven back towards Jacksboro. We were expecting to be attacked at every minute. However, we reached town without any molestation, and that night we again corralled the ponies in the stockade. The next day Slusher and I took the stock out about half a mile to let them graze. Here again I detected him fingering his six-shooter in a suspicious manner. I might have gotten the drop on him easily enough, but my compunctions were too strong against taking human life.

I now resolved to leave the outfit at the earliest opportunity and this resolve was strengthened by Rube taking me aside that evening and telling me that as I valued my life not to start up the trail with that outfit. My mind was greatly troubled. Here I was with very little money, and with miles of hostile Indian country in any direction I might turn. At times I was strongly tempted to secure a good gun, and mount one of Robbins' best horses and ride direct towards the home of the Kiowas and Comanches, and throw myself at their mercy. Then I realized that however I might justify myself in such a course I would be branded as a horse thief; a distinction which I did not fancy at all. Besides I was doubtful as to the reception my red brethren might give me. After a careful deliberation I determined to leave that night at all events. I retired with the others as usual, but not to sleep. I waited until two o'clock in the morning, when their heavy breathing told me that my companions were asleep, and taking a small bundle of clothing, I stole silently out of the cabin which was within the corral, and scaling the stockade I felt free once more. I knew, only too well however, that if I should be overtaken by Robbins' ruffianly followers that I need not hope for mercy, for in that lawless frontier country there were many who seemed to scruple no more at shooting a man than if he were a dog.

Hardly knowing which way to turn, I resolved to go to Fort Richardson, which was only half a mile from town and enlist in the regular army, knowing that with the "boys in blue" I might defy the hatred of those whom I had just left. I went nearly to the picket line, and there awaited impatiently for the dawn. When the sun at last appeared I advanced to the picket line and told the guard that I wanted to enlist. He directed me to the agent's quarters, and meeting that worthy, I made known my wishes. He informed me that I would have to wait about two hours until some other officer arrived. Before the two hours had passed I had thought of the long five years term for which I would have to enlist, to be domineered over by the petty, but pompous officials, so changing my plan, I sauntered leisurely out from the fort, for although there was a picket guard, their rules were not very stringent and citizens were allowed to pass with impunity. When I had reached a safe distance from the fort I quickened my gait, and leaving all roads, plunged into the forest and took a southeasterly course, being guided by heavier timber which bordered the Trinity. I suspected that should I be pursued they might naturally think I would take back towards the northeast, over the route we had come, hence I deemed it policy to take some other direction.

Travelling until nearly noon I suddenly came to a broad, plain road, which I rightly judged to be the road from Jacksboro to Weatherford, a town about forty miles southeast from Jacksboro. Taking this road I travelled on until about two o'clock keeping just outside of the dusty beaten track so as to leave as dim a trail as possible. I kept a sharp lookout towards the rear and suddenly saw two horsemen riding towards me on the gallop. I made an abrupt turn and gaining a rocky ravine I secreted myself behind a large boulder and watched them go by. I could not recognize them from my position, but I had no doubt that they were some of Robbins' gang, as they seemed to be looking for a trail as they rode along. When they were ahead a safe distance I came out nearly to the road, and followed them, keeping back in the scrub oaks, which skirted the road. They were soon lost to sight, but about two hours later they returned, and I once more eluded them by hiding in the bushes until they passed by. I then came out into the road and pressed rapidly on. About sunset I came to a rude cabin, which proved to be the home of an old hunter and his wife. Here I obtained a hearty meal, consisting of cornbread, milk and venison. I presumed that I must have astonished the folks with my appetite as I had eaten nothing since the night before.

They informed me that it was but a short distance to Jim Loving's ranch, so I resolved to reach it before stopping for the night. I arrived at the ranch soon after nightfall, and was hospitably received by the proprietor and half a dozen cowboys, who were just fixing up their outfits preparatory to starting out on a "round-up" on the following morning. I obtained a good night's rest, and in the morning tried for employment with the round-up outfit, but they were full handed so I went on to Weatherford, and hence to Fort Worth. Here I succeeded in finding employment with a herd of wild broncos. I had not been here long before I had received a kick on the head from one of the broncos while I was stooping down to pick up a halter. I was knocked senseless and did not recover for several hours. Although I was soon able to be around, I felt somewhat dazed, and concluded that I was not in a fit condition to work with wild horses. I felt that the best thing for me to do would be to go back to Kansas, so after a wearisome trip, riding and walking alternately I reached Red River and crossed over into the Choctaw Nation. I had been feeling quite feverish and had suffered with a violent headache for several days. Before I had gone far into the Choctaw country I gave way completely and was prostrated with a burning fever. I found shelter with a half civilized Choctaw family, who were very kind to me. My main want was plenty of cold water to drink and bathe my flushed temples. This they supplied, and after two weeks, which seemed like so many years, I concluded to try to travel once more. I succeeded in reaching Perryville, which was then the terminus of the Missouri, Kansas and Texas railroad. Here I was again compelled to stop, for the fever had taken a new hold on me. This time I found shelter in a railroad camp. I will never forget the kindness of a young Englishman by the name of Thomas Wall. He saw that I had clean clothing, and brought me many a little dainty such as I craved in my weak condition. I remained here several days after I was able to be around. The town was full of the "riff-raff," who always congregate at the terminus of a new railroad. There were Indians, half-breed gamblers, "bullwhackers," "muleskinners," Mexicans, and even Chinese besides one of the worst lots of white desperadoes that ever cursed a border town.

Here I met two noted outlaws who were known as "Tiger Bill" and "Curly," of whose desperate adventures I afterwards read many accounts in the newspapers. Perryville was, literally speaking, a city of tents. Merchants carried on business in tents and the gamblers gambled in tents while monte men flipped their cards on dry good boxes or wherever they could find a victim to bite at their delusive game. It was nothing unusual for a man to be found dead in the streets in the morning, with his pockets rifled and turned wrong side out. I frequently saw gamblers sit down to play, each with a huge six-shooter lying on the table before him. The state of affairs became so bad that the military were called upon for protection. A squad came from Fort Sill and one from Fort Gibson.

The morning after they arrived there was a great commotion in camp, for posted on numerous trees were notices for "Tiger Bill" and "Curly," and twenty five others to be out of town within twenty four hours under penalty to be hung to the nearest limb if they failed to obey the orders. I witnessed a gathering of the desperadoes and heard them argue whether to go or to stay; no notice being taken of my presence owing to my weak condition.

There were nearly thirty of them, long haired, heavy mustached, fierce eyed fellows, all heavily armed. Some were very vehement, and with bitter curses argued with their comrades to stay and fight the soldiers. The majority seemed to think discretion the better part of valor, for they decided to leave the country. This they did; some going towards Kansas and others toward Texas. "Tiger Bill" was killed at Short Creek, Kansas, during the great lead excitement at that place. A desperado from Granby, Missouri, came into the barroom of the hotel where Bill was sitting, and accosted him thus, "Are you 'Tiger Bill'?" He replied, "That's what they call me." "Then take that and that," exclaimed the Missourian, drawing a huge pistol and firing. "Tiger Bill" fell dead, without a chance for self defense. It was presumed that the stranger was "an avenger of blood." "Tiger Bill" was said to have killed several men himself, and in his death we find almost a parallel to that of "Wild Bill," who was slain in Deadwood, Dakota, about three years later.

I met Slusher only once after the events narrated. We shook hands at parting and agreed to "let bygones be bygones." Three years after my flight from Jacksboro I was walking down Main Street in Wichita, Kansas with my employer Captain Hughes of Uvalde, Texas, when Wiley Robbins came out from a hotel and joined us engaging in conversation with Captain Hughes. He failed to recognize me, and I thought best to "let sleeping dogs lie."

Now to return to my own adventures. Soon after the banishment of the outlaws, I decided to take a new start for home. I was in a very weak condition, as I had taken a severe cold in addition to the fever, and a racking headache which I endured, besides the wound on my head from the kick of the broncho had gathered and broken, causing almost inconceivable pain. My one great desire was to get home, to die as I thought. My small funds were nearly exhausted so I was compelled to walk a good part of the way. It was between two hundred and three hundred miles from Perryville to my home in Kansas, and how I ever accomplished it I hardly know. Suffice it to say that I at last arrived at my father's door nearer dead than alive. My poor mother screamed when I came to the door, I looked so pale, so wan and hollow eyed. I was sick nearly all that summer and did not regain much strength until late in the fall when I joined a party of buffalo hunters and spent several weeks on the old stamping grounds in the Medicine Lodge country.

The pure air, the wild game and the excitement of the chase seemed to be just the tonics I needed, for I returned home feeling much like myself again. During the following winter I attended the district school at Towanda. When spring time came again, with its birds and flowers, with the green grass covering the prairies, I was seized with a restless longing to be on the move again. There was a good sized pond just west of my father's claim. One night a party encamped by the pond with a herd of cattle bound for the west. Early on the following morning I went to this camp, and found that their destination was Colorado, and that they needed one more hand. The result was that in an hour's time I was in the saddle headed for Colorado.

My employer was a scarred and grizzled old miner, who had "raised a stake" in the northwest country where he had invested in cattle, and was now on his way to seek a ranch and range in Colorado. There were two others in the outfit; John Sullivan, a tall, strapping Irishman and a deserter from Custer's famous 7th cavalry as I afterwards learned, and Dave Rodebaugh, a smooth faced young fellow of about nineteen years. Dave drove the "mess wagon" and performed the culinary act for the outfit. Our route lay up the valley of the Arkansas. Great Bend was just springing into notoriety as a cattle market, and vast herds were grazing all around the place. Soon after we drove close to the base of the famous Pawnee Rock, then leaving Ft. Larned a few miles to our right we pressed on to Dodge city. We found it to be a typical frontier town; headquarters for gamblers, horse thieves, buffalo hunters and freighters. Fort Dodge, only five miles down the river, gave its share of the general "hurrah," for the "blue coats" were fond of whiskey and cards and made frequent visits to the city.

At old Fort Aubrey we met a famous character known as Prairie Dog Dave. He was a great hunter; he added to his income by trapping prairie-dogs and selling them in pairs to tenderfoot tourists for pets. He had an unique way of trapping the dogs. He would place a barrel over a hole, both ends of the barrel being removed; then he would fill the hole and about one third of the barrel with sand, put a cover on the barrel, and the trap was complete. Soon the dogs would try to dig out. They could easily come up through the sand, but when they reached the top of the sand there they were, for should they try to burrow down the sand would simply fall back into place and they could make no headway at all. So all Dave had to do was to remove the cover, reach in, and catch them. His usual price was $5.00 per pair.

From Dodge City to Coolidge, near the Colorado line, there was very little settlement, with here and there a water tank, and one or two boxcars, the latter being for the accommodation of the section men. Many of these stations were also supplied with a small detachment of soldiers, who acted as body-guards for the section men, as there was danger of Indian raids. We reached Granada, Colorado, after an uneventful trip.

This was about the last of June 1873. One day was particularly hot and sultry. About nightfall a black mass of clouds came rolling up from the west, nearer and nearer the clouds approached, jagged steaks of lightning shot athwart the sky, while the heavy crash and roar of thunder was almost incessant. The cattle moved restlessly and sniffed the coming storm, now and again giving vent to low moans of fear and apprehension; and soon the storm was upon us in all its fury. The rain fell in torrents. Soon it was intermingled with hail. The lightning kept almost a continual glare. What appeared like balls of fire stood on the tips of our horses' ears. In spite of our best efforts to hold the cattle, we drifted away with the storm. About eleven o'clock the storm subsided. Sullivan and I found ourselves miles away from camp but still in the lead of the cattle. At last daylight came and we headed toward camp which we reached about 9 o'clock a.m. tired, damp and hungry, just a little episode of cowboy life.

The Santa Fe railroad had just been completed to this point, and like Perryville, Granada was a city of tents. Here I met Captain "Dave" Payne, whom I had formerly known in Kansas. He afterwards became the famous "Oklahoma Boomer." We left this place on the third day of July, 1873, and moved about seven miles up the river, where good grazing was found, and it was decided to rest, and observe the National holiday. About noon on the Fourth, Jim Graham, my employer, and Dave Rodebaugh became involved in a quarrel, and high words led to blows. Rodebaugh soon put Graham's eyes "in mourning," and then, although he had by far the best of the encounter, he seized an ax which was lying nearby, and came rushing at Graham with it uplifted with both hands. Just as he was about to strike, Sullivan seized him from behind, pinning his arms to his sides with his vice-like grasp. At this juncture Graham wheeled, and grabbed a pistol which lay on the pistol seat. As he extended his arm to fire, I sprang forward and threw my arms around him and thus we held them until they agreed to drop the quarrel, and peace once more reigned supreme in camp.

On the morning of the fifth, we renewed our drive up the river. Gradually, we worked our way up the river until we reached a point not far from Las Animas. When we arrived at Mud Creek, a small tributary of the Arkansas on the south side, and about eighteen miles east of Las Animas, Graham left our outfit in camp and proceeded westward to look up a suitable location for a ranch. He returned in two or three days having failed to find anything better than we had passed, so we turned and took the back trail. He resolved to drive back nearly to Granada, and there make a permanent location. He is still there up to the present time, 1888.

When we reached the final camping place, Sullivan and myself being no longer needed were paid off. Rodebaugh remaining with Graham, not withstanding their late unpleasantness. Sullivan and I went to Granada, and there took the cars for Dodge City. Arriving at that place we found employment almost immediately with "Hank" Sitler, who had a large government hay contract. Sullivan being employed as a hand in the hay field, and I as night herder of the stock used in the contract. In a short time I was transferred to Fort Larned to serve in the same capacity there. I have never heard of Sullivan since we parted at Fort Dodge. When the hay contract was completed I was again paid off.

From Larned I proceeded to Great Bend, where I soon procured employment with a herd of Texas cattle owned by Peter Moore. He had several herds grazing in the vicinity, and employed quite a force of men. At this time he was shipping and selling, and as he reduced his herd he also reduced the number of herders. It was growing late in October and the boys from Texas were glad to start toward their southern homes. Finally the stock was reduced to about eight hundred head of cattle and seventy saddle ponies, with four riders and a cook to care for them. We moved our camp from the open prairie to a sheltered bend of the Walnut, just above old Fort Zarah.

One evening about four hundred Pawnee Indians camped about a quarter of a mile above our camp. They were on their way from Nebraska to the new reservation in the Indian Territory. Indians are always hungry, and never bashful about asking for something to eat, or anything else they happen to want. Several of them came to our camp, and we treated them very hospitably; giving them bread, beef, etc. One tall young buck, who was wrapped in a handsome red blanket, happened to see a new flannel shirt hanging on the wagon box. He at once let us know that he wanted it; saying, "Gimme, gimme." One of the boys said, "Give me that blanket?" In an instant the redskin threw the blanket to him and then stalked majestically into the chilled night air with scarcely anything to cover him. The blanket was sent back to him by another Indian but whether he accepted it or not I do not know.

The range becoming short we broke camp and moved about eight miles down the river, near the town of Ellinwood. One morning I rode up the river bottom between the Santa Fe railroad and the river in search of some of the ponies that had wandered off. Noticing a man walking down the railroad track with a bundle of blankets on his back, I approached him and asked if he had seen the ponies I was in search of. He replied that he had seen them about a mile up the river. Something about the man's face and voice seemed familiar, and as I rode away I tried to think where I had met him. Suddenly it flashed across my mind that he was the young Englishman, Thomas Wall, who had befriended me when I was so ill at Perryville in the Indian Territory. Turning I galloped back to him and asked if his name was Thomas Wall, and if he was not in Perryville about a year and a half before. He replied, "That is my name, but I don't know you." I asked if he did not remember the young fellow who had been kicked on the head by a horse, and lay sick in the camp at Perryville. He said that he did, but that he would never have known me and that he had never expected to see me alive again. I then asked where he had been and how the world had been using him. He told me that he had been prospecting in the San Juan country, and had raised quite a stake but afterwards lost it in prospecting, and now that cold weather was approaching he was tramping it back to Missouri where he hoped to find employment for the winter. He had bought some crackers and cheese that morning, and had just twenty cents left. Here he was, with twenty cents in his pocket, and a journey of three hundred miles before him. I said to him, "I haven't very much, but I will whack up with you what I have." I had six dollars with me and I handed him three of it. At first he refused to take it but as I pressed it on him he finally took it while his eyes filled with tears. He said that he little expected to meet a friend in that part of the country. We shook hands, I wished him good luck, and started after the ponies. I had not gone very far when the thought struck me that our cook had given notice that he was going to quit, and a man would be needed to fill his place. So I overtook my friend once more and invited him to go to camp and wait until I returned, and told him that I would lay the situation before them. Upon my arrival I found him in camp, and had no trouble in getting him installed as cook. The consequence was that when he left us he had over eighty dollars in his pocket, and instead of tramping it to Saint Joseph he returned by rail. I have never had the pleasure of meeting him since and do not know whether he is living or dead.

With the feed becoming very scarce and the weather very cold, it was decided to move the stock down the river below Hutchinson, at the junction of Cow Creek and the Arkansas, where there was an abundance of hay and corn. We reached this point about the middle of December, and I concluded to make a visit to my parents, as they were only fifty miles away, and I was weary of the cold and exposure. I had purchased a nice black pony, and made the trip on horseback. I found many a friendly greeting at home, and in the vicinity where I was acquainted. I had rambled too much however to be contented long in the quiet settlement, and before the winter had passed away, the fever of unrest was burning fiercely once more.

About the last of February I received a letter from Mr. Moore informing me that he was going to move the stock to the Medicine Lodge country, and offering me employment. Consequently I saddled my pony, bade my friends good-bye, and three days later was riding around the stock in the Arkansas valley. About a week after my arrival the outfit was ready to start. The company consisted of Peter Moore, my employer; a man by the name of Cheeney, who drove the mess wagon and acted as cook; a young man about my own age, Cy Davidson; and lastly myself.

It was the fore part of March that we started out across the eighty miles of bleak prairie, which lay between us and our destination. On this drive I met with a painful accident. A young calf died at one of our camping places, and its mother was determined to go back, and it was by a good deal of hard riding that she was kept in the herd. When we reached our next camping ground it was decided to neck her to a large steer, to keep her from leaving in the night. She had to be lassoed and thrown down, and the steer served the same way in order to get them together so we could perform the necking process. As I threw my lariat over his horns he plunged madly away. The other end of the lariat was fastened to my saddle horn, and just as the animal had taken up nearly all of the slack, my pony stepped over the rope with one of his front feet, and in the twinkling of an eye, pony and rider were hurled violently to the ground. A thousand sparks of fire seemed to flash through my brain, and then for an instant all was black as midnight. My left limb, which went down under the pony, was severely bruised, while the heavy wooden stirrup was smashed to splinters. I soon recovered, and we managed to complete the necking operation.

We were all very glad to reach the end of our journey, for there was quite a difference in the waste of prairie with its chilling blasts, and the sheltered timbered canons of the Medicine Lodge and its numerous tributaries. Our camp was established on Turkey Creek about a mile and a half above Sun City. The cattle were turned loose to range over a hundred hills and valleys. Cy Davidson and I would make a circuit around the range twice a day, turning the cattle back that were inclined to wander beyond the bounds. The country was full of game, so we carried our guns on saddles and had a great deal of fine sport mixed with rough living and hard riding.

I found a faithful friend in young Davidson. He was a quiet good natured fellow, full of grit, and everyone that knew him was a friend. There was a great deal of the rough element in that part of the country. The wild rugged canons afforded a safe retreat for lawless desperadoes and horse thieves, who were wont to prey upon the thinly settled portions of the country. They would not only run off stock, but if crowded upon or molested in any way, had no scruples about shooting a man.

Prominent among the outlaws were "Hurricane Bill," Bill Brooks, John Cole, and Joe Brown. They went in pairs as a rule, but "Hurricane Bill" was an exception, often having a gang of seven or eight desperadoes under his leadership. They would sometimes steal several hundred head of cattle and get away with them successfully. Early in May of '74, Jesse Evans, a prominent stockman, had thirty or forty head of ponies grazing at the mouth of Mulberry Creek, about two miles below Sun City. One Sunday morning some of the young men of Sun City shouldered their guns and sallied forth in search of buffaloes, as the community depended a great deal on this source for their meat supply. As the hunters entered the vicinity of Evans' ponies, they saw a man ascend a high point overlooking the valley, and after peering cautiously around, he descended into the canon from whence he had come. Satisfied from the movements of the man that he meant no good, they crept carefully to where they could see down the canon. There they saw five men and as many horses, while strewed around were saddles, blankets, saddle bags and a great variety of firearms. A camp fire was smoldering, and the men were lounging around in various attitudes. Being satisfied that the party was there for no good, the boys hastened back to town and raised a party of ten, returned to find out who the strangers were, and what they were there for.

As they drew near they saw that the strangers had saddled their horses and were about to take their departure. The Sun City party were decided on having an interview, so they advanced from their cover. They had no sooner showed themselves than the strangers began to mount and hurry off in the opposite direction. The Sun City boys requested them to stop, saying that they wanted to talk with them. No attention was paid to this request, and the strangers only seemed the more anxious to be off. As the last one of them was riding up a steep bank his horse stumbled and fell unhorsing his rider. With a muttered curse he picked himself off and wheeling around began to empty his Winchester toward the Sun City boys. Then began a lively fusillade. Finding that it was getting too hot for him the man followed his horse up the embankment, and remounted. Scarcely had he done so when his horse was shot and killed. This man was the redoubtable "Hurricane Bill." A moment after the horse fell, one of Bill's companions was shot from his horse. Bill hastened forward, and assisted him to mount, and then got on behind him, when the whole party rode off making their escape. The other party being on foot were unable to follow.

The wounded man was a brother of Bill Brooks, "Hurricane Bill's" partner. He afterwards died from his wound. His hat with a bullet hole through it was left on the ground. This little battle occurred in the line of my regular beat, and I arrived on the scene only a few minutes after it was over. The outlaws left a good part of their camp equipage. There were several pairs of new blankets; a quantity of flour, bacon and coffee; a pack of cards, an almanac, and strange to say a pocket Bible; besides a buckskin hunting shirt, the property of "Hurricane Bill"; a large quantity of ammunition; and the saddle on the dead horse.

Among the Sun City boys were Frank and Wilkes Whittaker; Milt Clemens; Rube Marshall and others whose names have been forgotten. In dividing the spoils, the hunting shirt fell to Frank Whittaker, who afterwards met its original owner under peculiar circumstances, which will be mentioned later on. Bill Brooks was captured and hung by the vigilantes sometime in the following summer.

Not long after this event occurred Jesse Evans' men were riding around the range and discovered the trail of a considerable number of cattle leading off from the range towards the south. Upon a close examination a number of horse tracks were found and it became evident that somebody had driven them off. Cowboys returned to camp and made a hasty round-up of the remaining stock, and found that about eighty head were missing. In a very short time about six well armed cowboys were galloping swiftly along on the trail. They followed it all day through a wild broken country, which lies between the Medicine Lodge and Cimarron. They camped when it became too dark to follow the trail, and waited anxiously for daylight to appear again. As soon as it was light enough to see on the following morning they once more took up the trail. It soon became evident that they were gaining on the stock, and the thieves who were driving them, and the pursuers pressed rapidly on. At noon, just as they neared a valley of the Cimarron, they descried a smoke curling up from among the trees. Approaching cautiously, they discovered the lost cattle and seven or eight Indian ponies grazing quietly in the valley, while a little distance to one side was a white man and a half dozen Indians having a regular barbecue over an animal they had butchered. The cowboys attempted to creep within easy shooting distance, intending to take the rascals by surprise. The wily savages proved too cunning to be taken in, their quick eyes had discovered the pursuers, and with a yell they fled for dear life. Two of them mounted one pony, while the rest escaped on foot. The cowboys determined to capture the white man if possible, as he was evidently the leader of the band. They fired shot after shot at the refugees. The white man, a notorious renegade called "Frenchie" who made his home or rather roamed with the Cheyennes, and Arapahos, finding himself hard pressed took refuge on a high, rocky bluff on the south bank of the Cimarron, and commenced to fire on his would-be captors, calling out to them, "Come on you d——n —— —— ——, I've got a Sharp's sporting rifle and a hundred cartridges," at the same time making the bullets sing in unpleasant proximity to the cowboys' ears. Knowing that he was in an almost impregnable position, and that some of them might lose their lives in trying to capture him, they were obliged to let him go. All of this transpired in a very few moments. While the boys were giving their attention to "Frenchie" the Indians had scattered like partridges, and in the rugged country it was useless to follow them. The boys were glad enough to recover the cattle, with the exception of the one they had killed. To atone for this loss they brought back several Indian ponies.

No one who was in southwestern Kansas at this time will ever forget the summer that followed the events just narrated. It was the never-to-be forgotten "grasshopper year," when an innumerable army of these pests filled the air and devoured every green thing that came in the line of their invincible march. Early in the summer the Indians went on the warpath. They murdered a number of settlers in the Medicine Lodge country and ran off their stock. To make bad matters worse the white outlaws, disguised as Indians, committed numerous atrocities, many of which were accredited to the Indians. Among the adventurous spirits who had located on the extreme outskirts of civilization, was a man by the name of Coon. He had built a log cabin on the banks of Big Mule Creek, about twelve miles southwest from Sun City. Here he lived with his family. They had a small herd of cattle which was their main dependence. Their son John, a lad of about fourteen summers, was the herder. He had a fine pony which was often admired by the Indians, who sometimes passed their ranch. On one occasion they asked the boy to give them this pony. Of course he refused, when they told him, "In spring, when grass so high," holding their hands a short distance from the ground, "we come, take pony and kill you." This was taken only as an idle jest, but alas it proved to be only too true, for in the following summer, '74, they came one evening as the boy was rounding the cattle in the corral, and getting between him and the cabin they charged upon him with wild yells. The poor boy knew not what to do, abandoning his pony he ran and tried to secrete himself in a clump of willows. The cruel demons rode right up to him; one of them placed a pistol almost against his head and sent a bullet crashing through his brain. Then each one took off a piece of the scalp and their hellish work was done. They then rode away down the valley, taking the pony with them. This occurred under the very eyes of the agonized family, who were powerless to aid as they knew not what moment they might share the same fate. This murder and others which were committed about the same time, spread consternation through the settlements, and nearly every family abandoned their claims and gathered together for protection.

At Sun City and Medicine Lodge stockades were built of logs set upright in the ground, forming large square enclosures, in which there were built stout log cabins well provided with loop-holes. There was also a stockade between the two places, known as Fort Woodward, from the settler in command, Dick Woodward. Here scores of families took refuge, and having no means at hand for earning a livelihood, they were supplied with rations by the state. The men were organized into militia companies, and made frequent scouting trips in every direction.

John Mosely, a genuine frontiersman, was lieutenant of the company at Medicine Lodge. His father had been shot and killed while standing in the door of his cabin, by a band of Big Hill Osages about three years before. John vowed vengeance against the murderers, and was only waiting an opportunity. It came at last, and in this way. John's company went on a scout east of Medicine Lodge. When they arrived at Sand Creek, east of the Cedar Hills, they found a large camp of Indians. In an instant every man prepared for an encounter.

It is probable that this was only a hunting party as they had their squaws and children with them. However, they belonged to the same band that had murdered Mosely's father. They were very much excited at the warlike demonstrations of the militia, and several chiefs and braves advanced to have "a talk." As they came they were gibbering loudly and making vehement gesticulations after the Indian fashion. Mosely had spent years among the Indians, and was the only man in the company who understood their language; hence he acted as the interpreter. Turning suddenly to Captain Ricker, his superior officer, he said, "They have given orders for them to fire on us." At once Captain Ricker ordered his men to fire. In an instant a volley thundered forth, and half a dozen redskins fell mortally wounded, among them three chiefs. The others were stricken with terror, and fled in a wild panic, some on foot and some on ponies, scattering all kinds of camp equipage down the Sand Creek valley. I was over the ground shortly afterwards and picked up a nice red saddle blanket, beautifully beaded. I mention this as it will have a bearing on incidents which occurred later on.

The cattle that had been wintered in this part of the country had nearly all been driven to the various shipping points, north and east, and finally ours was the only herd left in the Medicine Lodge valley. This left us doubly exposed to dangers from red or white outlaws, for if they needed meat or ponies they would have to take "Hobson's Choice."

Chapter 4

ONE EVENING IN THE FOREPART of June Mr. Moore returned from a trip to Great Bend. He informed me that he had seen several head of his cattle between the South Ninnescah and the Rattlesnake, and he thought best for me to make an extensive ride through that section of the country. I accordingly packed three days rations in my saddlebags and started early the next morning.

I camped the first night in a deserted dugout on the Ninnescah. After two days of hard riding I found one lone cow bearing Moore's brand. It was near night when I found her, and it was over thirty miles to camp, so I headed her towards home and she ran like a race horse. These longhorn Texas cattle became very wild if out of sight of a man for a few days. It kept me busy for a while to keep within sight of her, but after running probably five miles she came to some buffalo wallows, which were full of water and took a drink, then after going a short distance stopped to graze. It was now twilight, and I decided to camp by the water for the night. Securing my pony with a small iron picket pin, I gathered some dry weeds and buffalo chips and soon had a cheerful fire burning, over which I fried some bacon and boiled some coffee. This with some cold biscuit was bounteous fare to a hungry cowboy. After supper rolling myself in my blanket, with my trusty needle gun resting on one arm, for this was while the Indian excitement was at its height, I was soon wrapped in the arms of Morpheus. The night passed with no disturbing sounds except the howl of the coyotes, and the occasional lonely neigh of my pony.

In the morning I found the cow not far from where I left her when darkness intervened. After breakfast I once more headed her toward our range. The first few miles were passed very quickly, then my longhorned bovine changed her gait from a run into a trot and finally to a long swinging walk. About three o' clock we struck the head of Turkey Creek, six or seven miles from camp. Here I was startled to find the trail of a large number of cattle leading from our range out on the broad open plain, which stretched away to the northeast. Hastening to the range I found Davidson with the cattle. Rounding them up and counting them we found that nearly one hundred were missing.

Moore at this time lived with his family in Sun City. I did not take time to consult him, but caught a fresh horse, packed the saddlebags full of provisions, and hastened away on the trail. It was nearly sunset when I started. When the shades of night gathered round I still followed the trail by moonlight. About ten o'clock the moon disappeared, so there was no use trying to advance further until daylight.

As soon as dawn appeared I ate a hearty breakfast and was on the move again. Until noon I had a broad plain trail which I followed without any difficulty. Then it took an abrupt turn from the northeast to the northwest, and the light sandy soil turned to a regular hard-pan covered with a short growth of buffalo grass, where a hoof scarcely left any imprint visible to the eye. With difficulty I kept the trail until it reached the sand hills between the Ninnescah and the Rattlesnake, not far from the ground I had ridden over only two or three days before. It finally led me to the great Texas trail, over which many cattle had lately been driven, besides there were many buffaloes ranging in this section of the country, so it was utterly impossible to locate my trail any farther. After scouring the surrounding country for a long distance around and finding no sign of the lost cattle, the only reasonable conclusion I could arrive at was that they had been driven off with some Texas herd and enroute for Great Bend or Ellsworth. I resolved to visit these places and looked through the many herds that were grazing around them. This I did but with no success.

It was a pleasant relief from the monotony of riding over the lonely plains, to go from camp to camp, always meeting with a hospitable reception, for a cowboy is at home wherever he finds a cow camp.

Disappointed in my search, I resolved to return by way of Hutchinson, still hoping to find a clue to the missing stock. As I was riding across the plains between Hutchinson and the Medicine Lodge, I noticed a postal card lying in the grass. Curiosity prompted me to dismount, pick it up and read it. Its contents ran thus, "P. Moore, Dear Sir; — Your cattle were shipped from

Sedgwick City," giving the date of shipment, but having no signature. It had been mailed at a little obscure post office, the post mark on the back being Sedgwick City.

Here was a puzzle for me. I had never heard Moore intimate that he had any thought of shipping cattle, and the stock had been confided to my special care. And how came the card here on this lonely prairie?

I arrived at camp after an absence of about ten days. I resolved to say nothing about finding the card. Going down to Sun City I met Moore and related to him all the details about my trip. I fancied that he seemed chagrined at the course I had pursued. He informed that he had searched for the lost stock himself for about a week, and that he had been to Hutchinson, and had learned by some means that his cattle had been shipped by thieves to St. Louis, and there sold, but that he had obtained the information too late to do any good. It now became obvious to me that Moore himself had dropped the card upon the prairie. It afterwards developed that one, W. C. Edwards of Hutchinson held a mortgage on Moore's stock for about half their value, and to defraud him Moore had hired the outlaws, John Cole and Joe Brown, to run the cattle off and ship them for him. Under different pretexts he had sent both Davidson and myself away to give the thieves their chance to get the cattle. These facts finally leaked out through their boasting. It seems that they drove the stock about forty miles northwest, to about the point where I lost the trail, and then veered back to an eastern course, bringing up to the shipping point, Sedgwick City.

Moore at this time was president of a vigilance committee, whose object was supposed to be the putting down of lawlessness, and the punishment of evil doers.

The Indians had been committing more atrocities, and it was deemed unsafe to remain longer in the wild rugged canons, so we rounded up the stock, packed the "traps" in the wagon, and moved about thirty miles northeast to the South Ninnescah river, where the country was less broken, and the danger of Indian incursions lessened. Davidson and I enjoyed the change wonderfully. Before we had been obliged to ride hard nearly all the time, early and late, to keep the cattle within bounds, but now they grazed quietly in the valley, while we amused ourselves by chasing buffaloes which abounded here. Then there were ponds in the valleys in which fishing was excellent, and in which we often bathed and cooled our frames when weary. We remained here until sometime in July, when we became uneasy in regard to our wages, which had not been paid very promptly, so we decided to quit and have a settlement. This we did, obtaining the amount due us in cash, except for about thirty dollars, for which I took Moore's note. We then proceeded to Hutchinson, where I sold my note to W. C. Edwards, the man who held the mortgage on Moore's stock, at a discount of ten dollars.

Shortly after our departure Moore drove the whole outfit to Wichita and had effected a sale and was about to receive the money when one Cadwell, an agent for Edwards, appeared on the scene and stopped the deal. He telegraphed to Edwards, who came and took possession of the stock. He finally sold the entire herd, and after deducting what was due him, gave Moore the balance. Moore left immediately for New Mexico, and I never heard of him since.

I will now relate some of the adventures of John Cole and Joe Brown, and their tragic deaths. In the summer of '75 there was a great deal of freight to be transported from Fort Dodge to Fort Elliot, a new post which had been established in the Texas Panhandle. For a while the freighters made good wages, until a lot of Mexicans came with wagon trains, and cut down the prices charged for hauling freight to a very low notch. This made them many enemies among the white freighters, and the "greasers" did not stand in much favor with the white population in general. Taking advantage of this prejudice, the outlaws would steal their stock with impunity.

One evening a Mexican wagon train with about eighty head of work cattle camped near Oake's ranch, on Bluff Creek about twenty five miles south of Dodge. They turned their oxen out to graze in the valley. It seems that John Cole and another outlaw by the name of Ed Hays had followed them, having a covetous eye on their stock. About eleven o'clock they rounded the cattle up, and started them off. They drove hard all night and imagined that they had a good distance between them and the Mexicans. Who can picture their chagrin, when daylight appeared and they found they had driven in a circle all night, and were in plain sight of the now thoroughly aroused Mexicans. The latter gave chase and opened fire on the outlaws; Cole made good his escape, but Hays was shot through the leg and fell into the hands of his pursuers. They took him to Dodge and turned him over to the local authorities, which was almost equivalent to setting him free, for horse thieves, gamblers and desperadoes were among the elite of Dodge City at that time, and the offices were filled principally from this class. In a short time Hays "was on the turf again." Of his subsequent career I know but little, except that he was arrested at Great Bend for passing counterfeit money. What the result was I failed to learn.

We will now follow John Cole and Joe Brown to the Smoky Hill River, to a point east of Ellsworth, where they stole six head of horses from the settlers, and started for Dodge City where they expected to dispose of their booty. They traveled night and day until they reached Coon Creek, between Fort Larned and Fort Dodge, and about one hundred miles from where they started. They were weary from their long hard ride and here they prepared to take a short rest. Camping in a small hollow, one proceeded to a settler's cabin to get some food, while the other indulged in a nap, in the camp. A posse of enraged and determined men were on their trail. They had followed in a wagon drawn by a team of good horses, and came upon the sleeping outlaw and captured him before he realized whether he was awake or sleeping. They then concealed their outfit in a ravine and awaited the coming of the other outlaw. As he approached he was confronted by the muzzles of half a dozen guns, and at once surrendered. Putting their prisoners in the wagon, and tying the horses behind, the captors started on their homeward journey. They had reached the head of Plum Creek, fifteen miles southwest from Ellsworth, when the led horses became entangled in their ropes. While the men were busy disentangling them, Cole managed to slip his bonds from off his wrists and in a moment had cut those which held Brown. They then made a bold dash for liberty; Cole succeeded in making good his escape and the timber which fringes the banks of Plum Creek, but Brown was not so fortunate. The cold muzzle of a double barreled shotgun looking him in the face caused him to halt. He was once more secured and the party moved on about eight miles, to the head of Ash Creek. Here they claimed that Brown made another attempt to escape. Be that as it may, he was found by a passerby with the whole top of his head blown off, while his face was burned and blackened with the powder, so close had been the weapon when discharged. He had always been something of a dandy in his dress and took special pride in wearing a pair of high-topped boots made of alligator skin. A few days later a young settler had discarded his rough cowhide boots and appeared on the streets of Ellsworth in a pair of elegant ones made of alligator skins.

John Cole vowed vengeance against Brown's slayers, saying that he would "Crawl on my hands and knees, and eat buffalo grass, but what I'll have revenge." I heard but little of Cole after the events just narrated had transpired, until early in the spring of '76, when a band of horse thieves, Cole among them, stole eight head of horses from near Wellington, Kansas. As usual they headed for Dodge City. They disposed of part of the stock in that place, and took the others to Offerle, a small village on the Santa Fe railroad east of Dodge, where they completed the sale, and divided the profits. They then separated, each taking a route to suit his own inclinations. Cole went north to Saw Log Creek, eight or ten miles distant. Here a man by the name of Callahan was encamped. He was engaged in picking up buffalo bones and hauling them to the railroad, where they commanded a fair price. A frontiersman's camp being always open to everybody, Cole made himself at home, resting after the long ride and passing away the time by fishing and lying under the shade of the trees which bordered the stream. In the meantime a body of vigilantes had followed hot on their trail, men who were used to frontier life, and were filled with honest indignation that the hard working settlers should be robbed of their teams which were their main dependence for the support of their families, and the development of the homes which "Uncle Sam" had given them. Arriving at Dodge City they soon found and recovered the horses that had been sold there, and proceeding to Offerle they met with the same success there. Learning the direction taken by Cole, they at once proceeded to the Saw Log. Reaching the bone-picker's camp, they found Callahan there alone. He informed them that Cole had gone down the creek to catch a mess of fish. Part of the vigilantes remained in camp, while the others went down the creek in search of the young outlaw. After going a short distance, they saw him coming, fishing rod in hand. Lying in ambush they awaited his approach. As he drew near they stepped from behind the trees, and with weapons drawn told him to "throw up your hands." Fairly trapped, he complied with the orders. He was taken to the camp, and there with Callahan, was hung to a convenient limb. Callahan protested his innocence, but those frontiersmen were in no mood for drawing fine distinction. He had harbored a horse thief.

The hanging of Callahan created a great deal of dissatisfaction on the frontier where he was widely known, many saying that he was an innocent man. The vigilantes claim that he brought the thieves in his wagon to the locality where they stole the horses, and that he hauled supplies for them on their return trip. At all events he lost his life through being found in bad company. His father was a minister and lived not far from Topeka. When we consider that it is at least two hundred miles from Wellington to the Saw Log, by the way of Dodge City, and that within two weeks from the time of starting they were at home again, we can form some idea of the pluck and endurance of the hearty settlers who formed the vigilance committee.

Chapter 5

I WILL RETURN ONCE MORE to that part of my narrative which relates to Davidson and myself. After our arrival at Hutchinson we went through quite a transformation at the hands of a tonsorial artist, and then proceeded to the home of Davidson's parents, where I enjoyed a very pleasant visit. After resting a day or two we went about thirty miles southeast to some "through camps," where we each purchased a saddle pony. We then separated, Davidson returning home, while I went to Butler County on a week's visit to my parents. At the end of the week I started to Hutchinson, where I was to rejoin my comrade. On my journey I met the innumerable army of grasshoppers before mentioned. Behind, I had passed countless fields of waving grain, and prairies covered with blooming flowers, while all nature seemed to rejoice at the peace and plenty, but now what a change meets the eye; desolation and ruin on every hand, the very air blackened by the myriad hosts of the destroyers, vast fields of corn eaten down to the very ground, beautiful gardens laid waste, trees stripped of their foliage, and grasshoppers everywhere. They were on the houses, on the fences, in the air, and even the streams and ponds were covered with their dead carcasses. As I rode they would frequently strike me in the face and eyes. In fact, they were almost intolerable. I thought of the plagues of Egypt, and this seemed like a second edition. All over the state of Kansas they marched like invincible conquerors, as in fact they were. No one who lived in Kansas in '74 will ever forget the "grasshopper year." Think of the ruined hopes of the thousands of settlers who had staked their all on the season's crops.

Reaching the homes of my friends near Hutchinson I found they had not been spared from the general devastation. With saddened hearts, Davidson and I bade them adieu, and started for Great Bend, where we expected to secure employment with some of the many herds which were held in that vicinity. Being unsuccessful, we turned our faces toward Ellsworth, hoping for better fortune, but we were again disappointed. We resolved to return to Great Bend once more and try again. This time we were in luck, although we had to separate and work for different "outfits," which were several miles apart.

The monotony of camp life was varied occasionally by trips to Great Bend with cattle to ship. I often met old acquaintances in the city. Among them was Dave Rodebaugh. It will be remembered that he remained in Colorado with Jim Graham, after their fight on the Fourth of July of the previous summer. Dave had remained on the ranch about a year and then had driven from Colorado to Great Bend with a herd of cattle. Let us now endeavor to trace his subsequent career.

After the summer of '74 until the winter of '76 I knew nothing of his whereabouts. Then I was surprised to learn that he was one of a gang that "held up" an express train at Kinsley on the Santa Fe railroad. The would-be robbers met with poor success, scattered and fled with the hounds of the law close on their trails. Rodebaugh and his pals were captured in a cow camp near the line of Indian territory by Bat Masterson and another officer from Dodge City.

Mike Rourke, one of the leaders of the gang, was captured somewhere on the Kansas Pacific railroad; while part of the gang made good their escape. Rodebaugh turned state's evidence, and thus escaped the penalty of the law, but his life was endangered from those of the gang who escaped, so he left Kansas for new fields of adventure. He went to New Mexico, and soon became identified with a gang of outlaws headed by the notorious Billy the Kid. I heard of his being implicated in numerous crimes, and if I was correctly informed he was killed when the Kid's gang was finally broken up.

Among the well known cattlemen of the southwest was one Pepperd, who once had a ranch in Colorado, not far from Granada. In the autumn of either '73 or '74 he became involved in a difficulty over a horse race with a man named Kutch. Pepperd shot and killed Kutch, and was cleared on the grounds of self-defense. Shortly afterward he removed his stock to Kansas. For a while he held forth near Dodge City. While here he had occasion to shoot at a man in one of the numerous saloons. His weapon was a double-barreled shot gun. He missed his man, but left his mark on the bar which was riddled with buckshot. As an instance of the grim humor of this man, he had found a dead negro a few miles below Fort Dodge. There was a bullet hole through the darkey's head. Now Pepperd thought it would be improper not to have an inquest, so he cut off the head and put it into a gunny sack and carried it to Dodge City in order to save the coroner a trip down the river. Everyone in southwestern Kansas has heard of Pepperd's Ranch, on Big Mule Creek, where he finally located, and where he probably resides at the present writing. I had occasion once to stop at his ranch for the night. I found him a very kind and hospitable host in spite of his reputation as a shooter.

In the autumn Davidson and I were fortunate enough to secure employment together with a cattleman by the name of Simmons. He had wintered his stock in Colorado the previous winter, but the range becoming crowded had driven to the rich pastures of Kansas. As the winter of '74 drew nigh we were rejoiced to learn that the stock was to be driven to the Medicine Lodge country, so we would once more ride over the old familiar hills and valleys and meet many old friends and acquaintances. Not long before we were ready to start for winter quarters, I was taken with a severe attack of bilious fever, brought on by exposure and drinking alkali water no doubt. Our camp at this time was in the Sand Hills, twenty-five miles from Great Bend, and although there was plenty of good substantial food in camp, in my weak condition I turned from it with loathing. I longed for cooling fruits, and thought of shady groves and refreshing springs. One day "Old John," our darkey cook, said to me; "I knows what you need, leastwise dats what I always crave when I'se sick." I replied "What's that, John?" "Why a slice of bacon, a streak of lean and a streak of fat." It is needless to say that I did not have any desire for this luxury.

After I had been sick for about a week, my employer (who was once a physician) came out to camp. Seeing my condition he told me that he would send me some medicine the next day that would fix me up. The medicine arrived in due time and seemed to help me almost immediately and in a few days I was in the saddle once more.

We were now ready to start for winter quarters. About this time Jim Davidson, a brother of Cy's, came and secured employment with our outfit. I found him very different from Cy. While Cy had no lack of grit he was always genial, and very slow to anger. Jim, who had a great many years on the frontier, was reckless, quick-tempered and full of flash and fire, yet generous withal, as such men nearly always are. After a week's drive we reached the Medicine valley.

A man by the name of Rube Lake had a branding pen about six miles below Sun City. Rube was something of a character. He at one time ran the first and only saw mill in the Medicine valley, and now we find him a postmaster, a justice of the peace, hotel keeper, saloon keeper, merchant, farmer and proprietor of the corral and branding chute, where cattlemen could corral and brand their stock for a small price per head. We drove the cattle to this place to give them a fresh brand before turning them loose for the winter. Several stockmen had decided to put their stock together on a large range and establish a line of camps around it with plenty of riders to keep the stock within bounds.

This winter we had fifteen thousand cattle on a range forty miles square, with camps all around from six to ten miles apart, besides some camps scattered through the central part of the range. While the branding process was going on our camp was beside an old unoccupied shanty about two hundred yards from Lake's house. One morning Dr. Simmons told Jim Davidson and I that we could occupy a camp together on the north side of the range, and told us to go to the head of Elm Creek and select a location for it. We found a nice place in the thick growth of timber. After riding all day we returned to camp about dusk. We found no one at the camp except Old John the cook. Throwing the reins over our ponies' heads, we sat down by the camp fire. Seeing no preparations for supper, Jim inquired, "Have the rest of the boys been to supper, John?" John made no reply but looked sulky and went on washing some tin plates. Jim repeated his question with some emphasis. With a big oath, John slammed a tin cup and plate down in front of us saying "If you'se is all in such a hurry you can eat cold chuck." In an instant Jim was on his feet, drawing his pistol as he arose, saying, "You black ——, I'll shoot h——l out of you." Crash went a bullet through the old shanty just grazing the darkey's cheek, and cutting its way through his kinky locks. He staggered as if about to fall, and put his finger to his cheek and looked at it to see if there was any blood. He then took a "bee line" for Lake's house, where Doctor Simmons and the rest of our party were. Jim declared that he had no intention of firing and only meant to scare the old fellow, but that the pistol was discharged accidentally. We knew not how badly John might be hurt, and as Lake was a justice, we knew not how soon an attempt might be made to arrest him. At this juncture, Cy came riding into camp driving in the loose horses, his own being among them. We hastily caught Cy's pony and in a few moments had Jim mounted and provided with a Winchester in addition to his six shooter, all ready for fight or flight as the case might demand. It didn't take long for Old John to find that he was worse scared than hurt, for in a short time he returned and commenced to prepare supper. John was an old servant of Doctor Simmons, and Jim thought it might be unpleasant to remain after what had occurred, so the next morning he quit and obtained a settlement. I have never seen him since, but the last I heard of him he was mining in Colorado. The joke connected with this matter was that Old John had made the bullet that gave him such a close call. He had molded quite a quantity for me, and I had divided with Jim. In a few weeks I wanted more bullets, and said to him, "John, can you find time to run me a few more bullets this afternoon?" He replied, shaking his wooly head, "No Siree. Dis yere darkie done got tired of making bullets to be shot at hisself."

Jim Davidson's departure changed the program to some extent, and instead of being sent to one of the camps on the outskirts of the range, I was stationed in a cabin in the Medicine valley, about two miles below Lake's and in the midst of the settlement. The settlement to be sure was rather sparse, and there were no fences to interfere with the free ranging of the stock. Among the advantages presented by my location were the following: the post-office was very convenient, the woods were full of wild turkeys, and right on the line of my beat lived a family who had several bright-eyed daughters. They had a large old fashioned stone fireplace in the cabin, and I found it a capital place to stop and get warm, and it is a singular fact that I got cold on some very warm days.

For a while there was little excitement to break the monotony of camp life, except the occasional finding of a beef that had been slain by some hungry settler. It was the winter following the grasshopper raid, and we cannot blame them for being hungry. Suddenly we were startled by the information that the boys on the western border of the range had discovered the trail of several hundred cattle, and also quite a number of horse tracks following them toward the southwest, showing plainly that the cattle were being driven off by thieves. In a short time a party of eight men from the different camps were on the trail. They followed it about seventy miles, when to their intense chagrin they came upon a trail of a large body of Indians, and the signs showed that the thieves had joined them, and all had proceeded together. Although they knew they could not hope to cope successfully with the large force which the trail indicated, the pursuers still kept on hoping that some lucky accident might enable them to recover the stock, if they could not punish the thieves. The weather had grown intensely cold, and as they journeyed on they came to an old squaw, who had been left to die by her heartless people. She had grown too old to be of any service, so they had left her here in the bitter cold to freeze, starve or be eaten by the wolves as the case might be. Her feet and hands were badly frosted, and she was almost starved having eaten nothing but hackberries for two days. She was placed on a pack pony, and made as comfortable as possible, and the boys determined to return to the range. They had not gone far when they came upon a party of seven men; among the number was the notorious "Hurricane Bill." It was plain enough to the cowboys that these outlaws had stolen the cattle and turned them over to the Indians, then hovered along the trail keeping an outlook for the pursuers.

Among the cowboys was Frank Whittaker, wearing the buckskin hunting shirt captured from Hurricane Bill in the fight on Mulberry Creek the previous spring. Bill cast an evil eye on the shirt, and it looked for a while as if the chances were good for a little battle. Of course each party realized that being so evenly matched, and all well-armed, that several would be very apt to lay down their lives in case of any demonstration with their weapons, so the cowboys reluctantly withdrew after a brief conversation, and again took up the homeward march. They reached the range without further adventure. Some of them took the old squaw over to Sun City, where she was kindly cared for by the inhabitants until spring, when she was put into the hands of a party of her own tribe who were passing through. The stolen cattle, about four hundred in number, belonged to a man by the name of Quinlan. They were never recovered. The Indians were Pawnees, several hundred in number, on their way from Nebraska to Indian territory. Their meeting with the outlaws was probably an accident, and it is to be presumed that Indians and outlaws shared in this plunder when the stock was disposed of.

At this time Bill Anderson and "Clubfoot Tom," two noted thieves, were known to have a camp somewhere south of our range near the Cimarron River. They had half a dozen followers as reckless as themselves. Their ostensible object was hunting and trapping, but it was known that they were stealing ponies from the Indians and the stockmen were suspicious that their herds might suffer at their hands. Although their exact whereabouts was not known, frequent scouting parties were sent out to see if any stock had wandered, or been driven, from the range. In one of these parties there were five of us with three pack ponies laden with feed and provisions for a week's jaunt. After scouring the country for four days, we camped a little before sunset in a pleasant timbered valley on one of the small tributaries of the Cimarron. Shortly before dark, a solitary horseman was descried riding leisurely over a plateau about a mile to the northward. Two of our party resaddled their ponies and struck out to try to interview the stranger. Seeing this he quickened his pace, and soon disappeared in one of the numerous canons. The boys returned to camp, and we picketed our ponies in a circle in a small opening and about nine o'clock we rolled ourselves in our buffalo robes and blankets, within the circle, and were soon asleep. About eleven o'clock we were aroused by one of the boys saying, "Every fellow get to his horse, somebody's after them." In a moment each man was crawling snake-like through the grass with rifles tightly gripped ready for use. We were liable to have either white or red rascals to deal with, but fortunately we reached our ponies without molestation. We found that two of them had been cut loose, but instead of stampeding, the intelligent animals only rushed toward their masters, and their coming had aroused Doyle, who first raised the alarm. We brought the ponies all in and tied them to a tree, and stood guard by turns the remainder of the night. The night dragged slowly away with no further alarm. In the morning we looked carefully for signs of the intruder. About two hundred yards down the valley we found where a horse had been hitched to an oak sapling, and had gnawed the bark off, and pawed up the ground at the foot of the tree. We also found a man's tracks in the sandy soil. We easily concluded that our visitor was the solitary horseman we had seen shortly after going into camp.

We were in a wild rugged country, cut up and intersected by numerous timbered streams and canons. It may be imagined that we kept our eyes open as we rode during the day following our nocturnal visit. In the afternoon we descried five dark objects moving rapidly to the west of us. The distance, and the haze which hung over the landscape, prevented our making out what they were. We decided to find out at all events, so putting spurs to our ponies we dashed off at a lively gallop. We had not gone far until we came to a small stream with a sandy bed. The rest of the boys crossed it all right, but I thought to take a near cut. My pony leaped from the bank to the middle of the stream, and down he went midside in water and quicksand. I had to dismount in the slush and remove my saddle and trappings and carry them to shore. Two of the boys galloped on, while two remained to assist me out of my predicament. We hitched two lariats around my pony's neck, the other ends being secured to the saddle horns, I assisted by lifting what I could, while the ponies pulled with all their strength, and we soon had my steed on terra-firma once more. The moving objects proved to be buffaloes.

As it was near night and there was splendid grass for our ponies, we encamped not far from the scene of my mishap. We had seen no signs of any stock, so on the following morning we resolved to return to the home range. After a ride of a day and a half we reached one of our outposts on the Salt Fork. We found the boys full of bustle and excitement, for some of Evans' men had been on a scout and had discovered Bill Anderson's camp.

The next morning a party was to meet here and proceed to wipe out the outlaws, provided that any range stock should be found in their possession. Securing fresh ponies our scouting party prepared to return on the second trip. Early the next morning fourteen cowboys well armed and mounted sallied forth full of zeal for the work which might be before them. After a lively ride of five or six hours we came to a timbered stream which empties into the Cimarron. Evans' men, who acted as guides, informed us that the outlaw camp was on the bank of this stream, so we proceeded quite cautiously. Presently we came upon eight ponies with split ears, the Indian mark. A little farther on a smoke appeared curling up from a rude sod chimney on top of a dugout in the west bank of the creek. A halt was called and everyone got his weapons in readiness, and then all dashed down the valley at full speed, reining up at the dugout. We saw one man hasten from a small grove into the dugout, while another did not have time to gain its shelter, but stood before us calm and pale as death. They were Joe Watson, an old-time buffalo-hunter, and "Club Foot Tom," alias Thomas Hubbard, a noted rustler of Indian horses. Our leader asked "Club Foot Tom" what business they were engaged in. He replied that they were trapping wolves. He was then asked if they had any stock; he said that they had eight head of ponies, the ones we had seen up the ' valley. When asked if that was all he said, "Yes." Just at this instant five ponies came down the canon from another direction, thus giving the lie to the statement. When asked where Bill Anderson was, he said that he had gone to Dodge City. After some further conversation the young man went into the dugout. While we were questioning them, another man appeared on the scene, riding around a sharp point almost into our midst before becoming aware of our presence. That was Bill Tilghman. It is not to his discredit that he turned very pale as he sat his horse facing our party.

It was decided, after a short consultation, that we would go into camp close by, and while part of our forces would keep an eye on the dugout, the others would reconnoiter and see if any "rangestock" could be found. After a careful search nothing more was found, and our party were all assembled around the camp fire about 150 yards below the dugout. Then ensued an animated debate in regard to what should be done. Some argued, "That we came to find the outlaws and clean them out, and here they were. Why not do it?" Others were of the opinion that although we knew they were thieves, yet having no evidence that they had ever disturbed the stock on our range, we had no cause to disturb them. It was finally put to vote whether to lynch them or not, and a majority did not like having their blood on their hands. The following spring I met Bill Tilghman in Dodge City. We had a friendly talk. I told him of the balloting in our camp. He smiled and replied, in his quiet way, "Well, you might have got us, but we'd have got some of you while you were doing it." Do not criticize too severely the rustling of Indian horses, for to those who were familiar with their raids and atrocities, it seemed almost like a virtue to deprive them of their means of transportation.

We remained here overnight, keeping a picket out, and the next day returned to the range where we resumed the ordinary routine of range life. For a little variety we occasionally had a horse race or a shooting match. Through the rest of the winter but little happened worthy of note, and although springtime brought much harder work, all hailed its advent with joy, for the grand "round-up" brought together many old friends and acquaintances, and there was a good deal of life and excitement in the "cutting out" process, where the representatives of the different cattle owners separated their stock from the main herd, picking them out by their brands. Many a lively race took place between the horsemen and the longhorned, fleet-footed Texas steers. Frequently the pony would stumble, then steed and rider would sometimes pitch headlong to the ground. As a general rule both would be up and ready for business in a moment, but sometimes either horse or rider would have a sprain or broken limb, and I have known death ensuing from such a fall.

After the cattle were all separated so that each man had his own, the next thing would be to move into a more open country for a summer range. Then the cattle had to be guarded night and day, and the worse the weather the more men would be required to keep them together, and sometimes all the men in the camp would not be able to keep them, for in the darkness of night, in the midst of a storm, a sudden stampede would often occur and before one could realize it a whole herd would vanish as if swept away by a wind. Then there was likely to be hard riding to get the herd together again, for they would often scatter into several bunches and run miles in different directions, sometimes running into another herd and then cutting out would have to be done over again.

The cowboy was always in his glory, when after a long tedious winter and a hard spring's work, the cattle would at last reach the vicinity of the shipping point, generally about the month of June. Knowing his generous disposition, there were always plenty of friends awaiting his arrival at the cattle market. The saloon keeper, the gambler, the barber, the drummer for "Cheap John" clothing houses and others too numerous to mention all put on their blandest smiles, for well they knew how freely he would scatter his money abroad, unmindful of the hardships endured to earn it.

I have seen cowboys step up to a faro or monte bank with from one to four hundred dollars in their pockets, and never leave until the last dollar was gone. Then in a fit of desperation, the faithful cow pony, together with the saddle and bridle would be put up for the next stake; and when everything else was gone, as a last resort the much prized six-shooter would be staked. When that had been lost, the victim would wheel around and start for the door. Then the loving kindness and generosity(?) of the dealer would be manifested by his saying, "Come and have something before you go." I do not mean to intimate that all were so reckless and prodigal, for many were careful and prudent; some divided their earnings with their parents, while others invested in stock, and some of the wealthy cattle owners of today were poor cowboys at the time of which I write.

Chapter 6

I N THE SPRING OF '75, after the round-up was completed, our outfit headed towards Wichita, which was a great shipping point at that time. Leaving the rugged, hilly country behind, we arrived at Sand Creek, near a point well known as the "Nine Cottonwoods," named for nine large trees in a group isolated from other timber. It was decided to remain for a time, as there was excellent grazing and plenty of water—two great objects with the stockman.

Our camp was not far from where the Osage Indians had been slain the previous summer, as previously narrated. Parts of their skeletons still remained where they had fallen, and some of the boys secured bones of their fingers as mementos. After we had been here about two weeks we broke camp and drove over to the head of the Chikaskia. Here our herd was divided, and the two camps established about five miles apart. Doctor Simmons overseeing the lower camp, while I was placed in charge of the upper one. We had reached a point so near civilization that we had almost ceased to carry our Winchesters, that had been our constant companions through the winter, although most of the boys still clung to their six-shooters.

When our outfit was divided the guns were nearly all left at my camp. I carried a large Smith and Wesson pistol, and one afternoon I concluded to take my Winchester also, to shoot some prairie chickens which were very plentiful. I secured several of the fowls and had them tied to my saddle, and about sunset was making a final ride a mile or two outside of the regular range. Looking eastward, down the valley, towards the doctor's camp, I was startled to see a man, whom I recognized as the doctor, riding towards his camp at top speed, while only a short distance behind him were several horsemen riding like the wind; evidently bent on overtaking him. It required but a glance to tell me that they were Indians, there was no mistaking the grace with which they sat their ponies nor the blankets floating in the wind. I knew that the doctor was unarmed and I thought his fate was sealed. I was still more startled on turning towards the south to see six redskins galloping towards me. My first thought was of the bright beaded blanket on my pony, which I had picked up where the Osages had dropped it in their flight after the killing of their leaders by the militia. As I was on the old stamping ground, I thought very likely these might belong to the same band, and my having in my possession the peculiar blanket might make a special object for their vengeance. I had not long to meditate but putting spurs to my pony galloped to the top of a small round knoll, where I quickly let down my lariat to hold my pony by and dismounted. I stood holding my Winchester in one hand while I motioned them back with the other. They came on until they were only about a hundred yards from me, when I assumed a more threatening attitude. At this they came to a sudden halt and unfurled a large white flag having on its folds in large black letters, "Pawnees. Peace." Then one of their number advanced, bearing the flag. He came up to "have a talk." He informed me that they were Pawnees on their way from their agency in the Indian Territory to visit friends in Nebraska, and that they were friendly. I replied, "If you are friendly, why are those Indians chasing that man down there?" He grinned as he answered, "Makee Pawnee heap laugh. See white man run." I told him that they would not have laughed if that man had had his gun. He pointed to my gun, and then to the prairie chickens I had killed, and said, "Good."

I found them hungry as Indians are sure to be, so concluded that it would be better to take them into camp and feed and keep them overnight, where we could watch them, than to have them outside, where they might sneak around and steal our horses in the darkness. I told them to go ahead, and we would go to camp and get supper. They started out single file, I in the rear, keeping a close watch, for they were hard looking fellows, and I did not have full faith in their friendly assertions. As we neared camp I saw the boys run to the wagon and get out the guns. Then my red comrades did not seem inclined to advance much farther, so I rode ahead, and of course seeing me with the Indians relieved the apprehensions of the boys in camp, and we rode on in and alighted. We gave our visitors a hearty supper and invited them to remain all night but they would not hear to it; they said that they would "go camp with other Pawnees."

Knowing how poorly the other camp was off for weapons, I sent one of the boys there with two Winchesters. He found those who had followed Dr. Simmons encamped close to his camp, but the rascals we had fed did not put in an appearance at all. We kept our horses close that night, but were not disturbed.

We remained with the stock on the Chikaskia for some weeks, and then drove to Sand Creek, a small tributary of the Ninnescah, about thirty miles west from Wichita. Here we again pitched camp and remained for some weeks. It had been nearly a year since my last visit home, and as it was only fifty five miles away, I obtained a week's leave of absence and after a fair day's ride arrived at my father's house. As usual I met with a kindly welcome, not only from my own relatives, but also from a host of other friends and acquaintances. When my week's visit was at an end, it was not without feelings of regret that I bade adieu to my friends, and as I thought of the bright eyes and smiling faces that had greeted me during my brief stay, I was painfully reminded of the wild, rough associations that surround the cowboy's life, and there came a longing for something better, something more ennobling. I even wondered if someday after all the wandering and all the hardship, there might not be a quiet peaceful little home. But no, I thought, such things are not for me; I have chosen my lot and I shall live and die a wild, free rover of the prairie.

When I got back to Wichita, I met one Zach Potter, a man with whom I had had some difficulty. He was on his way from the range to where he had friends in eastern Kansas. I always tried to make it a rule not to hold enmity toward any man. It was near an ice cream saloon that I met Potter. I addressed him in a friendly manner, and invited him to have some ice cream with me. "All right," he said, and while seated at the table we discussed our past trouble, its cause, etc., and ended up shaking hands and parting as friends. I have always been glad that we did so, for not long after I heard of his tragic death. Shot to death over a game of cards. Zach had a wild, lawless brother, and not long after his death his slayer was found dead, pierced by a bullet. Although Zach's brother was not known to be in the neighborhood it was supposed to be his hand that directed the avenging bullet.

Returning to camp, it was not long after until our outfit was actively engaged in shipping cattle. Other outfits were similarly engaged, and many cowboys would meet in Wichita. Sometimes a dozen or more would join together to take in the town. Among themselves a spirit of general good humor prevailed. They were always ready to help each other in time of need. I remember once, when a cowboy was just on the eve of starting home to Texas, his pony was struck by lightning, leaving him on foot, and almost without money. As soon as it became known among the boys they chipped in a dollar apiece and bought him a good pony, and started him on his way rejoicing.

During the summer, while crossing a shipment of cattle, I came near losing my life in the Arkansas about two miles below Wichita. My horse drowned, and I was left in mid-stream to get out as best I could. I reached the shore in an exhausted condition. I lost my entire outfit, saddle, bridle and a suit of oiled ducking, which was tied behind my saddle. Not far from the time of the above event I was placed in charge of a herd of beef steers. Among the hands in my camp were Jack Dillon, and a boy named James Manning. Manning was only fifteen years old, and we all called him "Little Jim." Jack and Jim quit our outfit after a time, and went to Wichita, where they soon squandered their wages. At this juncture Jesse Evans was fitting up an outfit to go to the great Chisholm [Chisum] ranch in New Mexico to drive a herd of cattle from there to Dodge City. There was a lot of horses to be driven through to drive the cattle back with. Among the cowboys who found employment on this trip were Jack Dillon, "Little Jim," George Hill, Bill Dunlap, Texas Frank Anderson, who by the way prided himself on being "on the shoot," Louis Evans and Jim Ayers, and others whose names are forgotten.

Jim Ayers was foreman of the outfit. "Little Jim" was a high tempered boy, with flashing black eyes, and he was also quite careless, as boys are apt to be. It appears that several times on this trip he let his horse get loose, causing the other boys a good deal of trouble to catch it again. The last time this occurred was somewhere in New Mexico. Jim Ayers reproved him for his carelessness, telling him that if he allowed his horse to get loose again he would have to walk until they went into camp. "Little Jim" rode sullenly along for awhile and then galloped ahead about half a mile overtaking two of the boys who were riding in advance of the outfit. He asked one of them to lend him his six-shooter. Thinking he wanted to shoot a rabbit his request was complied with. As soon as he got the weapon he rode back to meet the outfit. Riding up to Ayers, he said, "I don't like the way you talked to me," and then commenced to fire on him. Before anyone fairly realized what was taking place, Ayers was pierced by two or three bullets and fell mortally wounded. That night they encamped by a deserted log cabin. "Little Jim" was placed upon a horse, with a noose round his neck. The horse was then led into the cabin, and the rope fastened to a beam. Then the horse was driven out, leaving the young murderer to hang until he was dead. "Little Jim" was the only son of a widowed mother who lived somewhere in Michigan. Ayers left a wife and two children near Coffeyville, Kansas. Before the trip was completed Jack Dillon and Frank Anderson became involved in a quarrel and Dillon shot Anderson, inflicting severe but not fatal wounds. It was well for Dillon that it was not fatal, for if it had been, very likely he would have shared the same fate as "Little Jim."

In the fall, my employers, having sold most of their stock, it became necessary for me to seek employment elsewhere. I found it with W. B. Grimes, then a heavy cattle driver from the Gulf Coast, but also a merchant on Delaware Street in Kansas City. At this time he had about ten thousand cattle, most of which he proposed to winter in the Medicine Lodge and Salt Fork Country. There were several brothers in his employ by the name of Walton. Their father was a farmer in Sumner County not far from Belle Plain. As corn was plenty down there I was sent with Lou Walton, in charge of fifty head of ponies to feed and get in good order for the winter range. Some of them were very thin in flesh, and a cold storm of rain and sleet coming upon them, quite a number were chilled to death.

I had a good time while at Walton's. Sundays I would hire one of the boys to take my place, while I went to Sabbath school, or horseback riding with their sister, Miss Ella. This was too good to last, for in about four weeks I received orders to return with the ponies, as the outfit was about to start for winter quarters. When I got back to camp I found it very cold and disagreeable. Our camp was on an open plain, and it was getting well along in November. We had long weary night guards to stand and all were anxious to get to a timbered region where the stock could be turned loose, and our night watching would cease.

A good many Texas boys could not stand the idea of roughing it so far north, so they drew their wages and departed for their southern homes. Among the number was Charlie Siringo, who afterwards immortalized himself by writing a book, entitled, "A Texas Cowboy, or Twenty Years on the Hurricane Deck of a Spanish Pony."

Our cattle were separated into six herds with five or six men to each herd. Accompanying the outfit was young Brady Grimes, a chip from the old block. He was evidently fresh from school, and was to be bookkeeper and general overseer of our outfit. I remember hearing him remark on one occasion, "It seems to me that these cowboys are pretty independent to be as poor as they are." And so we were, and why not? The broad prairie was our home, and we carried our law in our belts.

"Little Dick" Simpson, or as we called him, "the little sore eyed cook," on account of his eyes having been scorched by the blaze of the campfire, was a fair example of western independence. W. B. Grimes, Sr. once reproved him for some shortcoming, in rather a gruff manner; Dick straightened himself up and replied, "I don't care a d——n for you old Grimes, if you have got lots of money." Grimes had nothing more to say, but turned away with a smile on his grim old countenance. Poor Dick, the wild influences were too much for him. Before he reached his eighteenth year he took a man's life in Indian territory; fleeing, he was captured by United States marshals. They started to Fort Smith, Arkansas, with him but he succeeded in giving them the slip, and has never been apprehended.

To resume the regular course of my narrative. We reached the winter range about December first. The different herds were located within a radius of about twenty miles. The camp I was in was located near Elm Springs on the Salt Fork. While here I was sent out in company with Cal Marts to look for some mules and ponies that had strayed away. We searched through the country lying between our camp and the junction of the Medicine Lodge and Salt Fork.

At the mouth of the Medicine Lodge is a large grove of timber. We were somewhat surprised to see quite a smoke curling up from among the tree tops. We determined to find out the cause of it, so headed directly towards the grove. Our attention was momentarily attracted to the rear. When we again turned toward the grove we were startled to see a huge Indian standing, rifle in hand, directly in front of us. He was apparently immovable as a post. His face was daubed with paint, while his head was shaven close except for a roach or topknot extending from the forehead to the back part of his head, whence dangled the inevitable scalp lock. We rode straight up to him and greeted him with the customary "How." We received only a grunt in reply. He proved to be a picket or outpost for a camp of Big Hill Osages located in the grove. He had probably seen us when we were a long distance off, and had concealed himself to await our approach. He had chosen a moment when we were looking away, to rise up as if by magic, to add an air of mystery to his movements. Anyone familiar with Indian habits has noticed this characteristic. In the winter when the foliage is gray and dead an Indian will robe himself in a gray blanket, and it would require a keen eye to distinguish him from the dead grass in which he has concealed himself. If in summer he will don a green blanket to correspond with the foliage.

After an ineffectual attempt to draw "Mr. Lo" into conversation, we rode on to camp. We met with a very friendly greeting. The Indians all engaged in vehement conversation in their guttural jargon, in the meantime casting scowling suspicious glances in our direction. There were some halfbreed interpreters in camp, and to them we made known our business in the country. Night was near at hand, so we bade them goodbye, and started for Major Drumin's camp, a few miles upstream. We reached our destination soon after dark, and were hospitably entertained until morning, when we again started out in search of the lost stock. We arrived at our own camp in the evening after an unsuccessful trip.

Soon afterwards our camp was removed from Elm Springs to Little Mule Creek, about twelve miles southwest from Kiowa. Early one morning about a week after the visit to the Indian camp I started out alone to try once more to find the lost mules and ponies. I reached a point nearly twelve miles distant from the nearest camp or settlement, when I came across two horses grazing by a small stream. One was a very "scrubby" looking pony with a sore back, caused by saddle galls, while the other was a splendid specimen of the Equine genus. Jet black, with finely proportioned limbs, and a beautifully arched neck, he stood in marked contrast to his companion, and the ordinary pony which I bestrode. I wondered who they belonged to but concluded they must have strayed from some cow camp, and I quickly decided to take them to our camp, and keep them until I found out their owner. It was the work of a few minutes to pitch a lasso on the black horse and to change the saddle from my scrubby old cow pony to this fine looking steed. I then secured the sore-backed pony, and rode on my way leading the two ponies and feeling quite elated, for I thought no owner might ever appear to claim the stray horses, and I might be enabled to keep the best one at least, by right of discovery. This bright prospect soon vanished, for looking to the westward I saw two horsemen riding towards me at full speed. Their red blankets flying in the wind, told me that they were Indians, and then it looked as though I had serious trouble on my hands. For once I was careless enough to leave camp unarmed, and I readily guessed that the horses belonged to the approaching Redskins. For a moment I hesitated in regard to what course to pursue, then I turned and rode directly towards them. As they drew nearer they separated and circling around brought up abruptly on either side of me. I pointed to the horses and then to them, to inquire if they belonged to them; they nodded in the affirmative. I then explained as best I could how they came into my possession, and how I intended to take them to camp until I could find an owner. They held quite a conversation in their own language, and then I was relieved to hear one of them say, "Good white man, ketchem Indian pony, maybe so go home agents house, no ketchem." Then they dismounted and commenced to remove their saddles. I followed suit, and exchanged the handsome black for my old roan cow pony. They quickly saddled the two strays and were about to depart, when I produced some cold biscuits and beef from my saddle pockets and divided it with them. I knew that the way to an Indian's heart was through his stomach. We shook hands and said "Goodbye," and parted. They belonged to the band I had visited at the mouth of the Medicine Lodge.

They had left their agency without a permit, and were on the way to the panhandle country for a buffalo hunt. The two ponies had strayed away in the night, and were on the way back to the agency. There were forty-four Indians in the band all told, and when they got well out on the frontier we heard of numerous depredations committed by them.

In about five weeks they returned. The first we heard of them on their return, was when one of the boys from a camp about ten miles west of ours came and told us that the Redskins had killed two beeves in the presence of two of the boys, and had proceeded to camp, and notwithstanding the protests of the cook, had taken a quarter of beef which was hanging upon the limb of a tree. We were told that we might expect them on our range the next day. Early the next morning I rode over to Kiowa and purchased two hundred cartridges. One hundred for myself and the other for Dave Callahan, or "Old Dave" as he was familiarly known. Returning to the range I found Old Dave rounding in the cattle. We decided to ride in company the balance of the day. About one o'clock p.m. we had our cattle rounded in in good shape, and were about to start for camp, which was about a mile away, when Jim, a darkey who belonged to our outfit, came riding to us at topmost speed. He looked badly frightened as he said, "Marse Cal want you all to hurry up to camp. The Indians is up there just a raisin' h——l." We unslung our rifles and started up a narrow valley which led to camp. Just as we were about to round a point which jutted out into the valley, five Indians came galloping around from the other side. Seeing us with rifles in hand, in the twinkling of an eye they flung themselves to the ground, where they lay flat in the grass, with weapons in position for use. I almost expected to see a blaze of fire issue from their rifles, and feel the sharp twinge of a bullet piercing through me. Old Dave's black eyes flashed fire as he said, "Let's ride right onto them." We rode within about five feet of them, with rifles cocked, and every nerve strung to the highest tension. One of the Indians arose, leaving his gun lying on the grass, and with extended hand, explained, "How, How; good Indian, good Indian." We declined to shake hands, and Dave asked him what they were doing there, and what they wanted. He replied, "Want beef." Old Dave answered, "You can't get any beef here. We heard how you got beef at the other camp, but you can't come that on us, we're too well heeled." The Indians looked like so many scowling demons. We turned away, and rode to the top of a little knoll nearby, keeping a close eye on them all the time. After some parleying among themselves, they arose and mounted their ponies, and rode by us without deigning to glance our way. Sitting erect and haughty, and chanting, "Hi, yah; hi yah," expressive of their contempt for us. At the same time we saw their main party filing along the top of a ridge about a mile and a half away. My comrade and I headed for camp, not knowing what mischief we might find there. We found Cal Marts holding the fort in good shape.

He said that the five redskins we had just interviewed came riding up in front of the cabin and were about to dismount, when Cal leveled his carbine on them and told them not to get down. One of them would put one foot on the ground all the time insisting, "Good Injuns, good Osages, good Osages." Cal would say, "Just put that other foot on the ground and I'll let you have it." When Jim had started away, they took the hint that he had gone for reinforcements, so they left the camp taking the same direction.

Major Drumin's camp was located about ten miles east from ours. About sunset, the Indians all having rejoined the main party, came upon the major and one of his men rounding the cattle up for the night. They very insolently demanded a beef. The Major in reply told them that he had worked hard for his beef, and if they wanted any to go and do likewise. An interpreter told this to their chief, and after a short parley turned to the Major saying, "Chief says if you won't give us one we'll kill one anyhow." The Major replied, "and I'll kill the first red —— —— —— that does kill one." Then followed another conversation between the interpreter and the chief, then shaking his finger warningly, the former addressed Major Drumin, saying, "You be out of the Nation tomorrow morning by sunrise or we'll make it hot."

The Major's camp was across the line in the Indian Nation. That night apprehending danger of an attack, all hands had their best horses saddled and we did not think of retiring to rest. Although it was winter there had been no rain or snow for some time, and the grass was very dry. To the south of us along the Salt Fork valley was the heavy growth of grass. The wind was blowing briskly from the south. About nine o'clock three fires were started simultaneously to the south, southwest and southeast of us. The fire soon gathered great headway, and its crackling and roaring could be plainly heard, while the broad plain was illuminated for miles around. Our camp was on the north side of Little Mule Creek. We rounded our stock together and crossed them all over to the north side, and then we feared that the flames might leap across the narrow stream. Had they done so all our range would have burned, and probably a good deal of the stock. Fortunately the stream was sufficient to hold the flames in check, and they finally died out, leaving many miles of the best range a charred and blackened waste.

We saw no more of the Indians, but heard of them about fifty miles southeast, where Hubbard Wilcox was holding a small herd of cattle. One evening as he was about to start to camp after his afternoon ride he came upon two Indians who had shot down several of his cattle, and were in the act of skinning them. Not being seen Wilcox dropped back out of sight and securing his horse crept carefully to a point within easy range of the rascally redskins. Taking careful aim he fired dropping one Indian dead in his tracks. He quickly fired at the other one hitting him in the back. The wounded Indian is proverbial for his running and jumping qualities, and this one was no exception to the general rule. He made a wild break for the Indian camp. Wilcox returned to his horse, and mounting tried to overtake the fugitive to prevent his raising an alarm. In this he did not succeed; the Indian reached the camp just in time to fall in the agonies of death. Wilcox was obliged to round up his stock that night, and was fortunate in escaping with his outfit over the line into Kansas.

In the month of March Old Dave and I being worn out with our hard winter's work decided to quit, and after resting awhile to go to the southwestern part of the Indian Territory in search of wild horses, which were plenty in that section. We each had an excellent saddle pony, also good weapons, pack pony and general outfit. We spent two or three weeks very pleasantly about Sun City, Medicine Lodge, and visiting among old comrades in various camps. We were waiting for spring to advance far enough to insure good grass for our ponies.

We finally started down the Medicine valley. Arriving at Kiowa, we put up for the night in a log hotel, the only one in the place. While here circumstances occurred which caused me to take a trip about one hundred miles east. I expected to regain my comrade in about a week, but various difficulties prevented me from doing so. Very reluctantly I wrote him that I would be compelled to give up the trip, and for him to go on without me. I remained in the settlement until some time in April. I could not long remain quiet after my roving experiences, so I decided to start down the Texas trail, expecting to find employment with some outfit I might meet driving from Texas to Kansas. I met a herd belonging to Millet & Mayberry, William Lockridge in charge, between Skeleton and Wild Horse creeks in the Indian Territory. They were in need of an extra man, and I secured employment at once.

Three of the boys in the outfit were Arthur Mauping, a half-breed Choctaw, Matt Coates and a long haired fellow called "Doby." I soon felt at home in the new outfit. Lockridge had been a scout for General R. E. Lee through the rebellion. His face was deeply seamed and furrowed, telling the story of hardship and exposure. Travelling behind us, and often in sight, was a herd belonging to J. Driskill, in charge of his nephew Tillman Driskill.

Camping one night on Pond Creek, a terrific thunderstorm burst upon us, and the following morning a water spout burst about two miles above us, and an immense wave came sweeping down Pond creek threatening destruction to everything in its wake. We barely had time to move our wagon to higher ground when the spot where it stood was flooded. Driskill's wagon, with two men, was left upon an island until the flood abated.

Leaving Pond Creek, after several days drive, we reached the Arkansas which we crossed a few miles east of Great Bend. Thence we took the "Old Harker" trail, leading from Great Bend to Ellsworth. At Cow Creek, we encamped one night with the Driskill outfit about half a mile in our rear. That night one of Driskill's men went to sleep on guard and their cattle were scattered in every direction. Driskill sent to our camp the following morning for a man to help get the herd together, and I was sent with instructions to stay as long as I was needed, and then if I did not overtake our outfit on the trail to rejoin them at or near old Fort Harker.

Going to Driskill's camp, I rode in a circle until I struck a trail leading down Cow Creek. I followed this trail until about noon, when I came upon one hundred and eighty cattle with a Dutch boy herding them. He informed me that his father had taken up the stock and that I would find him at the house about half a mile distant. Arriving at the house, which was built of sod,

I found the family about to dine. I received and accepted an invitation to dine with them. Mine Host, a burly Teuton, informed me that he would require fifty dollars damages before he would let the cattle go. Finding him firm in this I could only return and report to Driskill. I found the outfit breaking camp to move on to the head of Plum Creek, about ten miles nearer Ellsworth. When I told Driskill the state of affairs he ordered two good horses caught and then went to the wagon and took out a Winchester, which he slung to his saddle, while he belted a pistol and a quantity of cartridges around him. Saddling the fresh horses we started for the Dutchman's ranch, while the rest of the outfit pulled on to Plum Creek.

When we came in sight of the cattle, instead of the boy herding them, there were nine men and large boys, all mounted and armed. My pistol being out of repair I had left it in Lockridge's wagon. Driskill unbuckled his pistol and handing it to me said, "If it gets too hot for us, that gray horse never knows when to stop running." He unslung his carbine, and we advanced on the hostiles. Driskill opened the conversation by asking, "Where is the man who took up these cattle?" The burly Dutchman, swelling with importance, answered, "I'm de man." Then the following conversation took place. "Have they done you any damage." "Yah, dey run across the corner of mine veat field, ont it dakes fifty tollar to settle it." "Well it's just like this; if they have done you fifty dollars worth of damage, you'll get fifty dollars, but if they haven't, you won't". "Vell I don't want to act de hog. I could get von tollar a head with de law, but you could have um for fifty." Driskill offered to give bonds to the value of the cattle and try it by law, or he would let the Dutchmen keep them until a case could be tried and settled, provided that he would give bonds for their safekeeping. Both propositions were rejected. Then Driskill said, "I have one more offer to make you, I'll give you twenty-five dollars rather than have any trouble," at the same time holding out the money. The Dutchman replied, "No. Nottings less don fifty tollars would settle it." Driskill then said, "Now I have made you all kinds of fair propositions and you won't accept any of them, so I'll tell you what we're going to do. We're going to take these cattle to camp or die right here with them, and when one of you fires the first shot, they'll be more dead Dutch lying around here than you ever saw before." He then said to me in a low tone, "Let's try a stampede on them." We accordingly dashed at the cattle yelling like wild Comanches. Away went the cattle like a whirlwind, but the Dutch were too many for them. Just as we were about to get the stock through their line, the big Dutchman managed to get in front and turn the leaders back in confusion. At this Driskill brought his Winchester to his shoulder and sent a shot whistling in close proximity to the Dutchman's head. He ducked his head in every direction, and quickly got out of the way. We were again just about to get beyond the German lines when some of them dashed into the rear of herd and cut off fifteen or twenty head and started them towards the house. Driskill yelled to me, "Shove on the main bunch, and I'll make these —— drop this bunch." I saw him present his carbine and they quickly got out of the way. I was driving the main bunch for all I was worth when the big Dutchman came galloping up to try to stop me. He had a big pistol in his hand, and was pounding his heels into his horse's sides to increase his speed. I reined my horse between him and the cattle and ordered him to stop. He still advanced when I levelled my pistol with a good deal of emphasis again told him to stop. This had the desired effect, he cried out, "Take de cattle; I try you now mit de law." In a few moments Driskill brought his little herd up, and then we had them together, and we pushed them rapidly across the prairie towards the head of Plum Creek, while the Dutch gathered together, an excited group, making wild gesticulations in our direction. Two of them left the others and followed a short distance behind us. When we reached the divide, about mid-way between Cow Creek and Plum Creek, looking back over the prairies we saw our enemies riding from cabin to cabin through the settlement, evidently trying to raise a larger force against us. I felt much relieved a little later to meet Bob Evans, one of the boys from camp, armed with a good Winchester. The two men who had followed us left when they came in sight of camp. It was nearly sundown when we reached camp and about dusk when supper was over. Driskill came to me and expressed his regrets for crowding so much upon me, but wanted to know if I could carry a letter to Ellsworth, a distance of fifteen miles. He said he would give me one of his best ponies to ride. I readily agreed to go. The fresh pony was caught and saddled, and handing Driskill his six-shooter I started out. In the meantime nothing more had been seen of the Dutch forces, although trouble was anticipated before morning.

A short distance below camp was a large grove of timber; the same in which Cole made his escape as narrated in a former chapter. When I was about half a mile from camp I heard a noise behind, looking back I saw by the dim twilight that a large party of men were issuing from the grove, and some of them were already between me and camp. A level plain stretched out before me for eight miles, until the trail reached the rugged breaks of Ash Creek. It seemed there was nothing to do but run for it. Loosening the rein, and giving my pony the word, he shot out like a race horse, and then the mob came tearing after me, yelling like hungry wolves. It seemed for a time as if they would certainly overtake me with their long-limbed farm horses. My steed had been a Cheyenne war pony that Driskill had purchased in the Indian Territory. The yells of our pursuers only quickened his pace, and he completely surprised me with his speed. However, I knew the chase would be a long one, and the outcome looked doubtful at best. I knew too well the spirit of a frontier mob to want to fall into their clutches. Oh, how madly I longed for a good Winchester to defend myself when the last pinch would come.

Presently I came to a sod shanty on the right-hand side of the road. I dashed up to the door and asked if they had a gun in the house. They answered, "No." On I went with my heart filled with desperation at the thought of having to yield my life to such a mob without a chance of defending myself. Soon I met an ox wagon with half a dozen people in it of both sexes. Again I inquired for a gun. Again I was answered in the negative. Soon after I overtook a solitary horseman riding leisurely along. As I dashed past him I yelled, "Look out for your top knot. There is a whole mob of Dutch after me, and they may take you in." I did not pause as I delivered this advice, and soon had the satisfaction of reaching the broken country at the head of Ash Creek. The faithful pony was white with foam. Leaving the trail I took a more moderate gait. I arrived at Ellsworth all right, and after stabling the pony, and seeing that he was well taken care of, I proceeded to the Central Hotel and delivered the letter to Mr. Mayberry, to whom it was addressed.

The next day I saw the solitary horseman whom I had passed in my flight, recognizing him by his horse, a spotted animal. He told me that when the mob came up to him, they gathered around with weapons leveled at him. He asked for an explanation, saying that he had done nothing to cause such actions. They replied, "What for you run so if you done nothing." He told them that he had not ridden faster than a walk. They then inquired if he had seen anyone pass on horseback. He informed them that he had seen a horseman, but that he was too far ahead for them to overtake him. They dashed ahead however until they came to the breaks of Ash Creek, when they realized that it would be useless to try to find me in that broken country.

The next day Bob Evans came into town, and I sent Driskill's pony back with him, while I rejoined Lockridge on Oak Creek near old Fort Harker, on the present side of Kanopolis, that great swindle of central Kansas. In a few days Lockridge was obliged to let one man go to cut down expenses. As I was the last man employed it fell to my lot to go. Lockridge informed me, however, that a job was open for me with "Till" Driskill's outfit, which by this time had arrived at Ellsworth. So without any loss of time I was once more in Driskill's employ.

Among the saddle horses set apart for my use was the one which had carried me so faithfully in my flight from the Dutch. The place selected for our summer range was about twelve miles north from Ellsworth. Our camp was located at the foot of a high bluff, known as Turkey Point. We found some of the settlers very hostile towards us, as they regarded us as intruders on their range, although our grazing ground was really on Uncle Sam's domain. One big fellow came into camp one day talking in a very blustering and insulting manner. Driskill very promptly knocked him down with a Winchester. A few days later we were notified that if we came down to our usual watering place we would find the creek lined with armed men. Accordingly all hands escorted the cattle to water, with weapons ready for use. As we neared the creek we saw two men sneak out from the timber, and make off across the prairie. We met with no disturbance, and everything passed quietly enough during the rest of my stay with the outfit.

In the latter part of August I determined to make a visit home. Going to Ellsworth I obtained a settlement, bought a pony and a new suit of clothes, and started for home. I stopped at Hutchinson to see my old time friend Cy Davidson, who was then stopping at home for a short time. From there I proceeded to Butler County, where I enjoyed a good visit with my own folks, and attended to some matters of business at the same time. Two weeks was about as long as I could stand it in the settlement at one time, so at the end of that time I saddled my pony and started for the southwest range by Wichita. In Wichita I met many old friends and comrades, had too good of a time for my pocketbook, so shaking the dust of the city from my feet I started westward.

W. B. Grimes was once more holding his stock on the Ninnescah, and I resolved to visit his camps where I would meet many of the old boys, and perhaps find employment. I was cordially greeted by old comrades and although there was no room for more help, I was invited to stay as long as I felt like doing so. There were three Mexicans in the outfit; Gabriel, Pancho, and Rosanna. It appears that a short time before Gabriel, or Gabe as he was called, had been in Wichita and in company with another Mexican named Philip had been on quite a "round-up" as the cowboys would term it. During their spree Gabe lost sixty dollars, which he carried in his pocket. He suspected Philip of stealing it. While I was stopping with the boys, two of them who had been to Wichita, returned on horseback and reported that Philip was coming out to camp with the provision wagon, which was on the road a few miles behind them.

When Gabe heard this he declared that he would shoot Philip if he came to camp. In a short time Gabe mounted his horse and rode out around the cattle. Soon afterward the wagon arrived with Philip on board. Philip was unarmed, while Gabe wore in his belt a large revolver. Presently I saw Gabe leave the herd, and come riding rapidly toward camp. Those in camp were all outside of the tent sitting around the campfire. Stepping toward the front of the tent I beckoned Philip to me. Stepping inside I pointed to Gabe and then touched my pistol in a significant manner. I then unbuckled my belt, which contained a Colt's forty-five and fifty cartridges. Placing them under the folds of a blanket I stepped out and joined the others around the campfire. I gave the Mexican this friendly warning because I did not want to see anyone shot like a dog without a fair show for defense.

For some reason Philip did not avail himself of my weapon. Gabe alighted from his horse and approaching Philip, extended his hand saying in the Mexican tongue, "How do you do, my friend." This was rather a surprise to me, for I did not then comprehend the Mexican nature as I do now. Gabe shortly returned to the herd, and the same afternoon Philip went out with Rosanna, the Mexican cook, to gather a wagon load of fuel. Now was the time for Gabe to accomplish his murderous purpose; approaching Philip he said, with an oath, "Now me going to killa you." He fired three shots in quick succession, one of which passed clear through Philip's body, while the others flew wide of the mark. Gabe fled at once and was seen no more; but that night a span of horses belonging to a settler disappeared, and it was supposed that Gabe took them. Notwithstanding a heavy bullet had passed clear through him between the first and second lower ribs, Philip was up and around in three weeks. Still looking quite pale however for a dark-skinned Mexican.

It is related of Gabe that a few years before this, while near Abilene, an officer came to serve an attachment on the cattle that he was with, when Gabe lassoed him and dragged him over the rough prairie until life was almost extinct.

Soon after the shooting of Philip I bade adieu to my comrades and went west to the Chikaskia River. Here I found a chance to drive to Sun City with Douglas & Son, merchants of that place, who had purchased a small herd of cattle with which they needed help. Arriving at Sun City I found employment for a few days roping and branding the cattle.

At this time Mr. J. Driskill was holding a large herd of cattle along the Cimarron, near the crossing of the Fort Dodge and Camp Supply trail. This outfit was in charge of his son, "Budd" Driskill. Winter was near at hand and I was desirous of getting employment for the winter. Having a good recommendation from Till Driskill, I decided to go to the camp on the Cimarron and strike for a job. I was successful in obtaining work and was gratified to find Bob Evans and J. W. McCaully, two of the boys from the Ellsworth outfit, located there for the winter.

The winter came and passed very quietly, with but little to vary the monotony. There were deer and plenty of antelopes, wolves, and now and then a small herd of buffalo, besides smaller game on our range; the pursuit of which added zest to the ordinary routine of range life.

With the advent of spring came one of the greatest sorrows of my life. Learning of the serious illness of my sister, who was about three years my senior, I decided to go home immediately. Drawing my wages, I mounted my pony and rode the entire distance, over two hundred miles, in five days. I reached home just five days too late to ever see her again in this world. They had laid her to rest where the wild prairie flowers might bloom over her grave. How sad was the greeting of my aged parents, and brother and sister. How sadly I contrasted the pure gentle life that had gone out, with my own wayward one. For a time I thought I would give up the roving life and stay and comfort my parents in their bereavement. A few weeks was all I could endure of the quiet and monotonous life in the settlement. There seemed to be a wild gnawing pain in my heart that would not be still. The boundless plains were ever arising before me, in my mental vision, and I longed to roam, I did not care where nor how far.

I had a splendid pony. Mounting him I proceeded to Dodge City. Once more I was among old companions of the range and trail. I found Matt Coates and Doby running a meat market; while a third partner named Charley Reed added to their profits by running a monte bank. Charley Reed was one of Millett's and Mayberry's old cowboys, who had gained quite a reputation for himself by a desperate fight in Fort Griffin, Texas. "Hurricane Bill," whom I have mentioned several times before, finally abandoned his old stamping grounds, and going to Fort Griffin in Shackleford County on the Texas frontier, was chosen sheriff, on account of his well-known reckless bravery. He soon gathered around him a crew of fellows as reckless as himself. He carried things with a high hand, bluffing and intimidating nearly everyone whom they came in contact with.

One evening Reed was playing a quiet game in a saloon, when Bill with four of his followers sauntered in, and addressed Reed in an insolent manner. He very quickly made them a cutting reply. In an instant all hands dropped to their weapons, and then ensued a terrible conflict, in which three of Bill's comrades lost their lives, while Bill himself was badly wounded. Reed escaped unharmed although a great number of shots were fired at him at short range.

Now I might as well follow Reed's career briefly to its tragic close. In the summer of '78 he in company with Matt Coates drove a herd of ponies to Cheyenne, where they sold them. Reed received the purchase money. They then started for Dodge City on horseback. When a few miles out from Cheyenne Coates proposed a division of the money. Reed only laughed at him, saying, "Do you take me for a tenderfoot?" Coates dropped his hand for his pistol, but Reed was too quick for him, and Coates fell mortally wounded, while Reed rode on to the southward. Coates lived just long enough to tell the story to some passerby, who hastened to Cheyenne, where a mob was quickly raised and started in pursuit of the murderer. They overhauled him, and he paid the penalty of his crime with a rope around his neck.

To return to my own wanderings. I had not been long in Dodge City until I had secured employment with one, George Littlefield, who had contracted to deliver a large number of cattle on Running Water, for the Sioux Indians, at the Red Cloud agency. In the herd I started with were forty-five-hundred cattle. Our party consisted of thirteen men, including the inevitable darkey cook. We had a long tiresome drive across the hot, alkali plains. Good water was impossible to obtain, and we suffered severely from thirst. What a pleasure it was when we would occasionally come to a small timbered stream, where choke cherries and wild currants grew in abundance.

Arriving at Frenchman Creek, we found a camp of the Olive Brothers, who have since become noted for burning two settlers named Mitchell and Ketchum at the stake. Many will remember this incident as "The Man Burning Horror of Nebraska." We crossed the South Platte at Ogallala, and proceeded across the divide to the North Platte, then our course lay up the valley of the last mentioned stream. Among the points of interest to me was Ash Hollow, once the scene of a terrible Indian massacre. After about two days drive up the river I was taken sick and was unable to proceed farther with the outfit. I had a burning fever, with fierce pains piercing through my body.

It was about six miles back to Ogallala, the nearest point where medicine could be obtained. I had turned my own pony in with the herd when I left Dodge, and having no work to do he had grown fat and frolicsome, so it was all I could do to manage him in my weak condition. However, with the assistance of my comrades I mounted him and started down the river. I did not ride far until I grew faint and dizzy. Crawling off my pony I laid down in the sand beneath the hot rays of an August sun. I know not how long I remained there, but I finally aroused and managed to remount. Several times throughout the day I had to dismount and lie down for a time. I reached a ranch about night where I rested until the following morning, when I again took up my journey. I reached Ogallala about noon. Here I obtained medicine, and after resting three days, although far from feeling well, I started down the trail for Dodge City. After riding a few miles I overtook five cowboys, who having delivered their cattle somewhere on the Platte were returning to Dodge City. They as well as myself had calculated on getting provisions at Olive Brothers camp on Frenchman Creek. After a hard day's ride we reached the creek about dark, and were disappointed to find that the outfit had moved away. We were tired and hungry, and the nearest supplies were miles away in a little sod store on the banks of the Republican. There was nothing for it but to go supperless to bed, or ride on to the store. We decided to ride on. We reached the store between nine and ten o'clock, and were disgusted to find no one about the premises. Upon examination we found that the door to the place was only an old wagon sheet hung over the opening. This was a small obstacle to a lot of hungry cowboys. We just went in and helped ourselves to crackers, oysters, canned fruits, etc. I am sorry to say that some of the boys filled their belts with cartridges from a large box which they found. In the morning it was decided to wait awhile and see if the proprietor would come around. About nine o'clock he came in. He had passed the night with some cowboys at a ranch about two miles up the river. When we asked him the amount of our bill, he said, "Oh, I guess three dollars will be about right." This was cheerfully paid, and we proceeded on our journey.

About noon one of the boys killed an antelope. We soon dressed it and packed it on a pony. Soon after we came to a settler's cabin on the banks of a small stream. He had some cows and quite a field under cultivation. We traded him antelope meat for milk, watermelons and roasting ears. We had quite a picnic. In a few days we arrived at Dodge City.

I soon found a party of the old boys from the Medicine Lodge country. They were encamped near the stockyards, just below town. They invited me to camp with them, and I accepted the invitation. At night I turned my pony loose on the river bottom with a number of others. In the morning he was not to be found. After searching up and down the valley, and not finding him I concluded that he might have gone to Jim Anderson's livery stable where he had sometimes been fed. I was riding a horse belonging to one of my friends. When I reached the stable and was in the act of riding in I was startled to see a man in the door of the office with a large pistol in each hand. He leveled them directly at me, saying while his eyes blazed like fire, "Get right down off from that horse." I replied, "What's the matter my friend?" He answered, "It don't make any difference. I am running this thing now." Then looking me over from head to foot he said, "Look here. I am a Texas cowboy, and I am in trouble here, and want to jump this d——d town. I only wanted you to get off so as not to attract any attention here until this —— —— —— gets my horse saddled." "Oh," I replied, "If you had told me that I'd been off long ago." I quickly dismounted, when he leveled his pistol at the stableman, saying, "Now you saddle that horse as quick as h——l will let you." The man hustled the saddle on pretty lively. Then he was ordered to lead him out, which he did. The man then proceeded to mount, keeping his eye on us with his pistol ready for instant use. When fairly out in the street he dashed his spurs into the steed, and turning to the south galloped across the toll bridge not stopping to pay toll. Riding in front of a sod ranch across the river, he called the proprietor, who soon appeared and handed him a bottle of whiskey. Taking a long pull at the bottle, he galloped away across the prairie to the southward.

There is a gradual rise from the river to a ridge which lies about three miles south of town. When he reached this ridge he stopped and looked back towards town. By this time there was a party of half a dozen well armed and mounted men galloping across the prairie in pursuit. It did not take long in those days to turn out the "shot-gun club" of Dodge City.

To deviate somewhat from the regular line of my story, the fugitive's name was Charlie Brady. He had killed a man in Arizona, and then fleeing to New Mexico had found employment with a herd of cattle enroute for Dodge City. He had formerly been a comrade of Jim Anderson in the Confederate army. Arriving at Dodge he rode right into town with two pistols in his belt, contrary to the regulations of that strictly(?) moral city. Joe Mason, of the police force, walked up to him, and without a word of warning knocked him down with a pistol. He then conducted him to the calaboose. A fine of twenty-five dollars was then levied against him, not having the money, Jim Anderson learning of his trouble, paid the fine, holding Brady's horse and pistols as security. No sooner had Brady been released than he proceeded to the stable. Anderson being out, he went into the office and obtained his pistols which were in a desk. At the moment that I appeared he was compelling the stableman to saddle his horse.

To return to the pursuit, which was headed by Jim Anderson. When Brady saw them coming he turned his horse and rode directly towards them. Within about half a mile of his pursuers he gave his horse free rein, and waving a pistol in each hand, approached them at a mad gallop. Anderson told his companions to stay back, and he would go out to meet him alone, and that he would bring him back without any trouble; but if all went some of them would very likely get killed, even if they succeeded in getting Brady. It turned out as Anderson had said, for desperate and reckless as Brady was he would not fire on his old companion in arms. He came quietly back with them, and when they reached town he was again assessed twenty-five dollars for his escapade. He was obliged to sell his fine horse, and finally left town on a scrubby old cow pony, going south to the old Indian Territory.

Returning to camp I was gratified to learn that one of the boys had found my pony. The next day I was pleased to meet my old friend, Till Driskill. He recommended me to a man named Scheedy, who had large herds of cattle up the river near Lakin, and was in need of an extra man. I soon made terms with him, and started for the camp the same day. It was about sixty-five miles away, and I reached it about three o'clock the next afternoon. I found a Texan named Gus Birdsell in charge. The boys were just about to start out for the evening ride around the range. They drove up the loose ponies and caught a large wild-eyed black one for me to ride. They informed me that "Coaley" had lately thrown one man breaking his collar bone, then another man had tried him, and he had reared and falling backwards had completely demolished the saddle, though the rider had escaped uninjured.

Birdsell said that I would not have to ride him but that he would like me to take him for one of my saddle ponies. I replied, "All right, I will try him." Turning my own pony into the herd I proceeded to saddle him. When my saddle was securely cinched I took a firm grasp on the side of the bridle with my left hand, and front part of the saddle with my right, placing my foot in the stirrup I made a quick move to vault into the saddle. As I raised from the ground, quick as a flash the fiery animal whirled to the right. He whirled around very rapidly several times, my firm grasp on the bridle and saddle kept me with him, standing in an upright position with my left foot in the stirrup. The moment he slackened up I threw myself fairly into the saddle, then giving him a sharp cut with my cuarte, or Mexican riding whip, he plunged away at a terrific speed. The other boys followed up, and I kept my wild steed going until he was thoroughly tired. Although he gave me an occasional shaking up I managed to ride him every third day.

I remained with this outfit until the fore part of November when I quit and went down the river to Dodge. I reached the city on election day, November 3rd. As I rode into town and neared one of the numerous dance halls I heard a great racket, and saw a crowd come pouring out of the door. Riding nearer I saw Ed Masterson, the deputy marshal, coming out pale and bleeding. It seems that one gambler tried to shoot another, when Masterson interfered and was himself fired upon. He drew his pistol, and was in the act of shooting when his opponent sent a bullet crashing through his right forearm and glancing between his ribs. He fell to the floor, but grasping his pistol in his left hand fired several shots, disabling the gambler and wounding a bystander. The gambler also wounded a bystander. So that in the melee four persons were wounded, but none fatally. Masterson kept his place on the street in spite of his wounds. Poor fellow, some time later he met his death while attempting to disarm two cowboys for wearing their weapons on the street.

The circumstances, as I recollect them, were about as follows; two cowboys named respectively Walker and Wagner came down from the Smoky Hill River. Masterson seeing them wearing their pistols walked up and demanded them. Wagner who wore two, handed over one of them, and immediately drew the other and commenced firing at Masterson, who was simply doing his duty as an officer. Masterson quickly returned the fire, Walker also joining in the affray. Batt Masterson, Ed's brother, hearing the shooting appeared on the scene and also joined in. Many shots were exchanged, and Ed Masterson and Wagner fell mortally wounded, pierced by many bullets. Walker also fell, having received six bullets, but none of them striking a vital point. He was taken to the Dodge House, and such was the indignation over Masterson's death, that a strong guard was required to keep him from being mobbed, desperately wounded as he was. He was the son of a wealthy Texas cattleman. The father receiving a telegram of his son's condition he managed to have him smuggled out of town, and he subsequently recovered. Nearly everyone who died "with his boots on" was buried on Boot Hill, as the

burying ground north of town was appropriately named. Masterson however was a general favorite and was buried with military honors in the military
cemetery at Fort Dodge. He was followed to his last resting place by a long
procession. Many fair but frail ones wept bitter tears over the brave man who
had fallen. Over his grave they sang the following sad refrain:

Lay him low, his work is done,
What to him is friend or foeman?
What to him since he is gone
Is hand of man or kiss of woman?

As man may he fought his fight.
Proved his truth by his endeavor
Let him sleep in solemn might,
Sleep forever and forever.

Batt Masterson who has been mentioned several times previously, has
since figured in a number of desperate encounters; has been since I first knew
him, a sporting man, dance house keeper, sheriff and editor of a newspaper,
and always noted for his reckless bravery.

Soon after arriving at Fort Dodge I met an old friend who was anxious to
have me join him in the search for some lost cattle, and I consented to do so.
Our pay was a certain sum per diem, with expenses, each man to furnish his
own horse and equipments. I purchased a good stout pony, in addition to the
one I already had, and we used him as a pack animal. Proceeding westward
we found seventy head of lost stock not very far from the Colorado line. We
returned with these to Dodge City. Winter being near at hand we decided to
start for Butler County to spend some time. Before leaving town my comrade
could not resist the temptation to imbibe some western "tanglefoot," and he
came to me in a condition which he described as being "as peaceful as a lion
and as harmless as a lamb." We fell in with a young fellow whose home was
near Cherryvale, Kansas, and we all started down the river together.

One day we camped for dinner close to a Mennonite settlement, which
was located between Great Bend and Larned. While the other boys made
some coffee and fried some meat, I went to a house to buy some eggs. There
was but one room in the house, with the ground for a floor. This one room

was a kitchen, dining room, bedroom and parlor combined. An old lady was busy churning with an old fashioned churn. Several white headed children were playing in a pool of water near the middle of the room while several half-grown chickens were drinking from the same pool, while others were perched on the footboard of a homemade bedstead. The old lady could not understand one word of English, but one of the youngsters had mastered the language enough to know what I wanted. They all went out back for the eggs, leaving me alone with the poultry. No sooner had they passed out when the feathered bipeds made a wild dash for the churn. Some flew from the pool of water to the top of the churn, alighting with their muddy feet in the cream which had gathered around the dasher. Of course I shooed them away. When the family came in, seeing the tracks in the cream the old lady took a dirty looking rag and gave a wipe or two around the churn and then went on with her work as calmly as the setting of the sun on a summer's eve.

By the time we had arrived at Great Bend I had changed my mind in regard to going home, and bidding my comrades good-bye, I turned my footsteps south toward the Medicine Lodge country. I visited many old friends in the towns of the valley—Sun City, Medicine Lodge and Kiowa, as well as in many camps on the range.

Among those that I had the pleasure of meeting were Tom Murray, Cy Davidson, Frank McAllister, Barney O'Conner, Old Dave Callahan, Frank Whittaker, and others too numerous to mention. At the present writing McAllister and O'Conner are partners in the livery business in Lakin, Kansas; Davidson lives on a ranch in New Mexico; poor Tom Murray sleeps beneath the sod, a victim of the fierce Cheyennes in their last great raid through western Kansas, an account of which I will narrate further on.

I met Old Dave in Kiowa, and after a hearty greeting he invited me to make my home at his ranch during my stay in that neighborhood. Wondering where the ranch might be I followed him across the river to a large log cabin, which stood in a grove of cottonwood timber. Here I was introduced to the proprietor of the ranch, Ed Withers, who gave me a cordial welcome. Withers was a striking personage. Tall, with broad shoulders, and piercing black eyes, with a mass of hair of raven blackness reaching down over his shoulders, while beneath a heavy dark mustache a set of even white teeth fairly glistened when he smiled. It did not take me long to discover that the ranch, and its inmates had a peculiar history. Withers appeared at the door wearing a pair of large pistols, and holding in one hand a Winchester carbine, while a huge fierce looking dog stood by his master eyeing me suspiciously. When he saw that his master gave me a friendly greeting he wagged his tail and leaped up to me, giving me to understand in his dumb fashion that he also welcomed me.

My tired ponies being well cared for, we went in to supper, which was served by an old darkey, whom I learned had long been a servant in the family. I noted that Withers sat down to the table with his Winchester across his lap. When a favorable opportunity arrived Old Dave explained the reasons for these precautions.

It appears that Ed Withers moved into northern Texas taking with him considerable stock, and settling in one of the border counties. It has been no uncommon thing on the Texas border for a northern man to have some false charge trumped up against him, in order that there might be some excuse for killing him and confiscating his property. Whether this was the case with old man Withers, I am not prepared to say. Suffice it to say that he was killed and his property confiscated, and his family harassed until they were compelled to flee over the line into the Indian Territory, and eventually from there to Kansas. It was charged that they added to their stock of horses in an unlawful manner. Old Dave told me that Ed had killed several of his father's slayers, and was in constant danger of being bushwhacked himself. At the time of my visit his mother and sister were at Fort Smith as witnesses against some of the old man's slayers. I remained at the ranch three days, resting my jaded ponies, and having a pretty good time after a cowboy's notion.

I found that there was a bitter feud between Ed Withers and Ez Iliff, an ex-convict who kept a small general store in Kiowa. One night while passing in front of Iliff's store, Withers fired a shot through the door barely missing some men who were standing around the stove. I did not approve of such cowardly conduct, and resolved to leave before I would meet the fate of "good dog Tray," from being found in bad company. Bidding my comrades adieu, I wandered restlessly around my old stamping ground for a week or two, and then decided to go home and spend a winter in civilization. It was well for me that I followed my judgment and left the Withers' ranch when I did, for three days later a posse of U.S. Marshals came up and captured Ed Withers and started with him to Fort Smith charged with stealing Indian ponies. They effected his capture in this manner. Gaining access to the house when its inmates were all away, they patiently waited for the coming of their intended victim. When he arrived he carelessly opened the door and stepped in, Winchester in hand; the moment he passed the threshold the cold muzzle of a Winchester was pressed against his temples from either side of the door, and there was nothing for it but to yield to the inevitable and submit with the best grace possible. Securing their prisoner the marshals started on their long journey to Fort Smith. Reaching a point well down in the Indian Territory, they encamped one night on the banks of a small stream. In some way Withers managed to slip his pinions, and he stole silently away in the darkness of the night. Traveling for quite a distance on foot he finally came to a herd of Indian ponies. Catching one of them, he mounted, and with neither saddle nor bridle, headed towards a locality where he had friends. A few days later the denizens of Kiowa were startled to see him ride boldly into town with a half a dozen armed and desperate looking men at his heels. He subsequently located in Colorado, where he met the fate of all desperadoes—"died with his boots on."

It was while at the Withers Ranch that my poetic genius burst forth in the following fashion.

I am a reckless cowboy,
The prairie is my home;
At the early age of sixteen
I first commenced to roam.
With two pistols in my belt
And a spur upon each boot,
I am a reckless cowboy.
You bet I'm on the shoot.

My first trip was from Texas,
In the year of seventy one,
When the boys all came to Newton,
And kicked up lots of fun.
Next summer found me ranging
On the raging "Arkansaw,"
Where we all grew wild and lawless
In the town of Wichita.

From there I drifted westward,
To a country wild and strange.
In the valley of the Salt Fork,
I found a winter range.
The winter was so dreary,
I thought it would never end
And when at last 'twas spring time
I drove up to Great Bend.

Next winter found me ranging
On the Medicine Lodge;
Headquarters for the last year
Was the reckless town of Dodge.
There gamblers shrewd and tricky
Are watchful as a cat
To trap some luckless "snoozer"
From Texas or the Platte.

Now I'm like an Indian,
I never can find rest,
For settlements keep pushing
Still farther toward the west;
So farewell friends and kindred,
And all I once held dear,
I am a reckless cowboy
Far out on the frontier.

Weary of the hardship and the tragedy incident to life on the plains, I started for home, which I reached in due time. I always received a kindly welcome from the young folks in the settlement. There were a great many social gatherings of various kinds. Old fashioned play parties, dances, literary societies, spelling school, and so forth etc. It is not to be supposed that I had wandered all these years heartwhole and fancy free, for I had had my dreams of love and home that ended with a rude awakening, and now at the age of twenty four I was growing cynical, and I had often exultantly declared to myself, "I will die as I have lived, a wild free rover of the plains." But there "is a providence that shapes our ends, rough hew them as we may." One day

I met a friend that gave me a pressing invitation to attend an evening party in his neighborhood a few miles north. I accepted the invitation, and now comes the crowning romance of my life. There were many bright eyes and pretty faces at the party, for Kansas is noted for her beautiful woman. Among the rest there was one pair of eyes that held a strange fascination for me. They seemed to wear a far away expression, and in their luminous depth there seemed to be a touch of ineffable sadness. Somehow the thought came to me, "Here is a woman that I might love, that might save me from the reckless life I have been drifting into." Then I laughed a bitter laugh at the idea. I asked myself, "What would she care for such as me?" I obtained an introduction and learned that the owner of the charming eyes was a recent arrival from Ohio. On my way home and in my dreams that night, I was haunted by those eyes. I tried to banish them from my thoughts and made up my mind to start back to the range again; but I could not break the chain that seemed to bind me. I sought for a better acquaintance with my fair charmer, and before the winter was over I had the pleasure of escorting her to a number of social gatherings, and I freely admit that I was head over heels in love.

I had planned all winter to go back to the plains in the spring, if not before, and now spring was here and I resolved to go in time to attend the spring roundup, and I determined to speak my mind and know the best or the worst, before I went. It may seem to some that I was rather hasty in this matter, but I had a restless impulsive nature that could illy brook any delay, when my mind was fairly set in any direction.

When I finally screwed up my courage to put the question, which would have such a bearing on my future, I did not get a direct reply, but was kept for some time in doubt, betwixt hope and fear. I insisted in my tempestuous manner on a decision one way or the other. The poor girl hardly knew what to do with me, and to make matters worse for me, several meddlesome old ladies warned her against "these here cowboys." While my affairs were in this condition, I again consulted the muse and this is the result:

> I had wandered sad and weary
> O'er the beauteous western land.
> All the world seemed void and dreary
> As desert waste of burning sand.
> Chains of wild unrest had bound me
> With links I could not break apart.

Sweet voiced birds sang all around me
Yet waked no echo in my heart.

Trusted ones had proved so fleeting
Fair faith and hope and love had flown
Ever was my heart repeating,
The sad old story, "lost and gone,"
Till I saw two brown eyes beaming
With a radiance sweet and rare
Then the star of Hope bright gleaming
Banished all darkness and despair.

Oh, will that star beam on forever?
Or will it quickly fade from sight,
Leaving me to rest, Oh, never,
Wandering through the vale of Night?
Oh, my heart is weary waiting,
Yet dreading most to know its fate;
Hope and fear, each alternating
Makes it so wearisome to wait.

Failing to get a definite answer, about the first of April (1878), I started for the range to be on hand for the spring round-up. I went not without hope, for my girl had promised to correspond with me. I went to the Driskill range on Bear and Bluff creeks, south of Dodge. I obtained employment at once. As usual I met many old friends and acquaintances, but somehow the old life had lost its charm, and it was with difficulty that I managed to stay on the range for about five weeks, when I settled up with my employer and started for home determined to see that girl if I never laid up a dollar.

I dedicated a few lines to the old plains life after the following fashion, borrowing a few words, and perhaps a portion of the sentiment from Joaquin Miller.

Adieu, adieu, to the western plain
I cinched my saddle and gathered my rein;
Then sprang to the back of my wild mustang
While my song of joy o'er the broad plains rang,

For my good steed's head was turned towards home
O'er the desolate waste no more to roam.

Dear ones at home so anxiously wait,
For fear that the cruel decrees of fate
Might drift the wanderer farther away;
And his absence be forever and aye;
So hasten good steed, swift bear me along
While I merrily sing my homeward song.

With the lasso coiled to my saddle tied,
With my trusty weapon by my side,
Once o'er the plains I loved to go
Chasing the wild horse and buffalo.
But the romance all has faded away,
So hasten good steed, no longer delay.

There's a bright eyed girl that I long to see.
I wonder if she is waiting for me,
Or will my one bright dream vanish away
As the bubble bursts on the storm tossed spray?
Now hasten good steed, I will go and see,
Farewell to our home on the prairies free.

I found my girl still a little chary about giving me much encouragement. I remained in the settlement about two months. One evening there was to be a party and I invited her to attend with me, but for some reason she refused to accept the invitation. Accordingly I took another girl, but I fear that I was rather a dull escort.

The next day I concluded that I was wasting my time in trying to win one who cared nothing for me, and without saying a word to her about my intentions, I started for the Indian Territory by the way of Wichita and Caldwell. Stopping at Wichita overnight I wrote her a letter, bidding her goodbye and expressing my regret that I had ever thought of casting the shadow of my wild and stormy life over her fair and bright one. The next day I started southward, with my whole being burning with the fierce fever of unrest. I headed for Fort Reno and reached that point with no adventure worthy of note.

Fort Reno is located south of the North Canadian River, while north of the stream is the Cheyenne and the Arapaho agency, only a mile and a half from the fort. On the reservation, scattered in villages in every direction, were six thousand Indians, men, women and children. Every other Monday was "Issue Day," when they would pour into the Agency from every direction, some on foot, sometimes two or three on one pony; sometimes a papoose with its head sticking out of a "sack," a kind of a double concern intended to hang across the saddle like saddle bags, with a dog in the sack on the other side to balance against the papoose. They presented a picturesque appearance indeed with their wild fantastic costumes and many colored blankets.

I soon found employment in a government hay contract, but the fierce heat of the summer sun and the malaria were too much for me and I came down with a fever which raged violently for several weeks. I did not fully regain my strength until cold weather came again. It was while I was here convalescent that the Northern Cheyennes made their terrible raid across western Kansas and Nebraska, which resulted in the death of many men, women and children, and the almost utter annihilation of the raiding band. They were part of the savage host that encompassed the death of General Custer and his devoted band in the summer of '76. They were armed with guns taken from Custer's dead soldiers. The Indians had kept them concealed when they finally surrendered in the Black Hills country, and when they removed to their new reservation in the Indian Territory had smuggled them through a few at a time.

It is known that for sometime prior to their outbreak in the Indian Territory they had kept secret runners passing to and fro in communication with their friends in Dakota. Being brought from the cold northern climate to the much lower altitude and warmer climate did not agree with them, and at the time of my sickness they were dying in great numbers of malarial fever. It is no wonder that their wild fierce natures became restless and discontented, and longed for the pure air and the bright waters of the north.

They asked permission of Major Mizner, the commandant at Fort Reno, to go on a buffalo hunt in the Texas Panhandle, saying they must have a change or they would all die. He told them that he could not let them go, that he could not trust them without an escort, and that he had no soldiers to spare for an escort. They then said that if he would not let them go on a hunt, they would go back to their old home in the Black Hills. Major Mizner told them not to undertake it, that he would have to take steps to stop them if they did, and that the troops might have to fire on them. They replied that they could fire too, and that they might as well die that way as to stay there and die of disease.

At the time of this parley there were about a hundred of them around the fort behaving in a very insolent manner. They turned their ponies loose to graze on the nicely kept parade ground, and when they would meet a white man they would scowl at him, and seem ready to pierce him through and through with the glare of their demon-like eyes. There was much apprehension felt at the fort, and there were indications of a general uprising of the Cheyennes and Arapahos.

About twelve miles northwest of the fort, they threw up breastworks, as if they intended to make a stand there and defy the soldiers. It was really only a blind however to cover the flight of the band who had started northward under the leadership of Dull Knife. Wild Hog and other subordinate chiefs were also in the band, which numbered not far from one hundred; eleven of whom were squaws and children.

As soon as their flight became known, runners were sent to Camp Supply and Fort Dodge, hoping that troops from these points might intercept them. In the meantime a squad from Fort Reno took up the trail and followed it as rapidly as possible. The troops were not successful in heading them off, but the three commands came together and joined the pursuit. The redskins being closely pressed laid an ambush in the sand hills south of the Arkansas River. They were concealed in a narrow pass, and a scout in advance of the troops rode right into the trap before he was aware of it. Seeing Indians concealed on either side of the pass he dared not make a sign to the soldiers, but seeming not to be aware of their presence he was permitted to ride on through and beyond the death trap, while the troops came unsuspectingly on. Suddenly a terrible fire was poured upon the soldiers, while the fiendish war-whoop echoed and re-echoed through the hills and valleys around them. Colonel Lewis of Camp Supply fell mortally wounded at the first fire, as did many others. The soldiers taken completely by surprise, were panic stricken, and broke into a disorderly retreat. The Indians separated into small squads, and they left a trail of blood behind them from there to the Nebraska line.

One party went through the Driskill range; going into one of the camps where there were three cowboys they pretended to be friendly, and the boys gave them some supper. The guns belonging to the cowboys were leaning against a tent, and after supper the Indians made a break for the guns and killed all three of the boys with their own weapons. They then drove about forty head of Driskill's horses off. At another of Driskill's camps, a young buck wishing to show his bravery, undertook to drive the horses by himself. Young Jesse Driskill seeing him, mounted his horse and after a hot chase succeeded in shooting him dead.

Tom Murray, whom I have previously mentioned, was returning from Dodge City to his camp at the mouth of Big Mule Creek, when he was met by a number of these bloodthirsty wretches. He was unarmed and they shot him to death, and tearing off his scalplock went galloping on their mission of death.

> *On the plains of western Kansas*
> *Neath a mild September sky*
> *A young ranger of the border*
> *On his mustang galloped by;*
> *And a merry air he whistled*
> *Time and distance to beguile,*
> *While the face so stern and rugged*
> *Had grown soft beneath a smile.*

> *He had left his home and Kindred*
> *Far away in Tennessee*
> *For a life upon the prairie,*
> *Western prairie, wild and free.*
> *He was thinking of his loved ones*
> *As he galloped o'er the plains*
> *Fondly dreaming of the future*
> *When they all might meet again.*

> *Little thought he of his peril*
> *Little dreamed that savage foe*
> *In the tangled thicket yonder*
> *Lurked to smite and lay him low.*
> *Now the quick eye sees the shadow*
> *Of the foeman dark and fell,*
> *And the stillness now is broken*
> *By a wild unearthly yell.*

Swift fell hand to ready pistol,
But alas, of no avail,
For a dozen deadly rifles
Showered forth their leaden hail.
See, both steed and rider stagger,
Both receive a mortal wound.
Yes, the gallant steed and rider
Sink together to the ground.

Now the cruel painted demons
Burst forth from their hidden lair,
While their fiendish yells of triumph
Rend the quiet autumn air.
Now they lift the gory scalplock
And their hellish work is done;
And their swift war-steeds now bear them
Toward the setting of the sun.

Weep, oh, father, sister, mother
In the far off eastern home,
For the dear loved son and brother,
Never more to thee can come.
Calmly sleep, oh, fellow ranger,
Comrade ever true and brave
Wintry winds are wailing dirges
O'er thy lonely western grave.

Several other cowboys were killed. The Indians crossed the Arkansas at Cimarron, a small station nineteen miles west of Dodge. Here they murdered men, women and children, and collecting what horses they could pressed on toward the north.

In northern Kansas, near Beaver Creek, they met a young man with two young ladies on their way to visit friends, who lived nearly a day's journey from their home. The young folks had taken their dinner along expecting to camp for noon on the prairie. They were traveling in a wagon. The Indians pretended to be friendly, and told them they were hungry, whereupon the young people gave them all the food they had. When the treacherous demons had eaten they cruelly murdered the young man, and then maltreated the young ladies in a horrible manner. But the coils were gathering around them. Dispatches had been sent to Camp Robinson in the northwestern part of Nebraska, and troops were hurrying from that point to meet them; while those from the southern posts were pressing along in their rear. Finally the troops were united, and the savages being cornered a desperate battle ensued. The Indians were overpowered, and those who were not slain were taken prisoners and conveyed to Camp Robinson, where they were confined in the military guard house. The woman and children were sent back to the Indian Territory in charge of Ben Clark, a well-known scout. I was at their Agency when they arrived, bearing the news of their disaster. Many of the warriors had left their squaws behind them, and their howling and wailings were something awful to hear. They would tear their hair in a frightful manner. They kept this up for some time, day and night. After the Indians had been in the guardhouse for about six weeks they undermined it, and all came out one night and killed three or four of the guards, and then fled in different directions. It happened that there was a light fall of snow on the ground, and the following morning all the cavalry had to do was to follow the trail on a gallop until they overtook the fugitives. When they were overtaken they turned on their pursuers, and fought like tigers with clubs and stones, until they were nearly all shot down. Only five, if I remember rightly, allowed themselves to be recaptured. Among this number were Dull Knife and Wild Hog. The latter committed suicide in the military prison at Fort Dodge. I am not informed as to the fate of the others.

After this raid, which terminated so disastrously, the Indians were more quiet, although sullen mutterings were occasionally heard. I remained about the post for some time, boarding at a citizen's "mess house." While there I met a noted character called "Colorado Bill." One day while seated at the dinner table Bill called upon a waiter for some article. The man made rather an uncivil reply, when Bill drew a large pistol and repeated his request, which was hastily complied with.

While here I attended a "chuckaway" dance among the Cheyennes and Arapahos. Chuckaway is their term for food, and a chuckaway dance is one that is given when several young fellows chip in and buy material for a supper. A large tepee will be cleared out for the dance, while the old squaws prepare supper over a campfire on the outside. The male dancers seat themselves upon the rush mats which are spread in a circle around the tepee, leaving a circle of bare ground in the center. The squaws partner by walking up and gently touching the one they choose with a toe of their moccasin. Two squaws dance with one man. The partners stand facing each other, each with a hand on the other's shoulder. Now the music commences. It consists of singing and pounding on a huge drum, which on a clear evening may be heard a long distance. The drum is made by stretching rawhide tightly over a barrel. The singing is a wild hi, yah; hi, yah; hi, yah; which all join in as they circle wildly around the tepee. I had the honor of dancing with Mrs. Molly Houser, a Sioux lady who was the wife of a government clerk at Fort Reno, also with her friend Ameahah or Cheyenne Minnie. Before Mr. Houser wedded his dusky bride he sent her to school at Leavenworth for a number of years where she obtained a good education. Her people lived on the banks of the North Canadian in the regular Indian fashion, and then she loved to throw off the style of civilization, and donning the savage costume of her people, she would often go and spend a week with them. It was during one of these visits to her people that I chanced to meet her at the dance.

It may seem to some that it was small business attending an Indian dance, but there is a certain novelty about such an entertainment that to the average young American is irresistible. And here I must say that with all my experience with Indians, and it has been quite extensive, I have scarcely ever seen anything in their deportment to shock the modesty of the most refined. I have slept in their lodges, and eaten by their campfires, and on such occasions it is hard to realize that when aroused and on the warpath they can be such monsters of cruelty, but the graves which are scattered here and there all over the vast plains but too truly attest their vengeful natures. Yet even when the mad thirst for the blood of the pale face seems to have taken hold of them, they have frequently been known to warn white men that they were going to "dig up the hatchet," and that they had better flee until the storm of wrath would pass over; and woe to the man that heeded not the warning but remained among them after receiving it.

When we consider what changes have been wrought in the last half century, or even the last twenty years, we need hardly wonder that the heart of the savage should be filled with vengeance. Twenty years ago the vast plains, which stretch from the British Possessions to the Gulf of Mexico, were covered with countless thousands of buffaloes, while deer, antelope and smaller game abounded, making the Great Plains seem like a very paradise to the Indians, many of whom were roving wild and free at the time. But now the game has been nearly wiped out of existence, hundreds of thousands of buffaloes have been slain for their hides alone. The Indians are cooped up on small reservations under the eyes of the military, with agents appointed to teach them the ways of the white man, ways that are hateful and repugnant to them. While we blame them for their cruel deeds, let us also sympathize with them in the wrongs which have been heaped upon them ever since our forefathers first took possession of their country.

[EDITOR'S NOTE: Half a page has been cut off and another page cut out.]

. . . and hemmed in on small tracts allotted to them by the Government. An outbreak among them is almost unheard of, and the soldiers of the regular army perform the monotonous rounds of post duty and grow fat through the lack of actual service. The range for stock has become so limited that hundreds of stockmen have quit the business, and thousands of cowboys have been compelled to choose some other calling.

Many of the old time boys are lying beneath the sod. Not a few of them have died as the average cowboy would have wished to die—game, with their boots on. The work of clearing a way through the wilderness for the approaching civilization has been accomplished, and heroes of the pistol and the bowie are no longer in demand as they once were. The border outlaws have been pushed to the remote confines of the frontier. Many desperate men may still be found in the mountain fastnesses of Montana, New Mexico, Arizona and other mountain states and territories, but the free rover of the plains is no more.

Thus far I have only given a brief outline of the adventures and wanderings of nearly ten years of life on the border. To return to the romance of my life, I will simply say that I married the one of my choice, and for nearly ten years she has been my faithful companion through joys and sorrows; ever striving to smooth over the rough points in my nature. On the margin of the sun-kissed plains over which I once galloped so restlessly, yet almost under the shadows of the snow-capped peaks of the Rockies we have pitched our camp, and life passes quietly and peacefully.

[EDITOR'S NOTE: Bottom half of the last page cut off.]

Part 2
Maynard's Poetry

A S A POET MAYNARD could count syllables better than most cowboy poets, while his rhymes were unforced and his syntax untortured. His twenty-two surviving poems (nineteen in *Rhymes of the Range and Trail,* two published in the *Colorado Springs Gazette and Telegraph,* and one unpublished), range in length from sixteen to one hundred lines. His favorite stanza, used in all but four poems, is the quatrain, or some variation thereof (an eight- or twelve-line stanza), usually rhyming *aabb, abab,* or *xaxa.* He also likes the ballad stanza. The content of Maynard's book ranges from realistic depictions of a cowboy's life to love poems for his wife. Some are pensive in tone, some humorous, some poignant. The joys and the melancholy of the lone wanderer figure prominently as well.

Maynard's most notable contribution to the heritage of the American West is without question his adaptation of what he called "The Dying Cowboy," and which most of the rest of the world knows as "The Cowboy's Lament" or, better still, "The Streets of Laredo." But Maynard's ranger (that is, a cowboy who ranged the prairies, not a lawman) was dying at the doorway of Tom Sherman's barroom in Dodge City, not on the dusty streets of a Texas border town. How the dying youth got to both places is described, if tangentially, in Maynard's own words, as recorded by Elmo Scott Watson in the January 27, 1924, *Colorado Springs Gazette and Telegraph:*

> During the winter of 1876 I was working for a Grimes outfit which had started north with a trail herd from Matagorda Bay, Tex[as]. . . . We were wintering the herd on the Salt Fork of the Arkansas river on the border

of Kansas and Indian Territory, waiting for the spring market to open at Wichita.

One of the favorite songs of the cowboys in those days was called "The Dying Girl's Lament," the story of a girl who had been betrayed by her lover and who lay dying in a hospital. I don't remember all of the song but it began something like this:

> As I walked down by St. James hospital,
> St. James hospital, so early one day, etc., etc.

I had often amused myself by trying to write verses, and one dull winter day in camp to while away the time I began writing a poem which could be sung to the tune of "The Dying Girl's Lament." I made it a dying ranger, or cowboy, instead of a dying girl, and had the scene in Tom Sherman's barroom instead of a hospital.

Tom Sherman was a noted character in the old cattle trail days. He first ran a dance hall and saloon in Great Bend in 1873, then moved to Dodge City, where he ran the same sort of place until some time in the '80s. All of the cowboys who came up from Texas knew Tom Sherman. He was a big, strapping fellow, six feet six or six feet seven tall. But to get back to the song—

After I had finished the new words to the song I sang it to the boys in the outfit. They liked it and began singing it. It became popular with the boys in other outfits who heard it after we had taken our herd to market in Wichita the next spring, and from that time on I heard it sung everywhere on the range and trail.

Although wrong about Tom Sherman's stay in Dodge City (he left in the mid-1870s), Maynard was unquestionably accurate on the methodology of the oral tradition: this is a real-life description of how a folksong evolves and is spread. Somebody with a musical or poetic bent alters the words to a popular song, then others hear it, like it, learn it, maybe make a few changes, and carry it with them to other regions.

The original of "The Cowboy's Lament" is a late-eighteenth-century Irish homiletic ballad, "The Unfortunate Rake," about a young soldier dying of the ravages of venereal disease acquired through riotous living. Once the ballad crossed the Atlantic early in the nineteenth century, the central character was switched from that of a misguided youth to a misguided maiden, her exact affliction left unstated. The resulting song became widely popular, both under its genteel title, "The Dying [or Bad] Girl's Lament," and by its more graphic appellation among the cowboys, "The Whore's Lament."

Others besides Maynard also asserted authorship of "The Cowboy's Lament," and given the wide set of variants in the lyrics there is no reason to doubt that what folklorists call independent re-creation might well have occurred. As Watson noted in his 1924 newspaper article, "The matter of authorship of a ballad is a perplexing one. . . . In a sense the ballad represents the contribution of a succession of bards rather than the work of a single poet." Still, Maynard's claim to have been the first to have changed the bad girl to a young ranger and to have placed the song in cowboy country is plausible.

Maynard's book of poems, as published in 1911, follows. Four of the poems included in his collection appear untitled in his memoirs, two of them virtually identical ("Twixt Hope and Fear" and "The Ranger's Last Ride") and two with revisions ("A Reckless Cowboy" and "Farewell to the Plains").

Rhymes of the Range and Trail by F. H. Maynard

AN OLD-TIME COWBOY

Preface

In presenting this little booklet to the public it is the purpose of the author to present, in a realistic manner, what were common phases of life on range and trail during the stirring days of the seventies.

It is with no hope of winning a place as poet Laureate, nor even as poet lariat, that these lines are written.

To those who have gathered around the same camp-fires; who have shared the same pleasures and privations, these rhymes are respectfully dedicated.

THE AUTHOR

On the Trail

It was down across the Brazos
That we rounded up to start,
With about five thousand cattle
For the busy Kansas mart;
There were just a dozen cowboys
With a greasy coon for cook,
Flour, coffee, beans, and bacon
Were the chief supplies we took;
And we thrived upon this diet,
For none of us grew pale,
But our hot, red blood ran riot
Upon the Texas trail.

It was in the rainy season,
There were swollen streams to cross,
But we boldly plunged into them,
And we suffered little loss;
There were long days' drives and weary,
As we pushed the herd along;
There were long night guards and dreary,
But we passed them with a song.
When at last, we reached Red River,
There was blowing quite a gale,
But we swam its turbid waters,
Ever onward up the trail.

What cared we for wind or weather,
For our hearts were young and gay,
And we all joined in together
For a good time on the way.
Now we traveled through a country
Where they little recked of law,
Indians and rustlers plenty

Till we crossed the Washita.
Yet the outlaws they were plenty,
Men who should have been in jail,
And we kept a constant vigil,
As we pressed on up the trail.

We had reached the north Canadian,
And everything seemed well,
Till at night the Redskins charged us
With a most infernal yell:
'Twas our cattle they were after,
And away in mad stampede
Went the herd of long-horned beef steers,
While we galloped for the lead,
And our foreman hoarsely shouted:
"Stay with 'em, do not fail."
And we circled 'em and milled 'em,
Upon the Texas trail.

Then the Redskins, disappointed,
Slyly sneaked off in the night,
And we kept our eyes wide open
Until dawn of morning light.
Then our trip was uneventful,
Till one evening just at dark,
Jim and Charley had a quarrel
And their guns began to bark.
Jim was quickest on the trigger
And his nerve it did not quail,
And poor Charley lies a sleeping,
Where we laid him by the trail.

Crossing Cimarron and Bluff Creek,
Soon Dodge City loomed in view,
Dodge, the wicked western city,
Painted oft a crimson hue,
There a horde of hard-faced gamblers
Waited each with sure-thing game,

To ensnare some verdant sucker,
And not anything was tame.
There was big Tom Sherman's dance-hall,
And Bat Masterson's, more swell,
And you need not go much farther,
For to find a little—well,
The least said is the better
About some things in this tale,
For conditions they were awful,
At the ending of the trail.

Now and then some foolish puncher
Would try to play Wild Bill,
And so quickly they would plant him
On a place they called Boot Hill.
But now all this is over,
For those wild days are no more,
Where once roamed the free Vacqueros,
There are homesteads by the score,
And perchance some pretty milkmaid
Goes singing with her pail,
Where we rounded up and bedded,
Upon the Texas trail.

On Boot Hill they've built a schoolhouse
And the W.C.T.U.
Holds an annual convention,
Where once corks and stoppers flew;
There are sermons, there is singing,
Where was pistol crack and flame.
Dodge, the erstwhile wicked city,
Has built up a better name,
And the lamb now skips and gambols
Where was heard the grey wolf's wail,
The survival of the fittest,
Marks the ending of the trail.

Bill Springer's Hand

Bill Springer, ranchman, lived south of Dodge,
He chose his bride from an Indian lodge.
He had a massive, athletic frame,
And a reputation for being game.

He often saddled and hit the trail,
And came up to town to get his mail,
As well as to meet some jolly pards
And enjoy a quiet game of cards.

They looked on the wine when it was red,
And drank quite deeply, so it was said.
Bill was known to have a handsome pile,
That he flung around in reckless style.

This caught the eye of a slick card shark,
Who thought he had found an easy mark;
With two of his ilk he laid a plan
To capture alive and skin their man.

They roped Bill into a game of "draw"
(Against which, in Dodge, there was no law).
The stakes for a time were very low,
In fact, the playing was very slow.

Till at last, all seemed to hold good cards.
And the card shark winked at cunning pards.
A "cold deck" deftly was brought in play,
And a great stake on the table lay.

Ten thousand dollars were there in sight,
Before they laid down their cards that night.
What have you? at last the card shark said,
And Bill Springer's face turned very red.

I hold four kings, he meekly replied;
I have four aces, the gambler cried,
And reached for the stakes on table spread,
But stopped dead short with a look of dread.

For a lurid light shone in Bill's eye,
He grabbed his Winchester standing by,
And, with a voice like an angry bull,
He roared, "But I've got a sixteen full";
"You fellers can just git up and git,
You haven't robbed old Bill Springer, yit."
They looked on the stern, determined face,
And quietly slunk out from the place.

Then old Bill, gathering up his pile,
Said, "Come up now, boys, and have a smile,"
And the hangers-on came up and drank.
And then he hastened off to the bank.

With his wealth all safely put away,
He cared no longer in town to stay,
But saddled and bridled wild "Comanch"
And galloped away to Springer's ranch.

Billy, The Kid

Perhaps you have heard of Billy the Kid,
And the numerous wicked things he did;
Of horses he'd stolen many a score,
And of cattle many a hundred more.
He gathered around him a reckless band.
And little cared he for mark or brand,
And woe to the ranger who crossed his path,
Who dared to arouse the young outlaw's wrath.

When his years had numbered but twenty-one
There were twenty-one notches on his gun,
And ever more reckless the course he ran,
As he mocked at the laws of God and man;
So at last with a price upon his head,
The officers sought him, alive or dead.
A deputy sheriff, Pat Garrett, by name,
Set out to capture the desperate game.

When he found where the outlaw had his lair,
He laid all his plans to capture him there.
He stationed himself in the Kid's bedroom,
And awaited him there in midnight gloom.
At last he detected a stealthy tread,
And he sat bolt upright on the bed.
The outlaw carefully opened the door,
As so frequently he had done before.

A mysterious something filled the air,
And seemed to warn him of danger there.
"Quien est?" (who is it) were the words he said,
As he comprehended the presence dread;
For answer there came a terrible roar,

And the outlaw fell backwards through the door.
His hand was clutched on his favorite gun
That was covered with notches, twenty-one.
But his sin-stained soul had winged its flight,
Out into the silent, sombre night.

Night Thoughts

The shades of night have gathered o'er me,
Afar out on the western plain,
Sad images loom up before me,
And fill this heart of mine with pain.

The stars above are shining brightly,
All nature seems to be at rest;
The winds are sighing softly, lightly,
The camp-fire burns with eager zest.

I sit and watch each dying ember,
Each spark that rises in the air,
And sadly, sadly, I remember
The flight of hopes as bright and fair.

I think of every fond ambition,
That in my bosom once did glow,
Of hopes that never find fruition,
All fleeting, melting, like the snow.

Oh, is there not some peaceful haven,
Some balm for heart-strings sick and sore?
Like Poe's grim, ghastly, croaking raven,
My spirit answers: "Nevermore."

Tho' by sad memories ever haunted,
Tho' o'er my path hangs midnight gloom.
Still onward I will go undaunted,
And laugh to scorn the darkest doom.

Colorado Joy

Did you ever go prospecting
   In the hills of Cripple Creek,
Scrambling up the rugged mountain
   With a shovel and a pick?

Did you ever find a fissure
   With the mineral in place,
And take some for an assay
   And never get a trace?

Did you ever dream of riches
   Laying Stratton's in the shade.
But in the end be busted,
   With a lot of bills unpaid?

Did you ever stake a placer
   Where some mountain streamlet ran,
Carrying black sand by the carload,
   But the stuff, it wouldn't pan?

Did you ever take a lease on ore
   That was quite "out of sight,"
Full of pyrites of iron,
   Causing tenderfeet to bite?

Or, perchance, it had real value
   And you shipped a car or two,
Making rich some mill or sampler,
   While, alas, you poorer grew?

Did you ever sink a shaft down,
   Feeling sure you had a "lead,"

But missing pay-streak by a foot,
    Seeming thus by fate decreed?

Then some new man takes the prospect
    And fires just a single shot,
Sells out at a handsome figure
    On the strength of what it brought?

Did you ever spread your blankets
    With the bright stars overhead,
Waking up in early morning
    With a snowdrift on your bed?

Did you ever flip a flapjack,
    Did you ever fry a spud,
Or ever build a cabin,
    With the cracks chinked up with mud?

Did you ever ride a broncho
    Who would stand upon his head,
Or sit back upon his haunches,
    Just to show how he was bred?

Did you ever pack a burro
    Over rugged mountain trail,
With a load that loomed above him
    From his ears back to his tail?

Did you ever rope a yearling,
    Did you ever shoot a buck,
Or ever try a sure thing,
    Just to find out you were stuck?

If not, come to Colorado,
    All these pleasures to enjoy;
Find adventure, trials, treasure,
    Purest gold without alloy.

The Call of the Wild

I have harked to the call of the wild,
And my soul echoes back the weird sound,
That my fancies have ofttimes beguiled,
When my fellows in slumber were bound.

I have harked to the call of the wild,
And so eager my feet press the trail,
By my foes I'm maligned and reviled,
But I'm soothed by the wilderness wail.

I have harked to the call of the wild,
'Tis a voice that's by few understood,
Yet revealed unto Nature's own child.
As he wanders o'er prairie or wood.

I have harked to the call of the wild.
It has sung me a wondrous refrain,
And ofttimes while listening, I've smiled.
Tho' its cadence is mingled with pain.

I have harked to the call of the wild,
It has lured me o'er mountain and wave,
It will lead me, though sad and exiled,
Till I sleep in a wanderer's grave.

The Ranger's Last Ride

On the plains of western Kansas,
'Neath a mild September sky,
A young ranger of the border
On his mustang galloped by.

And a merry air he whistled,
Time and distance to beguile,
While the face so stern and rugged
Had grown soft beneath a smile.

He had left his home and kindred,
Far away in Tennessee,
For a life upon the prairies—
Western prairies—wild and free.

He was thinking of his loved ones,
As he galloped o'er the plain,
Fondly dreaming of the future,
When they all might meet again.

Little thought he of his peril,
Little dreamed that savage foe
In the tangled thicket yonder
Lurked, to smite and lay him low.

Now, the quick eye sees the shadow
Of the foeman dark and fell,
And the stillness now is broken
By a wild, unearthly yell.

Swift fell hand to ready pistol,
But alas! of no avail,
For a dozen deadly rifles
Showered forth their leaden hail.

See, both steed and rider stagger,
Both received a mortal wound,
Yes, the gallant steed and rider
Sink together to the ground.

Now the cruel, painted demons
Burst forth from their hidden lair,
And their fiendish yells of triumph
Rend the quiet autumn air.

Now they lift the gory scalp-lock,
And their hellish work is done,
And their swift war-steeds now bear them
Toward the setting of the sun.

Weep, O father, sister, mother,
In the far-off eastern home,
For thy dear loved son and brother
Nevermore to thee can come.

Calmly sleep, O fellow ranger,
Comrade ever true and brave,
Wintry winds are wailing dirges
O'er thy lonely western grave.

The Black Cat

I've a black cat here in camp,
As black as black can be,
As bright-eyed, roguish scamp
As ever you did see.
I carried him fifteen miles or more
Upon Grey Eagle's back,
From Red Fork Ranch to our camp,
Tied in a buckskin sack.

Before I brought him into camp,
The mice ran riot o'er my head,
As I lay and dreamed of far-off home,
On my rough frontiersman's bed,
But now my slumbers are undisturbed,
For the cat a vigil keeps,
And woe to the mouse that ventures near
To where his master sleeps.

Alone on the Border

I'm camped tonight in a dark ravine,
Bordered thickly with timber round;
My weapons lie within easy reach,
My ear is awake to slightest sound.

I'm all alone except my good steed,
My kind, fleet-footed, faithful grey,
Anon he munches a tuft of grass,
Anon sends forth a piercing neigh.

From far on the evening breeze is borne
The famished grey wolf's mournful howl;
'Tis answered from a neighboring tree
By dismal hooting of the owl.

As I listen, and silently gaze
Into the camp-fire's ruddy glow,
My mind flies back o'er memory's track
To the diamond morn of long ago.

For I was a wayward, restless youth,
Weary of kindly restraints of home,
And went forth into the wide, wide world,
Over the desolate waste to roam.

Many have been the perils passed,
The tempests faced and torrents crossed;
Storm-beaten and worn I'm struggling on,
Still on life's tide my bark is tossed.

Oh, youth, filled with the wander lust,
Who long to leave home's sheltering nest,
Think well before you spread your wings,
For those who stay are happiest.

The Dying Cowboy

As I rode down by Tom Sherman's bar-room,
Tom Sherman's bar-room so early one day,
There I espied a handsome young ranger
All wrap[p]ed in white linen, as cold as the clay.
"I see by your outfit that you're a ranger,"
The words that he said as I went riding by,
"Come, sit down beside me, and hear my sad story,
I'm shot through the breast and know I must die."

Chorus:
Then muffle the drums and play the dead marches;
Play the dead march as I'm carried along;
Take me to the church-yard and lay the sod o'er me,
I'm a young ranger and I know I've done wrong.

"Go bear a message to my grey-haired mother
Go break the news gently to my sister so dear,
But never a word of this place do you mention,
As they gather around you my story to hear.
Then there is another as dear as a sister,
Who will bitterly weep when she knows I am gone,
But another more worthy may win her affection,
For I'm a young ranger—I know I've done wrong."

Chorus

"Once in my saddle, I used to be dashing;
Once in my saddle, I used to be brave;
But I first took to gambling, from that to drinking,
And now in my prime, I must go to my grave.
Go gather around you a crowd of gay rangers,
Go tell them the tale of their comrade's sad fate,
Tell each and all to take timely warning,
And leave their wild ways before it's too late."

Chorus

"Go, now, and bring me a cup of cold water,
To bathe my flushed temples," the poor fellow said.
But ere I returned, the spirit had left him,
Had gone to its Giver—the ranger was dead.
So we muffled the drums and played the dead marches,
We bitterly wept as we bore him along,
For we all loved the ranger, so brave and so handsome,
We all loved our comrade, although he'd done wrong.

A Rover's Thought

In a beauteous land, but lone,
Where Deep Fork and the Cimarron
Flow always on their winding way,
Where the treacherous "Mr. Lo,"
Armed with scalping knife and bow,
May take off your scalp-lock any day;
Where the eagle, wild and free,
Soars above the prairie lea;
Where the wily coyote makes its home
In the mystic Indian Nation,
Nearly out of all creation,
I am fated many days to roam.
Friendship's chain that once had bound me,
With its golden links around me,
I have long since severed all in twain.
Oft I think of those ties broken,
Of cold words that have been spoken
With regret, as I gallop o'er the plain,
Oft my spirit rages madly,
Then again I ponder sadly,
More than pen of mine can tell.
Oft I followed impulse blindly,
Yet, oh, friends, think of me kindly;
Deep within my heart I wish you well.

A Reckless Cowboy

I am a reckless cowboy, the prairie is my home,
At the early age of sixteen I first began to roam,
I drove from sunny Texas, in the year of seventy-one,
When the boys all came to Newton and kicked up lots of fun.

Next summer found me ranging on the raging Arkansaw,
Where we all grew wild and lawless, in the town of Wichita,
From thence I drifted westward, to a country wild and strange,
In the valley of the Salt Fork, I found a winter range.

The winter was so dreary, I thought 'twould never end,
And when at last 'twas springtime, we drove up to Great Bend.
Next winter found me ranging on the Medicine Lodge,
Headquarters for the last year, was the reckless town of Dodge.

There, gamblers, shrewd and tricky, are watchful as a cat,
To trap some luckless snoozer from Texas or the Platte.
Now, I am like an Indian, I never can find rest,
For settlements keep pushing farther toward the west.
So, farewell, friends and kindred and all I once held dear,
I am a reckless cowboy far out on the frontier.

The Exile

There's a wild and rocky canon,
Where the panther rears its young,
And where sombre, gloomy shadows
By the cedar boughs are flung;
There's no signs of human presence,
How e'er closely you may scan,
Yet within its dark recesses,
Dwells an exiled, ruined man.

Once his life was filled with pleasure,
And his prospects bright and fair.
But a wild, fierce storm of passion
Wrecked each castle in the air.
He once loved a fair young maiden,
Strove to win her for a wife,
But she smiled upon another,
And he took this rival's life.

Then he fled from home and kindred,
To a far and distant land,
With a restless, guilty conscience,
With the red stain on his hand.
Now he dwells within a cavern,
In the canon dark and deep,
Wild beasts furnish food and raiment,
And a couch on which to sleep.

There, surrounded by bad angels,
And by many a frightful ghoul,
Who can guess the awful anguish
Ever gnawing at his soul?

A Parody

In my prison here I sit, thinking Molly, dear, of you,
And the days when I roamed o'er the western plain;
If they would but let me out, how I'd dance and sing and shout,
And I'd never raise an Injun's hoss again.

Chorus:
Tramp, tramp, tramp, the guards are coming,
Even now I hear them at the door,
Fare you well, my Mollie, dear, I'm sent up for many a year,
And may never see my darling any more.

Their ponies were in camp when the fiercest charge we made.
And we dashed them off a hundred head or more;
Then away across the plain we drove with might and main,
Soon those Indians were following by the score.

Chorus

O, my darling, for your sake, I thought to raise a stake.
But they followed [on] my trail with eagle eyes;
And while I was asleep, upon me they did creep,
And they took me in, completely by surprise.

Chorus

Then they took me back to camp, and it was a weary tramp,
For on foot I was compelled to make the trip,
And a vigil they did keep, with eyes that would not sleep,
And I found no chance for giving them the slip.

Chorus

When we got back to the camp, I found marshals waiting there,
And with me, down to Arkansas they did steer;
Yes they took me to Fort Smith, where my sentence quickly passed,
Doomed to work within its walls for many a year.

Chorus

Tell my brothers there at home, if they are inclined to roam
From their father and their mother on the farm,
They would better till the ground, than to go a-roving 'round,
And the chances are they will not come to harm.

Chorus

Oklahoma, 1878

There's a land wild and free, far away in the west,
Where the deer and the antelope roam,
Where the soft sighing breezes are never at rest,
And one's roof-tree is heaven's blue dome.

There, the child of the prairie, unfettered and free,
On his fleet-footed steed dashes by.
A king of vast realms almost boundless is he,
Wild and fierce is the glance of his eye.

Little recks he of forms or society's creeds,
Full of grace, though untutored, is he
Strong and brave in his heart; small and few are his needs,
As he roams o'er the broad prairie lea.

Alas for the rover and the boundless domain,
For the vandal has come from afar,
Like a storm-cloud of wrath, he sweeps over the plain;
On the fair scenes of nature makes war.

See the deer and the antelope flee in dismay,
For the stag-hound is hot on their track,
They may seek a retreat in some land far away,
Ne'er again must they ever come back.

And the child of the prairie must seek a new home,
For the spirit, so proud, cannot bear
To be hemmed in and hampered, no longer to roam
O'er the broad plains that once seemed so fair.

But where shall he flee? For lo, on every hand,
The intruders environ about,
With insatiate greed to possess all the land,
There is not any chance to get out.

Far away to the west, o'er the vast boundless plain,
Where the great Rocky range rises high,
There the paleface has been in his mad thirst for gain,
Where, oh, where, shall his red brother fly?

To the North, to the South, to the East, to the West,
From Alaska to warm southern sea,
All in vain may he seek for a haven of rest.
Tell whither, indeed, shall he flee?

Far away o'er the range, lies a land broad and free,
Where his fathers have been gathered home,
To the fair hunting grounds, across life's troubled sea,
Ever longs the proud spirit to roam.

There, safe from the soldier's and settler's approach,
There he dreams he indeed shall be free;
There, none ever will dare on his rights to encroach,
Ne'er again from his foes will he flee.

Twixt Hope and Fear

I had wandered sad and weary,
O'er the beauteous western land,
All the world seemed void and dreary,
As desert waste of burning sand.

Chains of wild unrest had bound me,
With links I could not break apart,
Sweet-voiced birds sang all around me,
Yet waked no echo in my heart.

Trusted ones had proved so fleeting,
Fair faith and hope and love had flown,
Ever was my heart repeating
The sad old story, "lost and gone."

Till I saw two brown eyes beaming,
With a radiance sweet and rare,
Then the star of hope bright gleaming,
Banished all darkness and despair.

Oh, will that star beam on forever?
Or will it quickly fade from sight?
Leaving me to rest, O never
Wandering through the vale of night?

Oh, my heart is weary waiting,
Yet dreading most to know its fate,
Hope and fear each alternating,
Makes it so wearisome to wait.

Farewell to the Plains

Farewell, farewell, to the western plain!
I tightened my cinches and gathered my rein,
Then eagerly mounted my good mustang,
While full of joy was the song that I sang;
For my good steed's head was turned toward home,
O'er the desolate waste no more to roam.

Dear ones at home so anxiously wait,
For fear that the cruel decrees of fate
Might drift the wanderer farther away,
And his absence be forever and aye,
So hasten, good steed, swift bear me along,
While I merrily sing my homeward song.

With a lasso coiled to my saddle tied,
With my trusty weapons by my side,
Once o'er the plains I love to go,
Chasing the wild horse and buffalo.
But the romance all has faded away,
So hasten, good steed, no longer delay.

There's a bright-eyed girl I long to see,
I wonder if she is waiting for me,
Or will my one bright dream vanish away,
As the bubble bursts on the storm-tossed spray?
Now hasten, good steed, I will go and see,
Farewell to our home on the prairie free.

To My Wife

When life's tempests fierce sweep o'er me;
When the storm clouds gather black;
When the way looks dark before me
And so thorny is the track;
Who is there to cheer and guide me,
Nerve me for the coming strife,
Who so true, whate'er betide me,
As my loving, faithful wife?

When the world seems cold and dreary:
When the fleeting ones depart;
When my heart grows sad and weary,
And with anguish it doth smart;
Who is there to stand beside me,
Soothing all the ills of life,
While the mocking ones deride me,
Who, beside my loving wife?

Who on earth so kind and tender
As this precious wife of mine?
Who so strong, and yet so slender,
As my gentle, clinging vine?
Came she like a guardian angel,
Smoothing o'er my rougher ways;
Came she like a blest evangel,
Bearing news of brighter days.

I was too intensely human,
And mine erring feet had strayed;
But the love of one true woman
All my baser passions laid.
Now through life we'll go together,
Hand in hand we'll journey on;
Be there fair or cloudy weather,
Till life's pilgrimage is done.

When we reach the rolling river,
May we safely cross the tide;
May our loving, heavenly Father
Greet us on the other side.
May His loving smile beam o'er us,
May we hear the words, "Well done";
May we join the heavenly chorus
'Round the great Eternal Throne.

Come Home

Come back to me, dearest, I'm lonely;
Oh, why from my arms did you stray?
I'm longing for thee, and thee only;
Come back now, and cheer my lone way.

The robins are singing so gaily,
So happy each one with its mate,
But I pine for thee hourly, daily;
How long, dearest one, must I wait?

My heart still is loyally throbbing;
Still longing, my darling, for thee;
While the storm-cloud is drearily sobbing
And the chill wind sweeps o'er the lea.

So, come back with the sunshine of gladness,
No longer from me must thou roam,
For thy presence will scatter all sadness,
And with joy fill the desolate home.

Now the tears all unbidden are starting,
While I'm penning the words of my song,
For the anguish is not all in parting,
But in watching and waiting so long.

Come back, for the wide world is dreary,
Come back to the cot in the west;
If thy pinions with wand'ring are weary,
Fly back to my arms and find rest.

Poems from the *Colorado Springs Gazette and Telegraph*

The Night that Follows "The Day"

That Day* that you prayed for at last has come,
With the shrieking shell and the bursting bomb,
With the Zeppelins hovering o'er peaceful homes,
Or wrecking fair cathedral domes,
While the trenches are filled in dread array,
Oh, it must be indeed a welcome Day.

Yes, at last the terrible Day is here,
When pledges are broken with arrogant sneer.
See, the Uhlan prances in fiery pride
O'er patriot Belgians who have died,
Have died that their country might be free,
To uphold its sworn neutrality.

Hark! 'Tis the moans and groans and sighs
Of widows and orphans that reach the skies,
There are starving ones on every hand
Where the earth is seared with war's hot brand.
There are old and infirm who wait at home
For footsteps that never more will come.
There are awful forms of death and woe
For this is the "Sport of Kings," you know.

But what of the Night that follows "The Day,"
When ended shall be the war lord's sway,
When the Russian bear shall have filled his maw,
And the British lion shall bare his claw,
To tear and rend from the despot's hand,
Brave Belgium's plundered, desolate land,
And the eagles of France shall claim their prey,
Ah, what of the Night that follows "The Day?"

Oh, bitter the fruit of the war-mad lust,
When your sword is broken and covered with rust,
And the God that you pretend to trust
Shall hold unhindered the right of way
And the nations shall bow to his mighty sway;
Oh, ponder this question, kaiser, I pray,
What of the Night that follows "The Day?"

* German officers were said to offer the toast "Der Tag,"
referring to "The Day" when Germany and England
would meet on the battlefield.

Published December 21, 1914

Passing of the Old Frontier

Where are the stockmen bluff and bold,
Who pitched their tents on the far frontier,
Where wealth was not in bond or gold,
But in the long-horned Texas steer?
They gazed with delight on a fertile plain
On grazing ground, immense, so vast
That they felt like lords of a great demesne,
And they fondly dreamed it would always last.
They were harried by rustlers, red and white,
The wolves of the border who roamed the plain,
With many a foray by day and night,
Then up and away with ill-gotten gain.
A million buffalo had fattened and fed
On the range where the cowmen now held sway
But they melted away 'neath a hail of lead
Like balls of snow on a bright summer day.
Far away from the land they called their own
The Redskin is learning the white man's ways.
Unto the Great Spirit he makes his moan,
As the wild soul pines for the bygone days.
Where now are the boys who rode the range
In the far-off days when the west was young,
Who swore great oaths both loud and strange
And gay and wild were the songs they sung?
Where are the chums of sterling worth,
Those comrades ever so true and tried,
Where they measured a man not by size or girth
But by the way he could shoot and ride?
Many have crossed o'er the Great Divide,
Far from the scenes of border strife,
Some linger on with their hands applied
To the sober prosaic tasks of life.
Where are the girls, the painted ones

With the hollow cheek and the sunken eye,
Who would banter one with mocking tones,
And a laugh that was all a lie?
Full many are sleeping beneath the sod—
Let none their mournful fate deride;
They've pleaded their cause at the bar of God,
Those poor lost souls for whom Christ died.
The settlers came in a white-winged fleet,
And soon vast tracts of the range possessed,
And the cowmen's ruin seemed most complete,
As they pressed them farther into the west.
They now feed stock of the full white-face,
So good-by to the long-horned Texas steer;
For they now have little part or place
And gone are the days of the old frontier.

Published February 14, 1924

Unpublished Poem

My Faith

Fearless and unafraid
In peace or war,
Joyous and undismayed
I'll cross the bar.

I'll trust my all to Thee
For Thou wilt not fail,
Still thou wilt watch o'er me
To end of the trail.

When sinks life's setting sun
Far down in the west,
When life's fevered race is run,
There will be sweet rest.

Spite of man's tangled creeds
And their concepts odd
Thou still does fill my needs
Still Thou art my God.

Part 3
Maynard's Journalism

FOLLOWING HIS "DISCOVERY" by Elmo Scott Watson in early 1924, Maynard published five of his stories in the *Colorado Springs Gazette and Telegraph* under the heading "Maynard's Western Tales." Two other prose pieces were found in manuscript among Maynard's papers. The following editor's note prefaced the first article:

Mr. Maynard, who lives at 420 Cheyenne Boulevard, has lived an interesting life in the days of the pioneer west. In 1870 he was a buffalo hunter on the plains and from 1873 for many years was a cowboy in the great southwest, knowing intimately all of the famous characters. He will write several articles dealing with the great buffalo hunts and cattle drives of the early days.

The titles and publication dates, where applicable, are as follows:

"How Noted Peace Officer Tilghman Nearly Met His End in
 Roundup of Pony Rustlers," December 14, 1924
"1874 an Epochal Year," December 28, 1924
"A Tale of Two Rustlers," January 4, 1925
"A Hunting and Trading Trip," February 8, 1925
"A Trip to Texas," March 22, 1925
"A Trip to Colorado"
"A Reminiscence"

The last three published stories and the first of the two unpublished ones are essentially unchanged from Maynard's memoirs, but the first two have additional material and are included here, as is the final unpublished one.

1874 an Epochal Year

INDIAN RAIDS—THE FAMOUS
BATTLE OF ADOBE WALLS AND
EVENTS LEADING UP TO IT

P RIOR TO 1870, Indians of the great plains had roamed and
hunted over a vast expanse of territory that abounded in wild
game of many varieties. Buffaloes in countless thousands. Deer
and antelope in great numbers, while in the hills and along the
timber fringed streams were flocks of wild turkeys and quails,
rabbits, squirrels, etc., while the lush grasses that covered the earth furnished
abundant forage for any number of ponies. The Indians looked upon these
bountiful provisions of nature as being particularly their own. The buffaloes
they termed "Injun's cattle."

In the early '70s buffalo hunting was carried on in a desultory manner
and on a small scale. "Meat Pilgrims" and "Cornfield Sailors" as the cowboys
and other plainsmen dubbed the homesteaders who would go out in parties
numbering perhaps six or eight persons with three or four covered wagons,
would probably kill six or eight buffaloes and return to the settlement well
supplied with "winter meat."

In the winter of '72, Andy Griffin had established a hunting camp at the
junction of Turkey creek and the Medicine Lodge river where the village
known as Sun City now stands. Griffin employed a large force of hunters
at this time. The main object in killing the buffalo was for the meat which
Griffin smoked and dried in vast quantities. Most of it was destined for the
eastern markets.

The Indians, who had been placed on reservations, were becoming more
and more restless and furious at the encroachments of the paleface. During the winter they were "heap good Injuns." But when the grass was high
enough to provide feed for their ponies, they had an unpleasant habit of

breaking away from the reservations and scorning Uncle Sam's bountiful rations, they would sally forth in all their savage panoply of war and woe to the luckless hunter, cowboy or settler who came in the path of these wild riders of the plains.

Andy Griffin, altho handicapped by a wooden leg, was a skillful hunter, but for the most part he would ride out to locate the game and direct his hunters to the most favorable localities for their purpose. In the spring of '72 "he was found dead, lying behind his dead pony, at the mouth of Soldier creek, 10 miles west of his camp, while thickly strewn around him were empty cartridge shells which told the story of his desperate battle for life." The Indian casualties were unknown, as always, when possible, they would remove their dead.

About this time men everywhere were beginning to realize the value of buffalo hides, not only for use in robes but for leather and many uses. The settlers were constantly increasing in numbers and pressing further and further to the westward. The cowmen pitched their tents and ranged their herds beyond the far-flung borders of civilization, and now the wholesale slaughter of the enormous herds of buffaloes was on. Adventurous men from many walks of life took up the business of buffalo hunting. The professional hunters usually armed themselves with Sharp's "big fifties." The big fifty weighed about 13 pounds and carried a cartridge about four inches long, the bullet being one-half inch or 50/100-inch in diameter and using 120 grains of powder. From 700–1,000 yards was considered no unusual distance to bring down a buffalo, and hunters would frequently bring down 60 or 70 in a single stand. Soon the vast plains were covered with glistening carcasses denuded of their hides, the meat being left to shrivel and decay. As the awful slaughter progressed, the Indians became more and more enraged and many palefaces fell victims of their wrath. In the spring of '74 a reign of terror was inaugurated. Many murders were committed all along the border of Kansas and Indian territory. A homesteader and his wife were killed and scalped and their stock stolen at the mouth of Bitter creek, only six miles from Sun City. On Big Mule creek, 12 miles southwest from Sun City, John Coon, a boy of 12, was shot and scalped before the eyes of his parents who stood in the door of their cabin watching him drive in their little bunch of cattle. And so it went all along the border. Space is too limited to make mention of, or go into full detail of the many tragedies.

Later on in the summer, the Cheyennes and Arapahos assembled at their favorite place for "making medicine," 12 miles above Fort Reno on the North Canadian river. Old Minimic, the great medicine man, knew that an eclipse of the sun would occur at a certain time so he addressed the war-bedizened host as follows: "O, my children, we have gathered here to make medicine, and to learn what is the will of the Great Spirit concerning us. Not many moons ago we were free to go where we could over our vast hunting grounds. There were countless herds of buffalo as well as deer and antelope in great numbers. The redman killed only what was needed for food, while the hides were used for clothing and to cover our teepees. Our squaws were happy and contented. Our papooses played around our teepees and bathed in the streams and everywhere was plenty. And then came the paleface in such great numbers that we have been herded like so many cattle on the reservations and forced to feed at the hands of our enemies. The plains are strewn with the rotting carcasses of thousands of buffaloes, and still the awful slaughter of our cattle goes on. The cabins of the palefaces have taken the place of our teepees. Their spotted cattle are fast spreading out on the grazing grounds where our cattle fed in peace.

"Shall we sit like squaws and submit to the wrongs that have been heaped upon us? We are a race of warriors. The Great Spirit is not pleased that his children should quietly submit to these great humiliations. To prove that my words are true, tomorrow he will hide his face from us. The sun will cease to shine, but then if in that dark hour we shall decide to go forth in our might and destroy our enemies, the Great Spirit will again smile upon us. His Sun will again shine upon us in all its glory."

The eclipse came in due time and the wily old medicine man harangued them in a dramatic manner.

"See! The medicine is good, the Great Spirit has spoken. He has hidden his face in anger, but if we will be men, and not squaws, and shall this moment decide to take to the warpath he will smile upon us once more."

He was answered by the beating of the tomtoms and the savage war chant was taken up by all present. At that moment the eclipse slowly passed and again the sun shone unobscured.

"See!" cried Minimic, "the medicine is good. Away to the west the pale-faced hunters are slaughtering our cattle. They have built a strong house where they plan to take refuge in case of attack. Now, if we strike them on a certain day we will surprise them, and their bullets will fall from us as peas thrown by the hand of a child."

Then a great band of picked warriors, variously estimated at from 500 to 1,100, including their allies, the Kiowas and Comanches, struck out for the Texas Panhandle. Ere they reached the adobe walls, the keen eyes of the hunters in outlying camps discovered their approach and warning was quickly passed to other camps with the result that all but two, and some say three hunters, who were asleep under their wagons and failed to receive the warning, were barricaded behind the walls of the adobe, which gave the fort its name. Now, seeing they were discovered, and having full faith in the medicine, the redskins threw aside all caution and charged right up to the very doors of the fort, only to meet with a withering fire from the heavy rifles of the brave defenders. Time after time they charged en masse, striving to force an entrance by sheer weight of numbers. Indians and ponies were piled in heaps against the walls of the fort. At length, deciding that the medicine was "no good," they hastily withdrew, rushing pell-mell to get beyond the range of the great guns of the hunters. Soon they passed over a ridge about one mile from the fort. There, one brave wishing to show his contempt for the pale-faces, stood erect upon his pony and made insulting gestures. Clearly silhouetted against the skyline he presented an admirable target even at that great distance. A hunter, Billy Dixon, having a telescope sight on his rifle, said, "I'm just going to try that chap for luck." At the crack of the gun the Indian threw out his arms and toppled over to the ground. The rest fled in a complete panic. Their dead were estimated at from 70–100, while no one will ever know the number of wounded, while the brave defenders lost only two of their little band within the walls. They only numbered 28, including one woman, to start with.

Old Minimic barely escaped lynching at the hands of his followers and saved himself by saying they were one day later than the time set for making the attack, hence, "the medicine was no good."

Thus passed into history the battle of "Dobe Walls," one of the most desperate battles, and heroic defenses in the annals of the west.

In June 1924, there were only two survivors of that battle, Andy Johnson of Dodge City and Fred Leonard of Salt Lake City.

How Noted Peace Officer Tilghman
Nearly Met His End in Roundup
of Pony Rustlers

"Lay him low, his work is done,
What to him is friend or foeman,
What to him since he is gone
Is hand of man or kiss of woman?"

T HE DEATH OF "BILL" TILGHMAN while trying to arrest a man who was disturbing the peace has received a great deal of notice in the press. Having known him for many years, I wish to add a few words to what has been written.

In the early '70s we hunted buffalo on the same range west of Wichita, Kan. Later, in 1873, I met him in Dodge City, which was destined to become famous as the "wickedest city in the west." There one would meet the most conglomerate mixture of humanity in existence. Buffalo-hunters, mule-skinners, bullwhackers, cowboys, gamblers, long-haired scouts as well as soldiers from Fort Dodge, five miles down the river, all added to the picturesqueness of this frontier population. Here Bill Tilghman, a youth of about 20, looked out with wide, questioning eyes upon the turbulent scenes that were being enacted around him. At this time he was employed at various odd jobs that came to his hand.

Then, for a time, I lost track of him. Our next meeting was unexpected and in a far different setting. It was in the winter of 1875. Several cattlemen had turned loose about 15,000 cattle on a range about 40 miles square. A line of camps was established on the borders of this range, and in addition to the regular riding around the boundaries, at intervals, small parties of cowboys would make long scouts or out-rides to catch any stock that might have drifted out in the blizzards. On one of these out-rides the boys accidentally discovered the rendezvous of Bill Anderson and his band of rustlers. Anderson had long been suspected of rustling from the cattle range, but so securely was his retreat hidden in the wild, rugged country adjacent to the Cimarron that its existence seemed almost mythical. Soon after its discovery a posse was formed for the avowed purpose of cleaning out the gang.

There were 14 of us, each man armed with Winchester and six-shooter. We rode about 30 miles south the first day, camping for the night about one mile from the outlaws' camp. In the morning, after an early breakfast, horses were saddled, the cinches given an extra hitch, with rifles in hand and six-shooters hitched well forward, we laid aside all attempt at secrecy and dashed down upon the camp, bringing up short at the very door of their dugout. Two men came out, looking very much surprised and anxious at their unexpected visitors. They were Joe Watson, an old-time buffalo-hunter, and "Club Foot Tom," alias Thomas Hubbard, a noted rustler of Indian horses. While we were questioning them, another man appeared on the scene, riding around a sharp point almost into our midst before becoming aware of our presence. That was Bill Tilghman. It is not to his discredit that he turned very pale as he sat his horse facing our party. They (the rustlers) claimed to be "wolfing" (trapping and poisoning wolves). A large number of Indian ponies around their camp told a different story. We saw no sign of any stock from our range. After a thoro investigation, we decided to camp close by, which we did, keeping out a picket when night came.

Some of the "hard-boiled" ones of our party were insistent on wiping out the gang, in fact, the question was put to vote three times that night, but the majority ruled that, as we found no signs of their having molested our range, we had no right to molest them. At the time of our visit, Bill Anderson and others of his band were out on a raid.

The following spring I met Bill Tilghman in Dodge City. We had a friendly talk. I told him of the balloting in our camp. He smiled and replied, in his quiet way, "Well, you might have got us, but we'd have got some of you while you were doing it." Do not criticize too severely the rustling of Indian horses, for to those who were familiar with their raids and atrocities, it seemed almost like a virtue to deprive them of their means of transportation.

I need not comment on the career of Bill Tilghman as a peace officer, and legislator in the subsequent years. Many years had elapsed after our meeting in Dodge City before I saw him again for the last time. It was in December,

1920, while in Wichita Falls, that I saw posters announcing the coming of Bill Tilghman, the noted peace officer, with his moving picture show entitled "The Passing of the Oklahoma Outlaws." I met Bill in the lobby of the theater where we talked over old times. He presented me with a little book under the title of "Oklahoma Outlaws," which is now one of my much prized mementos. He also gave me a pass to his show.

Poor Bill; he has realized the poet's dream of life as expressed in four short lines:

> "A cry of pain new-born from baby lips,
> A cheery laugh as brave youth starts the race,
> A stern set look that knows its hopes eclipse,
> A smile upon a dead man's dreaming face."

A Reminiscence

P ROBABLY THERE are few westerners who have not had more or less experience with either forest or prairie fires.

There is something indescribably grand and fascinating about a great prairie fire. How the billows of flame leap and bound and how swift is their approach, "terrible as an army with banners."

It was in the winter of '78 that we were holding a bunch of cattle on the Cheyenne and Arapaho reservation.

Our range lay about 18 miles out from Ft. Reno. We were permitted to occupy this range by virtue of tribute paid to one Jimmie Morrison, a white man who had gained an Indian head-right by marrying a squaw.

The Indians were in a very restless mood, and viewed the encroachments of the pale-face with jealous eyes. Now everything went well with us until about mid-winter.

There had been but little rain or snowfall and everything was dry as tinder. One day about mid-afternoon three fires sprang up simultaneously, to the south, southwest and southeast of us. Hastily we rounded up the cattle and pushed them to the northward and then began a battle with the flames.

A rude sled upon which was placed a barrel of water was brought to the field of action. Backfires were started all along the line. Each man was supplied with a gunny sack soaked in water. Often it required desperate effort to keep the backfires under control, to keep them from racing away in the wrong direction.

All that afternoon, through the long night, and until nearly noon the next day we battled with the devouring element. We fought with all the energy of desperation half expecting to see silhouetted against the flame-lit horizon the dark forms of vengeful riders. Often the issue was in doubt. The very lives of the herd were at stake. There was the double danger of famine and fire.

But at last we were victorious. The last backfire had met the last head-fire and together they leaped madly toward the sky and died.

Miles away to the south farther than the eye could reach was a scene of ruin and desolation. We stood and gazed upon it with blood-shot eyes, with parched lips and smoke grimed faces.

As I surveyed the desolate waste I thought how like the lives of many: lives that were once fair and bright with the sunshine of happiness, but over whom the fierce fires of passion have swept leaving only a blackened, ruined waste.

A few short months elapsed, and warmed by the generous rays of the sun, and watered by the vernal showers that dreary waste was transformed into a field of delight, covered with green grass and interspersed with flowers of wondrous beauty. So, warmed by the sunshine of love and hope, and watered by showers, of mercy, even lives that were charred and wasted may rise from the ashes, to bloom, and to ripen into glorious fruition.

Maynard's *American Magazine* Contest Entry

Colorado Springs, Colorado
February 13, 1925
Contest Editor
American Magazine
381 Fourth Avenue
New York City, N.Y.

Dear Contest Editor:
Enclosed herewith please find letter about, "The Best Loved Person I Ever Knew."
Whether it wins a prize or not it will be a tardy tribute to one who was worthy of all affection.

Yours sincerely,
F. H. Maynard
420 Cheyenne Blvd.
Colorado Springs, Colorado

The Best Loved Person I Ever Knew

My Mother

As a young bride she came from Ohio to Iowa by covered wagon in 1848. For a number of years she endured all the hardships and privations incident to pioneer life. Later she moved into Iowa City where Father engaged in the grocery business. Came then the great panic of '57 which wrought such ruin all over our fair land. She saw the death of hopes and the loss of worldly goods, accumulated by unremitting toil, yet I've often been told how patiently and uncomplainingly she bore the loss and changed conditions.

The next move was to a little ten acre farm about six miles north from the city. Soon came the Civil War. Father answered the call of country. He came home and said, "G—— I've enlisted." She bowed her head on his shoulder and silently wept. Then came days of anxious watching and waiting, of unceasing toil, for women and children did men's work.

How calm and patient Mother was. Other wives and mothers were passing thru the same bitter ordeal of those war days. Often they'd come to my Mother for comfort in their hours of sadness. She loved little children, and many a weary night watch she put in by the bed-side of a sick neighbor or neighbor's child as the case might be.

Mother had a slight fragile form, but what wonderful endurance, what wonderful resiliency. She was kind to everyone so was loved by all. I saw her last near Seattle, the year the World War closed. The worn hands were resting from toil for the dear eyes were sealed by total blindness. She lived to the age of 91. Two years after I last saw her found me amid the turbulent scenes of the great oil fields along Red River.

A letter came in saying, "Mother is dead."

I retired to my room, flung myself on my cot and wept bitter tears for the best loved person I ever knew, My Mother.

F. H. MAYNARD

Glossary of Names

Ameahah A Cheyenne woman at Fort Reno with whom Maynard danced at a "chuckaway" in 1878.

Anderson, Bill An outlaw who led a band of horse thieves operating in southern Kansas and the Cherokee Outlet in Indian Territory during the mid-1870s. (*Medicine Lodge Cresset*)

Anderson, Jim A liveryman in Dodge City who helped catch Charlie Brady when he was trying to escape from the law. Anderson may also have been the bystander who was wounded in a shooting scrape between Bat Masterson on one side and A. J. Peacock and Al Updegraff on the other. (O'Neal, *Encyclopedia of Western Gunfighters*, 221–22; Miller and Snell, *Great Gunfighters*, 173)

Anderson, "Texas Frank" A cowboy who was part of the Evans & Hunter crew that went to New Mexico in 1875 to drive cattle from the Chisum Ranch to Dodge City. In 1878 a man named "Texas Frank" stole some horses near Medicine Lodge and was a short time later arrested at Sedgwick. (*Barber County Mail*)

Arp, —— A farmer or small rancher in north Texas east of Jacksboro.

Arp, Hub Arp's son.

Arp, Rube Arp's son. A cowboy who was on a drive with Maynard in 1872, taking horses for Wiley Robbins from winter pasture in Kansas back to Jacksboro, Texas, for use in driving cattle to Kansas.

Ayres, Jim James Ayres lived in Louisburg Township near Coffeyville in Montgomery County, Kansas. Born in Missouri, he was thirty-three at the time of his death in 1875 and left behind a thirty-two-year-old wife and two sons, aged fourteen and three. (Census records)

Billy the Kid Perhaps the best known of all the outlaws of the American West.

Birdsell [or Birdsall], Gus A Texas cowboy who was range boss for Dennis Sheedy (spelled Scheete in Records and Wheeler, *Cherokee Outlet Cowboy*) near

Lakin in 1877 and near Kinsley in 1878. (Records and Wheeler, *Cherokee Outlet Cowboy*, 63)

Brady, Charlie A Texas cowboy who got into difficulty in Dodge City. On September 3, 1877, Bat Masterson, Marshal Lawrence Deger, and a citizen named Anderson apprehended a horse thief; most likely the thief was Brady and the citizen, Jim Anderson, as related by Maynard. A man named Charles H. Brady was one of John Chisum's gunslingers in a range war in New Mexico in the late spring of 1877. (Miller and Snell, *Great Gunfighters*, 173; Nolan, *Lincoln County War*, 123)

Brooks, Bill Brooks was both lawman and outlaw, serving as marshal of Newton and a policeman in Ellsworth before being lynched for horse theft near Caldwell. (O'Neal, *Encyclopedia of Western Gunfighters*, 47–48; Miller and Snell, *Great Gunfighters*, 41–47; Wright, *Dodge City*, 166; Drago, *Wild, Woolly, Wicked*, 233–35)

Brown, Joe An outlaw who ran with Hurricane Bill Martin, Bill Brooks, and John Cole. He was killed in 1875 trying to escape from an Ellsworth posse. His moral character would seem to match the Joseph Brown who was arrested in Wichita in July of 1870 (the same year and month that Wichita was incorporated) on a charge of drunkenness in a privy. Brown, following a night in the saloons, seems to have established squatter's rights in the outhouse of a man named Carter and would not allow any of the family members into the facility the following morning. (Miner, *Wichita*, 46)

Buchanan, James Fifteenth president of the United States.

"Buckskin Joe" Edward Jonathan Hoyt, born in Canada in 1840, was a Union veteran of the Civil War, a circus performer, a musician and band organizer and director, a gold prospector, a Wild West showman, a deputy U.S. marshal, and a genuine frontiersman. He arrived in Kansas in 1870, making the Arkansas City area his headquarters for the next twenty years, which included ventures in show business and prospecting in Colorado, Nova Scotia, and Honduras. He sold his properties in Kansas and Oklahoma in 1909 and moved to California, where he died in 1918. (Shirley, *Buckskin Joe*)

Cadwell, —— An agent for Hutchinson businessman W. C. Edwards. Possibly Curtis Cadwell, a cousin of Laban Records. (Records and Wheeler, *Cherokee Outlet Cowboy*, 254)

Callahan, [John] John Callaham was lynched, most probably wrongfully, with John Cole for horse theft on Saw Log Creek near Dodge City on April 8, 1876. (Miller and Snell, *Great Gunfighters*, 23; Wright, *Dodge City*, 185)

Callahan, "Old Dave" A cowboy in the Gypsum Hills with Maynard, 1875 to 1877.

Cheeney, —— Chuckwagon cook for the Peter Moore crew in moving some cattle from the Wichita area to the Gypsum Hills in 1874.

"Cheyenne Minnie" *See* Ameahah.

Clark[e], Ben Ben Clarke, an able frontiersman, was chief of scouts for General Miles. (Berthrong, *Cheyenne and Arapaho Ordeal*, 281; DeArment, *Bat Masterson*, 52–53; Haley, *Buffalo War*, 41, 131)

Clemen[t]s, Milt Clements, who helped fight Hurricane Bill's horse thief gang in the Gypsum Hills in 1874, lost his legs as a result of a blizzard in which he and Rube Marshall were caught during the winter of 1874–75. (Records and Wheeler, *Cherokee Outlet Cowboy*, 329)

"Club-foot Tom" *See* Hubbard.

Coates, Matt Cowboy for Millett and Mabry on a herd being driven from Texas to Ellsworth in 1876. He ran a meat market in Dodge City in 1877 and was killed by Charley Reed east of Cheyenne after being cheated in a horse deal in the summer of 1878.

Cole, John Outlaw and horse thief, lynched April 8, 1876, on Saw Log Creek near Dodge City by a posse from Sumner County. (Miller and Snell, *Great Gunfighters*, 23)

"Colorado Bill" A "noted character" Maynard met at the Fort Reno Indian agency in 1878.

Coon, —— A settler in the Gypsum Hills near Sun City.

Coon, John Coon's son, killed by Indians on the family homestead in 1874.

Cord, [Thaddeus] One of three men who stole horses from the Osage Indians in 1872 and was apprehended by Buckskin Joe and Hard Rope and taken to Wichita for trial. He was convicted in 1873 and sentenced to seven years in the state penitentiary. He served six years, with time off for good behavior. *See also* Omett and Wolsey. (Court records, Kansas State Historical Society)

"Curly" An outlaw Maynard met in 1872 in Perryville, Indian Territory.

Custer, George A. Famous American military leader in the Indian wars on the Great Plains, killed with most of his command at the Battle of the Greasy Grass (Little Bighorn) in June 1876.

Davidson, Cy Born in Illinois in 1853, he was the son of Reno County farmer C. B. Davidson and his wife S. C., who farmed near Hutchinson in the mid-1870s. Cy Davidson was a line rider for the Texas Land and Cattle Company in the Cherokee Outlet in 1878. (1875 census records; Records and Wheeler, *Cherokee Outlet Cowboy*, 93)

Davidson, Jim Cy Davidson's brother, two years older. (1875 census records)

Dillon, Jack A cowboy who worked with Maynard near Wichita in 1875. While on an Evans and Hunter cattle drive from John Chisum's ranch in 1875, he shot "Texas Frank" Anderson.

Doby, —— A long-haired cowboy on the Millett and Mabry drive in 1876 who ran a meat market in Dodge City in 1877 with Matt Coates. A John Doby, born in Canada and aged thirty-nine in 1880, ranched in Barber County, Kansas. (1880 census records)

Douglas and Son Brothers S. B. (age thirty-three) and C. H. (age thirty) Douglas are listed as merchants at Sun City in 1875. (Douglass in 1875 census records)

Douglas, Stephen A. Political opponent of Abraham Lincoln.

Doyle, [John] A cattleman who helped organize the Comanche Pool in 1879. (Records and Wheeler, *Cherokee Outlet Cowboy*, 62; Yost, *Medicine Lodge*, 49, 56)

Driskill, Budd Son of J. L. Driskill. (Miller and Snell, *Great Gunfighters*, 284–85; Chrisman, *Lost Trails*, 150; Haywood, *Cowtown Lawyers*, 93; DeArment, *Bat Masterson*, 211–12)

Driskill, J. [L.] Driskill and Sons were well-known Texas cattlemen who established a ranch in Clark County, Kansas, in 1876. (Berryman, "Early Settlement," 568; Haywood, *Cowtown Lawyers*, 125; Hunter, *Trail Drivers*, 872; McCoy, *Historic Sketches*, 58–59)

Driskill, Jesse Son of J. L. Driskill. (Hunter, *Trail Drivers*, 872)

Driskill, Tillman Nephew of J. L. Driskill.

Drumin, Major Major Andrew Drumm was the first cattleman to graze stock in the Cherokee Outlet, establishing a ranch there in 1870 after having made his fortune in the California gold fields. He was also one of the first to use barbed wire fencing, having built a drift fence two hundred miles long at the north end of the Strip about 1880. (Brown, *Bury My Heart*, 305–306; Freeman, *Midnight and Noonday*, 101; Rainey, *Cherokee Strip*, 165; Records and Wheeler, *Cherokee Outlet Cowboy*, 301; Savage, *Cherokee Strip Live Stock Association*, 35)

Dull Knife A Northern Cheyenne chief who helped lead the Cheyenne Outbreak of 1878. (Berthrong, *Cheyenne and Arapaho Ordeal*, 33; D. Brown, *Bury My Heart*, 325)

Dunlap, Bill A cowboy active in Kansas and Indian Territory during the 1870s and 1880s, Dunlap was cattleman William Quinlan's foreman in 1883. He later moved to California. (Records and Wheeler, *Cherokee Outlet Cowboy*, 334)

Edwards, W[illiam] C. An entrepreneur who came to Kansas in 1870 at age twenty-three and established lumberyards in various towns, including Hutchinson. He was a founder of Edwards County, which was named after him. He and his brother, Rufus Eugene, were bankers as well as lumber dealers and also had a cattle ranch in Comanche County. (Andreas, *History of the State of Kansas*, 561; census records)

Evans, Bob A cowboy who rode for Texas cattleman J. L. Driskill on a drive to Ellsworth in 1876. Later that year he worked for Driskill's son, Budd, who was in charge of wintering cattle on the Cimarron River.

Evans, Jesse With Robert Hunter, a major cattleman during the trail-drive era. In one well-known deal the firm of Evans and Hunter got the best of John Chisum, who often signed notes for Texas cattle but didn't always pay them off. Evans hired fifty tough cowboys from Dodge City to round up the cattle while Hunter handled the paperwork, then they paid Chisum with his own notes, which they had bought for pennies on the dollar. This episode may well be the one Maynard relates in which Jim Ayres was killed. Evans and Hunter also had major cattle interests in the Gypsum Hills area, where Evans was one of the first to herd cattle in Comanche County. There was a different Jesse Evans who rode and fought for Chisum in various range wars. (Chrisman, *Lost Trails*, 180–85; Hunter, *Trail Drivers*, 240, 289, 936; Nolan, *Lincoln County War*, 346; Records and Wheeler, *Cherokee Outlet Cowboy*, 332; Wright, *Dodge City*, 262; Yost, *Medicine Lodge*, 49, 56)

Evans, Louis One of the cowboys who went on the Evans and Hunter drive to the Chisum Ranch in New Mexico in 1875.

Frenchie Most likely James S. "Frenchy" French, who was a whiskey trader to the Indians and involved in cattle and horse theft in the country between the Canadian and Salt Fork Rivers in the mid-1870s. (Lillibridge, *Red Fork Ranch*, 12)

Gabriel, "Gabe" A Mexican cowboy working for W. B. Grimes herding cattle on the Ninnescah River in 1876. He shot another Mexican cowboy, named Philip.

Graham, Jim In 1871 James and Martin Graham established a ranch south of the Arkansas River near what would become, two years later, Granada, Colorado. During the 1880s it was one of the largest private ranches in the area. (Betz, *Prowers County History*, 74)

Griffin, Andy Griffin located his trading post in the midst of Indian country and the buffalo range, west of Medicine Lodge, in the winter of 1871–72. He was killed in Indian Territory during the summer of 1872. (DeArment, *Bat Masterson*, 14; Yost, *Medicine Lodge*, 37–38)

Grimes, William B. A Texas cattleman who had a packing plant on the Gulf Coast in Texas in the late 1850s and also sent thousands of cattle to the Kansas market. He maintained a ranch in Clark County, Kansas, as late as 1899. (Dary, *Cowboy Culture*, 106, 256; Hunter, *Trail Drivers*, 405, 488, 643, 866–67)

Grimes, Brady Son of W. B. Grimes.

Hard Robe, or Hard Rope Chief of the Heart-Stays band of the Osages who fought against the Confederates in 1863 and a scout for Custer at the Washita in 1868. By 1870, however, he was ready to unite with the Kiowas, Kiowa-Apaches, Comanches, Cheyennes, and Arapahos to resist the encroachments of Euro-Americans onto the plains. Although defiant and martial by nature, he was also wise enough to know when fighting was futile. In 1880 he was elected lieutenant governor of the Osage Nation when the tribe adopted a constitution modeled on that of the Cherokees. (Mathews, *Osages*, 640–41, 643, 669, 679–80, 687, 689, 698)

Hays, Ed A cattle rustler and horse thief. He was arrested by Mike Meagher and Wyatt Earp in Wichita in November 1875 for horse theft. (Miller and Snell, *Great Gunfighters*, 83, 356)

Hickok, "Wild Bill" Perhaps the most famous gunfighter and lawman in the Old West.

Hill, George A Texas cowboy of this name was active on the Kansas trails during the 1870s. (Hunter, *Trail Drivers*, 103, 137–38, and 306–308)

Houser, —— According to Maynard, a government clerk at Fort Reno in 1878. Perhaps Herman Hauser, married to an Indian woman whose English name was Amy, who had a farm on the Cheyenne-Arapaho reservation. (Berthrong, *Cheyenne and Arapaho Ordeal*, 122–23, 176–81)

Houser, Molly According to Maynard, a Sioux woman married to Houser at Fort Reno in 1878. Perhaps Amy Hauser, a Cheyenne or Arapaho woman married to Herman Hauser. (Berthrong, *Cheyenne and Arapaho Ordeal*, 122, 176–81)

Hubbard, "Club Foot" Tom Tom Hubbert, with his cohort Bill Anderson, was notorious for stealing horses in the Gypsum Hills area. The two were headquarted in Kiowa, Kansas, in 1874. (*Medicine Lodge Cresset*)

Hughes, Captain A Texas cattleman for whom Maynard worked near Wichita in 1875. Hughes had four herds of cattle, numbering fourteen thousand head, driven to Wichita in 1875. (Hunter, *Trail Drivers*, 763)

"Hurricane Bill" *See* Martin.

Iliff, Ez A merchant and liveryman in Barber County who, with his brother-in-law, J. W. McNeal, bought the *Barber County Mail* in 1879 and changed its name to the *Cresset*. Iliff was an admirer of Milton, who in *Paradise Lost* had used the term *cresset* to describe the light fixtures in Hell. Iliff came to Barber County as a cowboy in 1873. ("Osage Troubles," 50; McNeal, *When Kansas Was Young*, 82; Roach, "Memories of Frontier Days," 616; Yost, *Medicine Lodge*, 54)

Jackson, Andrew Black cook and wagon driver for Wiley Robbins in 1872.

Jim Black cowboy for W. B. Grimes in the Gypsum Hills during the winter of 1875–76. Before the Civil War, Grimes, like many east Texas ranchers, had made extensive use of slaves as cattle workers. After the war many of these former slaves (who have often been recorded in history, if at all, by a first name only) continued to work as cowboys. (Durham and Jones, *Negro Cowboys*, 16)

John *See* Old John.

Ketchum, [Ami] A Nebraska settler killed in December 1878 by cattleman Print Olive in revenge for the death of his brother Bob. (Abbot and Smith, *We Pointed Them North*, 34–35; Chrisman, *Ladder*, 249ff.)

Kutch, —— Killed by C. C. Peppard near Granada, Colorado, in a dispute over a horse race in 1873 or 1874.

Lake, Reuban A rancher in the Gypsum Hills and founder, in the summer of 1873, of Lake City. Lake was involved in a near fatal buffalo hunt in the winter of 1873 when he was separated by a blizzard from his party. He wrapped himself in a freshly skinned hide to keep warm and was immobilized when the hide froze around him during the night. He was rescued by his companions the following day. In 1875 he was sheriff of Barber County. ("Osage Troubles," 48; Yost, *Medicine Lodge*, 38–39)

Lee, Robert E. Leader of the Confederate Army.

Lewis, Colonel Commander at Camp Supply during the Cheyenne Outbreak of 1878. (DeArment, *Bat Masterson*, 167)

Lincoln, Abraham Sixteenth president of the United States.

Littlefield, George A prominent Texas cattleman during the trail-drive era. (Hunter, *Trail Drivers*, 188, 570, and 700–702)

Lockridge, William Trail boss for Millett and Mabry on a drive to Ellsworth in 1876.

Loving, Jim A rancher in north Texas and son of Oliver Loving, cofounder of the Goodnight-Loving Trail. (Hunter, *Trail Drivers*, 870–71)

Lowe, "Rowdy Joe" A saloon keeper and, with his wife, Rowdy Kate, a bawdy-house keeper in various cowtowns, including Ellsworth, Newton, and Wichita. (O'Neal, *Encyclopedia of Western Gunfighters*, 196; Miller and Snell, *Great Gunfighters*, 151–68)

Maberry, [Seth] Major Seth Mabry (variously spelled Maberry or Mayberry) was a Texas cattleman and sometime partner of Captain E. B. Millett. Mabry, who hired over a hundred drovers every spring, was said to have been able to remember every one of them by name and place and date of hiring. (Hunter, *Trail Drivers*, 478, 539, 704; McCoy, *Historic Sketches*, 70–73; Wright, *Dodge City*, 270)

Manning, James "Little Jim" Fifteen-year-old hot-tempered cowboy from Michigan who, in 1875, shot and killed Jim Ayres.

Marshall, Rube A hunter from Sun City who helped fight Hurricane Bill's horse thief gang in the Gypsum Hills in 1874. While hauling freight for the government during the winter of 1874–75, he and Milt Clements got caught in a blizzard; they survived but lost their legs. Marshall went on to homestead in the Cherokee Strip near Kingfisher. He rode a mule, which he had trained to walk up to a platform so that he could mount. (Records and Wheeler, *Cherokee Outlet Cowboy*, 27, 329)

Martin, "Hurricane Bill" An outlaw, lawman, buffalo hunter, bootlegger, and horse thief. One of his buffalo hunting companions was Bill Tilghman. Hurricane Bill's theft of horses from the Indians, as well as his proclivity to scalp any white man he had killed, thus causing Indians to be blamed for the atrocity, did much to unsettle the southern frontier in the 1870s. His reputation was such that Wichita lawmen Sam Botts, Bill Smith, and Wyatt Earp were hesitant to arrest him, but Sim Tucker, a lawyer, took him into custody on July 6, 1874. He was later both a lawman and an outlaw in Texas and New Mexico. (DeArment, *Bat Masterson*, 130; Drago, *Wild, Woolly, Wicked*, 199 and 203–206; Haley, *Buffalo War*, 45–47; Lillibridge, *Red Fork Ranch*, 12–15; Thrapp, *Encyclopedia of Frontier Biography*, 948–49)

Marts, Cal A cowboy for W. B. Grimes in the Gypsum Hills during the winter of 1875–76 who had a scrape with some Osages.

Mason, Joe A respected law officer in Dodge City. (Miller and Snell, *Great Gunfighters*, 171, 203, 205, and 220; Chrisman, *Lost Trails*, 100; DeArment, *Bat Masterson*, 80–81 and 97–98; Wright, *Dodge City*, 239)

Masterson, Bat One of the best known of Western lawmen.

Masterson, Ed A brother of Bat Masterson and marshal of Dodge City, where he was killed on April 9, 1878, by Jack Wagner and A. M. Walker. (O'Neal, *Encyclopedia of Western Gunfighters*, 215–16; Miller and Snell, *Great Gunfighters*, 178–84; Wright, *Dodge City*, 305)

Mauping, Arthur A half-Choctaw cowboy for Millet and Mabry on a drive to Ellsworth in 1876.

Mayberry *See* Mabry.

Maynard, Georgia [or Georgiana] F. H. Maynard's mother, born in Ohio in 1829. (Butler County census records)

Maynard, Horace F. H. Maynard's father, born in Ohio in 1822, died at Towanda, Kansas, in 1890. (Butler County census records; Butler County cemetery records)

Maynard, [Mary A. "Nettie"] Maynard's older sister. She died on May 1, 1877, a week after giving birth to a son, Ernest M. Ross, who died on September 13 of that same year. *See also* Ross, George. (Butler County marriage and cemetery records)

McAllister, Frank A cowboy Maynard knew in the Medicine Lodge country in

1877–78. In 1874 Frank McAlister signed a petition requesting that a local militia be established in Barber County to protect citizens from Indians. Nine years later he saved a young boy from drowning in a flood on Spring Creek. He was also a major dealer in Texas horses, trailing them to Kansas for sale. ("Osage Troubles," 5; Records and Wheeler, *Cherokee Outlet Cowboy*, 114, 335; Yost, *Medicine Lodge*, 114)

McCaully, J. W. A cowboy working for Budd Driskill on the Cimarron in 1876.

Miller, Joaquin Colorful California poet.

Millett, —— E. B. and Alonzo Millett were prominent cattlemen from Seguin, Texas. Among their numerous business partners during the great cattle drives to Kansas was Seth Mabry. (Hunter, *Trail Drivers*, 478, 539, 704; McCoy, *Historic Sketches*, 111–13)

Mitchell, [Luther] A Nebraska settler killed in December 1878 by cattleman Print Olive in revenge for the death of his brother Bob. (Abbott and Smith, *We Pointed Them North*, 34–35; Chrisman, *Ladder*, 249ff.)

Mizner, Major [J. K.] Commander at Fort Reno at the time of the Cheyenne outbreak in 1878. (Berthrong, *Cheyenne and Arapaho Ordeal*, 7, 32–33)

Mooney, Volney P. A buffalo hunting and Indian trading companion of Maynard. His father, Isaac, officiated at the marriage of Maynard and Flora Longstreth in 1881. Mooney was later a judge in Butler County and author of a history of the county (see Bibliography).

Moore, Peter A cattle owner who "arranged" to have his cattle "rustled" in 1874 in order to evade the mortgage held by W. C. Edwards.

Morrison, [James S.] "Jimmie" A white man married to an Arapaho woman. In 1883 he secured lease rights to 138,000 acres in the Cheyenne-Arapaho Reservation. (Berthrong, *Cheyenne and Arapaho Ordeal*, 94, 97)

Morrow, "Prairie Dog" Dave Coming to the plains as a buffalo hunter, Morrow became an early settler, respected citizen, and sometime policeman of Dodge City. In 1872 he killed a white buffalo, which he sold to Dodge City merchant Robert Wright for a thousand dollars. He received his nickname from his practice, at the Hays City railroad station, of selling prairie dogs as pets to tourists. (Wright, *Dodge City*, 177, 197; DeArment, *Bat Masterson*, 17, 87, 89–90, 211–12, 262; Miller and Snell, *Great Gunfighters*, 212, 213, 284, 286; Dary, *Buffalo Book*, 215–17)

Mosely [Mosley], John An Indian fighter at Medicine Lodge. His father, E. H. Mosley, built a trading post on the Medicine Lodge River near the Indian Territory line in the spring of 1872 and was killed by a band of Osage Indians on July 30 of that year. Two years later the Osages were accused of killing two farmers, although the killers may have been white men disguised as Indians (see Martin, "Hurricane Bill"). In response to this trouble and other Indian unrest, Kansas governor Thomas Osborne authorized local militias or home guards. The Barber County Guards were commanded by Captain Ricker, with John Mosley second in command. According to one version of the encounter, later in the summer of 1874 Barney O'Connor, then seventeen, was carrying mail to Wichita when he spotted about fifty Osages camped on Sand Creek. He returned to Medicine Lodge, where Ricker and Mosley mustered the militia, which then attacked the camp, killing half a dozen Osage men. The Osage perspective of the encounter was different: About thirty Indians, ten of them women and children, were hunting buffalo near Cedar Springs eighteen miles southeast of Medicine Lodge. There they were attacked by a quasi-military force of white men who seemed to propose a parley before suddenly killing four of the Osage men, the rest of the group fleeing. When the Osages returned later, they found three bodies, two of them scalped. All of the Indians' camp gear and equipment was taken, including fifty-four horses and mules. The authorizing of the militia was later postdated to make the killings legal. (Mathews, *Osages*, 709–12; "Osage Troubles," passim; Yost, *Medicine Lodge*, 37, 40, 46–48)

Murray, Tom One of Maynard's fellow cowboys in the Medicine Lodge country, noted for never carrying a gun. He was killed in the Cheyenne Outbreak of 1878 while herding cattle by himself in Comanche County. (McNeal, *When Kansas Was Young*, 87; Records and Wheeler, *Cherokee Outlet Cowboy*, 63; Yost, *Medicine Lodge*, 52)

O'Connor, Barney A cowboy whom Maynard knew in the Medicine Lodge country. Throughout his life O'Connor was active in the cattle business, later becoming an important influence in the Kansas Livestock Association. He was best known in his home town for having been instrumental in capturing Henry Brown, marshal of Caldwell, who in 1884 robbed the Medicine Lodge bank and killed two bankers. Brown and his three fellow outlaws were captured after a running gunfight through the Gypsum Hills, then later lynched. *See also* Mosely. (O'Neal, *Encyclopedia of Western Gunfighters*, 48–53; Miller and Snell, *Great Gunfighters*, 56–64; Yost, *Medicine Lodge*, 47, 88, 95–96, and 103)

Omett [Ohmert, Simon K.] A sometime law officer in Wichita who was convicted in 1873 of stealing horses from the Osage Indians and sentenced to seven years in the state penitentiary. Despite efforts from friends to win him a gubernatorial pardon in 1875, Ohmert served six years, with time off for good behavior. *See also* Cord and Wolsey. (Miller and Snell, *Great Gunfighters*, 346–47; court records Kansas State Historical Society)

"Old John" Black cook for Dr. Simmons in Gypsum Hills during 1874 who was nearly shot by Jim Davidson.

Pancho A Mexican cowboy working for W. B. Grimes herding cattle on the Ninnescah River in 1876.

Payne, Dave Well-known leader of the Boomer movement to open lands in Indian Territory to white settlement. (Mathews, *Osages*, 168; Shirley, *Buckskin Joe*, 162)

Pepperd, [Christopher Carson] A cowboy and rancher who had a reputation for rascality. After a falling out with a trail boss surnamed Allen, Pepperd tried to shoot him in a Dodge City saloon, then turned him in to the authorities for the murder of Pepperd's black cook. When authorities refused to act because there was no physical evidence of murder, Pepperd exhumed the body, cut off the head, and brought it back to Dodge City as evidence. He gave up the prosecution in disgust, however, when the court continued the trial until the rest of the remains could be brought to town. Pepperd was one of the Dodge City crew of jokesters who liked to haze tenderfeet by pretending to be Indians and attacking them when they rode outside town. When he was nearly shot one time when the dude didn't run, however, he gave up the practice. When the open range ended, he moved to Texas, where he died in poverty in 1921. (Haywood, "Comanche," 166–90; Wright, *Dodge City*, 180 and 207)

Philip A Mexican cowboy working for W. B. Grimes herding cattle on the Ninnescah River in 1876 who was shot and killed by another Mexican cowboy, named Gabriel.

Potter, Zach An antagonist of Maynard's for an unspecified quarrel. Maynard bought him some ice cream in Wichita in 1875 and resolved the quarrel. Perhaps a member of the Potter family that ranched on the Cimarron River. (Lillibridge, *Red Fork Ranch*, 64)

"Prairie Dog Dave" *See* Morrow.

Quinlan, [W. C. "Bill"] A cattle owner in an early ranching pool in the Gypsum Hills in 1874 who lost four hundred head to rustlers. Originally from Texas, Quinlan established a ranch in the 1870s in the Cherokee Outlet north of the Cimarron River near the present site of Enid. (Records and Wheeler, *Cherokee Outlet Cowboy*, 297, 348)

Reed, Charley A cowboy, gambler, and gunfighter who was lynched by a mob in Ogallala, Nebraska, sometime about 1883 after he had shot and killed a man named Dumas. (O'Neal, *Encyclopedia of Western Gunfighters*, 260)

Richards, [Ephiram G.] A Butler County neighbor of Horace Maynard's who farmed in Fairview Township near Towanda. (Butler County 1880 census records)

Ricker, [Cyrus M.] An Indian fighter and commander of the local militia at Medicine Lodge in 1874. *See* Mosely. ("Osage Troubles," passim; Yost, *Medicine Lodge*, 46–47)

Robbins, Milt Brother of Texas cattleman Wiley Robbins.

Robbins, Wiley A horse and cattle owner near Jacksboro, Texas, and staunch anti-Yankee. Maynard worked for him in 1872 and was in danger of getting killed because he was from Kansas. Maynard met him on a street in Wichita in 1876 but was not recognized.

Rodebaugh, Dave *See* Rudebaugh.

Rosanna A Mexican working as a chuck wagon cook for W. B. Grimes on the Ninnescah River in 1876.

Ross, George Most likely H. G. Ross, the only person with that surname listed in the census records for Fairview or Towanda townships during the period of Maynard's memoirs. On February 7, 1875, H. G. Ross married Maynard's older sister Mary, also known as Nettie. Isaac Mooney, Vol Mooney's father, performed the ceremony. A month later the 1875 census listed Ross as a thirty-six-year-old butcher who had been born in Massachusetts. His wife, listed only under the initial N., is recorded as a twenty-five-year-old teacher. The couple lived on an eighty-acre farm along with a twenty-year-old hired hand, W. A. Stone. Shortly after the death of his wife in childbirth, Ross disappeared on a cattle buying trip and was not heard of again. (Butler County census records)

Rourke, Mike An outlaw active in southern Kansas during the 1870s. He was reputed to have been the leader of the gang that attempted to rob the Santa Fe train at Kinsley on January 27, 1878. He was caught seven months later at Ellsworth and received ten years in the penitentiary. *See* Rudebaugh. (Miller and Snell, *Great Gunfighters*, 216–22, 421, 422; DeArment, *Bat Masterson*, 92–95)

Rudebaugh, Dave Sometime after helping trail cattle to Colorado for Jim Graham in 1873, Rudebaugh turned outlaw. He was one of several men who unsuccessfully attempted to rob a Santa Fe train at Kinsley on January 27, 1878. By the next year he had relocated his operations to New Mexico, where, after a stint as a policeman in Las Vegas, he joined with Billy the Kid and was captured by Pat Garrett and sentenced to hang. He escaped from jail and fled to Mexico, where he had his head cut off in a barroom fight in 1886. He is said to be the only man Billy the Kid was afraid of. (O'Neal, *Encyclopedia of Western Gunfighters*, 269–71; Miller and Snell, *Great Gunfighters*, 220–22; Nolan, *Lincoln County War*, 482–83; DeArment, *Bat Masterson*, 89–92, 94–96)

Scheedy, [Dennis] A cattleman active in southwest Kansas during the late

1870s, Sheedy was proud of being a self-made man, but his thriftiness as an operator who skimped on food and supplies for his cowhands earned him a parody in cowboy nightherding songs. (Atherton, *Cattle Kings*, 104–05; Chrisman, *Cimarron*, 150; McCoy, *Historic Sketches*, 388–96)

Simmons, Dr. [A. S.] A Texas cattlemen who was living on a ranch near Lake City in Barber County, Kansas, in 1875. Although he owned only 160 acres, he had personal property, including forty horses and thirty-two hundred cattle, valued at $39,420. (Barber County 1875 census records)

Simpson, "Little Dick" Cook for W. B. Grimes' winter crew in the Gypsum Hills, 1875. Before he was eighteen he had killed a man in Indian Territory. He escaped from marshals taking him to Fort Smith, and Maynard never heard of him again.

Siringo, Charlie A working cowboy whose contemporary writings about his experiences on the plains were the first to be published, in 1885. In the mid- to late 1870s he was active in southern Kansas. (Records and Wheeler, *Cherokee Outlet Cowboy*, 195)

Sitler, Hank An early businessman in Dodge City. (Wright, *Dodge City*, 272, 308)

"Slusher" An Arkansas man employed by Wiley Robbins in 1872. He threatened to kill Maynard over a dispute about a kicking horse shot by Maynard, but the two reconciled in later years.

Springer, Bill A rancher who served as president of the Barber County Livestock Association in 1878. (Records and Wheeler, *Cherokee Outlet Cowboy*, 89)

Sullivan, John A cowboy who, along with Frank Maynard, helped Jim Graham drive cattle from near Towanda, Kansas, to Granada, Colorado, in 1873. Dave Rudebaugh was the cook for the crew. John Sullivan helped William Butler drive a herd of cattle to Abilene in 1868. Ten years later he was foreman for John Gobie on a trail drive from Dodge City to Barber County. (Hunter, *Trail Drivers*, 717; Records and Wheeler, *Cherokee Outlet Cowboy*, 65–66)

"Tiger Bill" A Texas outlaw run out of Perryville, Indian Territory, in 1872. In 1873 he was shot to death in Short Creek (that is, Galena), Kansas, a lead mining boom town, by a band of Missourians who were attempting to redeem a pocket watch given in security for a ten-dollar bottle of champagne in the Round Top Saloon, where Tiger Bill functioned as a de facto, although in this case ineffective, enforcer for the saloon owner. (*Pen-Lens Views*, 10)

Tilghman, Bill A buffalo hunter, race horse owner, possible outlaw, and lawman. Arrested for train robbery and horse theft, but not convicted on either charge, Tilghman became a highly respected marshal of Dodge City, the first of many towns he helped to tame. In 1924 he was shot and killed at age seventy by a drunken rowdy in Cromwell, Oklahoma, a boom town where he was serving as marshal. (O'Neal, *Encyclopedia of Western Gunfighters*, 323–26; Miller and Snell, *Great Gunfighters*, 420–37; Wright, *Dodge City*, 309)

Vandeberg, —— One of Wiley Robbins's cowboys who threatened to kill Maynard at Jacksboro, Texas, in 1872. A Bob Vanderbert was one of several men who hassled Luke Short out of Dodge City in 1883. (Miller and Snell, *Great Gunfighters*, 379)

Wagner, [Jack] A Texas cowboy, killer of Ed Masterson. (O'Neal, *Encyclopedia of Western Gunfighters*, 216; Miller and Snell, *Great Gunfighters*, 178–84; DeArment, *Bat Masterson*, 103–107)

Walker, [Alf M.] A Texas cowboy, killer of Ed Masterson. (O'Neal, *Encyclopedia of Western Gunfighters*, 216; Miller and Snell, *Great Gunfighters*, 178–84; DeArment, *Bat Masterson*, 103–107)

Wall, Thomas A man who nursed Maynard back to health at Perryville, Indian Territory, in 1872. Maynard got Wall a job as cook for the Peter Moore crew near Great Bend in 1873.

Walton, [J. C.] A farmer, born in Virginia in 1815, who lived near Belle Plaine in Sumner County, Kansas. (Sumner County 1875 census records)

Walton, Ella Daughter of J. C. and Sarah Walton, born in 1862. (Sumner County 1875 census records)

Walton, Lou A cowboy working for W. B. Grimes in 1875 and son J. C. Walton, Belle Plaine, Kansas.

Watson, Joe A suspected horse thief in the Gypsum Hills in 1875, part of the Bill Anderson gang.

Wells, Professor Maynard's school teacher in Iowa.

Whittaker, [Francis A.] "Frank" A cowboy from Sun City, born in 1850. (Barber County 1875 census records)

Whittaker, [Wilkerson] "Wilkes" A cowboy from Sun City, born in 1857. (Barber County 1875 census records)

Wilcox, Hubbard A cattle owner who shot an Indian in the Cherokee Outlet and had to hurriedly get his cattle over the line into Kansas during the winter of 1875–76.

Wild Hog A Northern Cheyenne Indian involved in the outbreak of 1878. (Berthrong, *Cheyenne and Arapaho Ordeal*, 33; D. Brown, *Bury My Heart*, 325)

Wilson, Emma A girl Maynard knew in Iowa.

Wilson, May A girl Maynard knew in Iowa.

Withers, Ed Along with his brother Bill, Withers consorted with rustlers in the Kiowa area. Ez Iliff helped lawman Mike Meagher arrest Ed Withers, which was the cause of their quarrel. Withers was later killed in New Mexico. (Records and Wheeler, *Cherokee Outlet Cowboy,* 77)

Wolsey, —— One of three men who stole horses from the Osage Indians in 1872 and was apprehended by Buckskin Joe and Hard Rope and taken to Wichita for trial. This man might have been Jerry Williams, an associate of known horse thieves Hurricane Bill Martin and Bill Brooks. According to papers associated with the pardon petition for Simon Ohmert, Williams was involved in the theft but not brought to trial. *See also* Ohmert and Cord. (Freeman, *Midnight and Noonday,* 167; Miller and Snell, *Great Gunfighters,* 46)

Woodward, Dick A buffalo hunter who established a hide camp on a mound (later called Dick's Peak) near Bitter Creek west of Medicine Lodge in the fall of 1872. During the Indian scare of 1874 his wife and son went into the stockade at Forest City (probably what Maynard calls Fort Woodward), but Woodward remained outside and supplied the settlers with bison meat during the siege. In 1874, the only year in which Woodward kept track, he killed seventeen hundred bison. After the buffalo were gone he became a freighter, hauling bones to Wichita. (Yost, *Medicine Lodge,* 38, 47, 50–51)

Bibliography

Abbott, E. C. ("Teddy Blue"), and Helena Huntington Smith. *We Pointed Them North*. Norman: University of Oklahoma Press, 1984. (Orig. pub. 1939.)

Adams, Andy. *The Log of a Cowboy*. Lincoln: University of Nebraska Press, 1964. (Orig. pub. 1903.)

Andreas, A. T. *History of the State of Kansas*. Chicago: Andreas, 1883.

Atherton, Lewis E. *The Cattle Kings*. Bloomington: Indiana University Press, 1961.

Barber County Mail, December 19, 1878.

Barry, Phillips. "The Cowboy's Lament," *Bulletin of the Folklore Society of the Northeast* 7 (1934): 18.

———. "Some Aspects of Folk-Song," *Journal of American Folklore* 25 (1912): 276.

Berryman, J. W. "Early Settlement of Southwest Kansas," *Kansas Historical Collections* 17 (1926–28): 568.

Berthrong, Donald J. *The Cheyenne and Arapaho Ordeal*. Norman: University of Oklahoma Press, 1976.

Betz, Ava. *A Prowers County History*. Lamar, Colo.: Prowers County Historical Society, 1986.

Brown, Dee. *Bury My Heart at Wounded Knee*. New York: Bantam, 1972.

Brown, Jean M. *More About Kiowa and Other Stories*. Newton, Kans.: Mennonite Press, 1993.

Cannon, Hal. *Cowboy Poetry: A Gathering*. Salt Lake City: Peregrine Books, 1985.

Chrisman, Harry E. *The Ladder of Rivers: The Story of I. P. (Print) Olive*. Denver: Sage Books, 1962.

———. *Lost Trails of the Cimarron*. Denver: Sage Books, 1961.

Dary, David. *The Buffalo Book*. New York: Avon, 1975. (Orig. pub. Chicago: Swallow Press, 1974.)

———. *Cowboy Culture.* New York: Knopf, 1981.

DeArment, Robert K. *Bat Masterson: The Man and the Legend.* Norman: University of Oklahoma Press, 1979.

Drago, Harry Sinclair. *Wild, Woolly, Wicked: The History of the Kansas Cow Towns and the Texas Cattle Trade.* New York: Clarkson N. Potter, 1960.

Durham, Philip, and Everett L. Jones. *The Negro Cowboys.* New York: Dodd, Mead & Company, 1965.

Fife, Austin E., and Alta S. Fife, eds. *Songs of the Cowboys by N. Howard ("Jack") Thorp.* New York: Clarkson Potter, 1966.

Freeman, G. D. *Midnight and Noonday: The Incidental History of Southern Kansas and the Indian Territory.* Ed. and intro. by Richard L. Lane. Norman: University of Oklahoma Press, 1984. (Orig. pub. 1890.)

Haley, James L. *The Buffalo War: The History of the Red River Indian Uprising of 1874.* Norman: University of Oklahoma Press, 1985. (Orig. pub. New York: Doubleday, 1976.)

Haywood, C. Robert. "Comanche County Cowboy: A Case Study of a Kansas Rancher," *Kansas History* 4, no. 3 (Autumn 1981): 166–90.

———. *Cowtown Lawyers: Dodge City and Its Attorneys, 1876–1886.* Norman: University of Oklahoma Press, 1988.

Hunter, J. Marvin. *The Trail Drivers of Texas.* Austin: University of Texas Press, 1985. (Orig. pub. in 2 vols., 1924.)

Lillibridge, John L. *The Red Fork Ranch and Its People.* Ocala, Fla.: Greene's Printing, 1990.

Logsdon, Guy. *The Whorehouse Bells Were Ringing and Other Songs Cowboys Sing.* Urbana and Chicago: University of Illinois Press, 1989.

Lomax, John. *Cowboy Songs and Other Frontier Ballads.* New York: Sturgis and Walton, 1910.

Mathews, John Joseph. *The Osages: Children of the Middle Waters.* Norman: University of Oklahoma Press, 1961.

McCoy, Joseph G. *Historic Sketches of the Cattle Trade of the West and Southwest.* Kansas City: Ramsey, Millett and Hudson, 1874.

McNeal, Thomas A. *When Kansas Was Young.* New York: Macmillan, 1922.

Medicine Lodge Cresset, February 6, 1880.

Miller, Nyle H., and Joseph W. Snell. *Great Gunfighters of the Kansas Cowtowns, 1867–1886.* Lincoln: University of Nebraska Press, Bison Books, 1967. (Orig. pub. Topeka: Kansas State Historical Society, 1963.)

Milner, Joe E., and Earle R. Forrest Milner. *California Joe, Noted Scout and Indian Fighter, with an Authentic Account of Custer's Last Fight by Colonel William H. Bowen.* Caldwell, Idaho: Caxton Printers, 1935.

Miner, H. Craig. *Wichita: The Early Years*. Lincoln: University of Nebraska Press, 1982.

Mooney, Volney P. *History of Butler County Kansas*. Lawrence, Kans.: Standard Publishing Company, 1916.

Nolan, Frederick. *The Lincoln County War: A Documentary History*. Norman: University of Oklahoma Press, 1992.

O'Neal, Bill. *Encyclopedia of Western Gunfighters*. Norman: University of Oklahoma Press, 1979.

"The Osage Troubles in Barbour County, Kansas, in the Summer of 1874." The State Government and the Indian Bureau. Topeka, Kans.: State Printer, 1875.

Pen-Lens Views of the Galena-Empire Mining Camp. N.p.: The Pen-Lens View Company, 1899.

Rainey, George. *The Cherokee Strip*. Guthrie, Okla.: Co-Operative Publishing Company, 1933.

Records, Laban Samuel, and Ellen Jayne Maris Wheeler. *Cherokee Outlet Cowboy: Recollections of Laban S. Records*. Norman: University of Oklahoma Press, 1995.

Roach, Mrs. S. T. "Memories of Frontier Days in Kansas: Barber County," *Kansas Historical Collections* 17 (1926–28): 606–17.

Savage, William W., Jr. *The Cherokee Strip Live Stock Association*. Columbia: University of Missouri Press, 1973.

Shirley, Glenn, ed. *Buckskin Joe: Being the Unique and Vivid Memoirs of Edward Jonathan Hoyt, Hunter-Trapper, Scout, Soldier, Showman, Frontiersman, and Friend of the Indians, 1840–1918*. Lincoln: University of Nebraska Press, 1966. Reprint, Bison edition, 1988.

Sires, Ina. *Songs of the Open Range*. Boston: C. C. Birchard, 1928.

Siringo, Charles A. *A Texas Cowboy, or Fifteen Years on the Hurricane Deck of a Spanish Pony*. Lincoln: University of Nebraska Press, 1979. (Orig. pub. 1885. Introduction by J. Frank Dobie, 1950.)

Thorp, N. Howard (Jack). *Songs of the Cowboys*. Boston: Houghton Mifflin, 1921. Orig. publ. 1908.

Thrapp, Dan L. *Encyclopedia of Frontier Biography*. 3 vols. Lincoln: University of Nebraska Press, 1991. (Orig. pub. Glendale, Calif.: Arthur H. Clark Co., 1988.)

Tinsley, Jim Bob. *He Was Singin' This Song*. Orlando: University Presses of Florida, 1981.

Watson, Elmo Scott. "Springs Man Claims Authorship of Famous Old Cowboy Ballad," *Colorado Springs Sunday Gazette and Telegraph*, January 27, 1924.

Wright, Robert M. *Dodge City: The Cowboy Capital and the Great Southwest*. Wichita, Kans.: Wichita Eagle Press, 1913.

Yost, Nellie Snyder. *Medicine Lodge: The Story of a Kansas Frontier Town*. Chicago: Swallow Press, 1970.

Young, Harry. *Hard Knocks: A Life Story of the Vanishing West*. Portland, Ore.: Wells and Company, 1915.

Index

Page numbers in *italics* refer to illustrations.